THE EROTIC ENGINE

ƐR⊙TIC

engine

PATCHEN BARSS

DOUBLEDAY CANADA

Doubleday Canada and colophon are registered trademarks

Library and Archives Canada Cataloguing in Publication

Barss, Patchen
The erotic engine : how pornography has powered mass communication, from Gutenberg to Google / Patchen Barss.

ISBN 978-0-385-66736-4

1. Sex in mass media. 2. Pornography—Technological innovations. 3. Pornography in popular culture. I. Title.

HQ471.B37 2010   306.77   C2010-902496-6

Book design: Terri Nimmo
Printed and bound in the USA

Published in Canada by Doubleday Canada,
a division of Random House of Canada Limited

Visit Random House of Canada Limited's website: www.randomhouse.ca

10 9 8 7 6 5 4 3 2 1

For Andrea

Contents

INTRODUCTION

A deep link exists between pornography and the tools and techniques of human communication. For forty millennia, pornography and sexual depiction have been a powerful source of creativity and innovation that has spurred the development of many new media. Creators and consumers of sexual content have been the driving force behind communications developments as diverse as streaming Internet video and the concept of "beta testing" software. In other cases—for example, the VCR, cable television and many Internet applications—pornographers were the technological pioneers who figured out how to make money from a new medium before the mainstream saw any profit potential. The pornography industry has also played an important role in familiarizing people with new media—motivating them to figure out how to use their cable box or UHF dial, or to master the intricacies of a modem or a webcam. Those who work in the pornography industry have also been business innovators, developing customer service models, secure transaction systems, distribution networks and marketing tools that mainstream companies later emulated.

Pornography's powerful influence over communications—a driving force of innovation that I refer to as the Erotic Engine—has contributed to many of the great tools and toys that consumers enjoy today. You might never have looked at a dirty picture in your life, but if you use search engines like Google and Yahoo!, online retailers like Amazon and eBay, video- and photo-sharing sites like YouTube and Flickr, and many other integral components of modern media, you have benefited directly from pornography's influence both on the infrastructure of the Internet itself and on specific technological and business innovations. Video games, smartphones, media players—each owes its own debt to pornography.

In the modern era, the reason for this link seems straightforward. Consumers of pornography like to buy and use their product anonymously. Every recent advance in technology has made media consumption more private and more convenient. It's small wonder that pornographers were early adopters of the VCR, which meant that customers no longer had to venture out to triple-X cinemas, which were often located in rough neighbourhoods and always came with the risk of being spotted. It makes sense that cable television would benefit from being able to pipe pornography directly into people's homes. And the Internet, of course, offered such convenience and secrecy that pornography couldn't help but dominate its explosive development.

There is more to the pornography–technology link, though, than coming up with better ways not to get caught. For one thing, pornography has played a major role in many media in ways that have nothing to do with anonymity or convenience. Photography, for instance, had barely come into existence before people started to make and sell erotic pictures. Pornography drove the growth of the photographic industry not thanks to better privacy but because it offered a new kind of erotica—voyeuristic, realistic and unlike any form of sexual representation that had come before. Photography was inherently exciting (to a certain market) because it was a new means of expressing one of the fundamental forces of human nature: sexuality, passion and intimacy.

Since at least the 1840s, when the first erotic photographs appeared, the link between pornography and communications has been financial. Pornography consumers have a greater-than-average willingness to try out new technologies and to pay a premium to get their product in a new way. From photography forward, that willingness helped support many new technologies through their "pornographic years" until other, slower-developing non-sexual applications could gain a popular foothold. In the past half century, this influence has become so pronounced that one business model holds that any new communications technology should consider appealing to the pornography market in its early days. Pornographers are "early adopters" who will see a new medium through its rough early stages until it is ready for mainstream markets.

Pornography's influence goes back even further, though, and has affected innovations in communication in ways that go even beyond money. In fact, from the earliest known examples of human beings using a medium to express themselves—painting, carving, drawing—sexual representation has been at the heart of advances in communication. It has never stopped. Media that have been influenced by sexual depiction include (but are not remotely limited to) forty-thousand-year-old cave drawings, six-thousand-year-old Mesopotamian reliefs, traditional Japanese woodblock prints, Hindu temple carvings, medieval European music, early output from the Gutenberg press, millennia-old Chinese sculptures, drawings, oil paintings, watercolours, daguerreotypes, photographs, dime novels, films, videos, velvet paintings, DVDs, phone-sex lines, cable TV, video-on-demand services, playing cards, video games and every nook and cranny of the Internet.

Throughout history, across cultures, and in every part of the world, whenever a new means of communication emerged (with the possible exception of smoke signals), people adopted it and adapted it so as to find new ways to produce, distribute and consume pornography.

In the world of fine art, where styles, media and methods change from generation to generation, nudity and sexuality have never diminished as a driving creative force. Folk tales, ancient legends and religious myths are laced with sex, ribaldry and passion. Modern sex shops and websites carry such quantity and variety of pornography, it seems impossible that portraying the act of sex could still lend itself to new themes and variations— and yet there is never a shortage of new product. This never-ending stream of innovation speaks to something deeper and more fundamental about pornography that extends beyond the basics of prurience and business. Even in the modern era, some of the most interesting ways that pornography shaped the Internet and other high-tech developments had less to do with money than with a widespread and powerful desire to find new ways to manifest sexual expression.

The links between pornography and communications innovations are complex enough on their own, but they are further muddled by the strong feelings the subject matter often engenders. Advocates of pornography sometimes treat the matter with a wink and a nod, and sometimes with no small amount of bitterness. Many who work in the porn industry decry the hypocritical mainstream for dismissing and marginalizing pornography while reaping the benefits of their technological contributions. Time and again, entrepreneurs who hone their technologies, techniques, skills and business models in the adult-entertainment world must conceal this past before selling these tools to the rest of the world. At the same time, many tell tales of mainstream companies like Google, Yahoo! and even Disney hiring from within the adult industry in a bid to find employees at the bleeding edge of new technology.

Critics of pornography, on the other hand, sometimes regard the material as so destructive and offensive that they can't or won't accept that the industry has even an iota of merit. "If it were not for the subject matter, pornography would be publicly praised as an industry that has successfully and quickly developed, adopted, and diffused new technologies," writes Jonathan Coopersmith, one of the foremost researchers on pornography's influence on media technology, in "Sex, Vibes and Videotape." "But because the subject matter was pornography, silence and embarrassment have been the standard responses."

Standard, but not universal. Some members of the mainstream media do acknowledge pornographers as technological trailblazers. Adult content was the first "in cable TV, it was first in home video and on the Internet," said Larry Kasanoff, a producer of such Hollywood blockbusters as *Mortal Kombat* and *Terminator 2: Judgment Day*, in the marketing weekly *Brandweek*. "So while we're all wondering what types of entertainment people will like on the Net, some guy named Rocco down the street is making $24 million a year [selling porn]. And not because he reinvented entertainment, but because he gave it to the public in a better way. So you know what? Porn is great for all of us. We should all study it."

Easier said than done. Because it is a widely reviled and marginalized industry that often operates in an ambiguous legal shadowland, the pornography industry is inherently prone to hyperbole and misinformation. Analysts can't even agree on straightforward questions like how much pornographers make in a year. The only real consensus is that the modern porn industry is a major economic force. Exactly how major, though, is unclear. *Variety*, Hollywood's trade magazine, tracks sales for movies, TV, theatre and music. It monitors only mainstream productions, though. Neither can the industry be tracked via the stock market—only a few publicly traded companies, among them Playboy Enterprises and Private Media Group, can be measured this way.

The two main groups who do publish statistics on how much money changes hands for sexual content are the pornography industry itself and the religious organizations, political conservatives and businesses dedicated to fighting porn. Both sides have a vested interest in skewing the numbers on the high side.

The organization Family Safe Media, which sells products that filter and block adult content, pegged global pornography revenues in 2006 at $97 billion, $13 billion of which came from the United States. (China, Japan and South Korea each reportedly have higher revenues than the U.S.) The pornographic yin to Family Safe's puritan yang is *Adult Video News*, a pornography-industry trade journal. Its estimates tally with Family Safe's. Both sides love to trumpet the statistic that revenue from American pornography exceeds the combined revenues of all professional baseball, football and basketball franchises plus the three major television networks.

Many other sources accept these figures. They have been used in much academic and business analysis. Frank Rich wrote in *The New York Times*, "At $10 billion, porn is no longer a sideshow to the mainstream like, say, the $600 million Broadway theater industry—it *is* the mainstream."

Forbes gazes witheringly upon such claims. In 2001, when the porn and anti-porn sides were both estimating revenues of well over $10 billion in the U.S., the business magazine's analysis put the industry's turnover at closer to $4 billion. That's still big, but not as big as the adult industry—or its detractors—would have you believe.

Another estimate comes from former *Wall Street Journal* writer Lewis Perdue, who developed and conducted his own methods for analyzing the industry. He says that porn consumers and distributors spent $2 billion in 2001 just for Internet bandwidth. He reckons that American pornographic businesses account for $13.1 billion.

In 2002, the National Research Council in Washington, D.C., put the value of just the online adult industry—which does not include bricks-and-mortar sex shops, cable television or DVD rentals—at $1 billion. This report also estimated the number of adult pay websites available that year at more than 100,000 in the United States and three times that in the rest of the world. Even the NRC, though, added caveats about how difficult it is to get reliable statistics about Internet pornography.

An additional ambiguity arises from the fact that consumer spending can't be cleanly divided into pornographic and non-pornographic categories. People can buy a modem or upgrade their Internet connection, for instance, both because it makes it easier to access pornography and because it allows them to do their banking more conveniently. Pornography can be the determining factor in a decision to invest in new technology, but that will never show up in measurements of actual porn sales. This suggests that, however large the pornography industry really is, its financial influence on technological development is even larger.

Another ambiguity arises from the language we use to describe sexual material. With such a long history, and with ever-changing social values, vocabulary can be tricky. When it first gained widespread usage in the nineteenth century, "pornography" meant specifically "writing about prostitutes." The term expanded over time to encompass sexually explicit material of all sorts. It also often carries a connotation of condemnation, as do many other commonly used terms such as "smut," "filth" and "obscenity." Almost every related word comes with its own baggage and connotations. "Porn" and "porno" are usually uttered by fans with a little more relish, while "erotica" hints at some sort of artistic merit or other redeeming quality. People in the industry tend to use "adult" (both as noun and adjective) as a euphemistic term that helps distance them from the less seemly and highly illegal world of underage subjects and users. "Sexual representation" is the broadest means of describing the subject matter. While the neutrality of this term is sometimes an asset, it can also fail to capture the strong emotional and physical responses people have to the material. In this book I use most of these terms not quite interchangeably—I try to apply them as best suits their context.

Those who work in the industry have no trouble with the term "porn." Historically, people in the business have been reluctant to speak with mainstream journalists, fearful of being misrepresented and judged by the broader community. Times have changed. Partly because pornography itself has become more mainstream, and partly because pornographers have become fed up with apologizing for their career path, most are eager to tell their stories—especially when it comes to their role as early adopters of new technologies.

Almost everyone I approached in the industry was more than happy to go on the record. True, a culture of pseudonymity pervades the sex industry, but its purpose has evolved. Porn performers, directors and reporters used to use pseudonyms because they didn't want to be outed to mainstream friends, families and colleagues. Today a good pseudonym is less about disguise and more about branding. While some people requested that I use their *nom de porn*, this generally had as much to do with seeking publicity as it did with avoiding unwanted attention. The overwhelming sentiment was a kind of "porn pride." More than one porn business seminar I attended opened with one CEO or another saying something along the lines of, "Hey,

I'll admit it—I like my product. I like to jack off as much as the next guy." (The audience always responded with good-natured mock praise for such honesty.) The great wall of silence that some writers have found characterizes the industry has been replaced by over-communication.

When I set out to really understand the relationship between pornography and media technology, I was especially curious about those who worked behind the scenes in low-profile jobs— the web designers, marketers and tinkerers who are responsible for the nuts and bolts of working with technology. One of the things I expected to be able to say was that, except for the product, this was an industry like any other, and the people who worked in it were pretty much like their counterparts in any other type of business. It turned out that this is not the case. True, plenty of people working in the pornography sector bring the same professionalism, focus and savvy as anyone else in mainstream work. I interviewed a woman who was both a porn performer and the CEO of one of Spain's largest and most respected adult websites. It was a difficult interview because she spoke only a few hundred words of English and I speak no Spanish. Prominent in her limited English, though, were "know-how," "synergy" and "professionalism." Like many people I spoke to, she talked about the same business principles, the same marketing strategies and customer service models, as your average mainstream online content provider.

But you don't have to dig very deep to reveal how different the adult industry really is. In ordinary jobs, people complain about having to work late, not getting the recognition they deserve, the boss taking credit for someone else's PowerPoint presentation. A Brazilian porn-actress-turned-tech-entrepreneur explained to me why she preferred to work for herself rather than one of the many male-run companies. While many people worry about getting metaphorically screwed at work, it was quite literal for her. "I opened my ass to three cocks, and he wants to keep all the money? I don't think so."

Occasionally I encountered people who were marginal even among the marginal—people whose opinions shock even others in the industry. It is a strange culture, full of contrasts and contradictions. The world of pornography is sometimes about grotesquery and exploitation. It is also about liberation, education, entertainment, curiosity, creativity and pleasure. Through researching this subject, I have met feminists, misogynists, geniuses, kooks, blowhards, wallflowers, tech-heads, entrepreneurs, megalomaniacs, intellectuals and more. It is an extreme subculture that attracts extreme personalities. It is hard to reconcile some of these personalities with their contributions to mainstream media. But somehow, out of this strange mix of people has come a steady stream of technological progress.

To put that role in perspective, imagine how the last sixty years might have gone if there were no pornography. The VCR might never have launched successfully, which would have meant that its descendants, DVDs and Blu-ray, would never have come about, or would have developed much more slowly. Cable television and in-room hotel movies would have faced potentially crippling obstacles. We might not yet have seen the emergence of streaming Internet video, e-commerce or peer-to-peer file sharing. Video games would have taken a very different developmental path. Broadband wireless and the fundamental infrastructure of the Internet itself might not yet have developed to the point where they could support eBay, iTunes, BitTorrent, CNN.com, Flickr, Amazon, YouTube and Google. Facebook and Twitter might never have had the chance to evolve out of early bulletin board systems, newsgroups and chat rooms.

Pornography's influence over new media has steadily increased. Today, media evolve more quickly than ever before. For media entrepreneurs, one of the most effective ways to keep ahead of the game is to pay attention to what is happening in the world of pornography. If the history of communications tells us anything, it's that pornography can indicate, or even determine, which technology is the next success story and which is a passing fad. For ordinary consumers, the story of the relationship between pornography and communication may not always be comfortable, but it contains a surprising amount of passion, creativity and warmth. This "dirty secret" of technology history connects to more than just salacious motivations—it speaks to the fundamental reasons why it matters so much for us to connect to one another.

PART ONE

Drawing, Painting, Carving, Writing

The Oldest Impression

I typed "cave drawings" into Google's image search engine. In four one-hundredths of a second, I had access to thousands of pictures that seemed both strange and familiar: digital representations of the first known examples of recorded human expression, displayed using the most advanced consumer technology available. These two media—stark images created by humanity's artistic pioneers, and the modern marvel of information storage, cataloguing and retrieval—are tied together by much more than the fact that I can now use one to display the other. They are the alpha and omega of a forty-thousand-year-long story about how representations of sex and sexuality have driven human beings to find new ways to express themselves.

These ancient images, which populate caves in southern Spain and France, as well as other parts of Europe, maintain their vivid hues forty millennia on. The black of the carbon and dull red of the ochre mix with the tones of the rock walls to provide an earthy glimpse of the life lived by those first visual artists. A stag frozen in mid-bound. A bison dying from a spear-inflicted thoracic wound. A man, perhaps a shaman, with the head of a bird. A naked woman. A giant erect penis.

These last two examples don't get talked about as much as the animals. But they are not exceptional. The very same caves that have given us so many iconic images of how our caveman ancestors lived—how they hunted, how they ate, their religious practices and their communities—also contain hundreds of images of penises, vaginas, buttocks and breasts. From the very start, recorded human expression and scenes of sexuality have been two mutually dependent parts of the same history. Nobody can say if anyone was bartering or paying for such images in the early days, but what we do know is that from the caves of France's Dordogne Valley to the software of Silicon Valley, there was never a time when sexuality was not a driving force in communication.

In anthropological and archaeological circles there are great debates about what these ancient images mean. How were they used? What did they symbolize? What was the context in which they were created? These questions are important and fascinating, but they should not distract from a plain truth that exists independently of the answers: from the moment human beings developed tools for expression, they used them to satisfy a desire to represent human sexuality for others to experience.

Many scholars say these cave images were part of a shamanic tradition—that they were either depictions of the gods and goddesses of fertility and power or the product of rites performed by holy men to supplicate to such powers.

Not everyone agrees. R. Dale Guthrie, a professor emeritus at the University of Alaska Fairbanks, thinks that, while some of these drawings might have been accompanied by the sounds of ancient chants and prayers, many others were created with snickers and giggles not unlike what you'd hear in a high-school lavatory today. "In schools all over the world, you go to the toilets and far enough back in the toilet booth you'll start seeing these same sexual images," he wrote in his controversial book, *The Nature of Paleolithic Art*.

Some scholarly reviewers attacked Guthrie's ideas about Paleolithic prurience as "wishful thinking" and exaggerations of the drawings' sexuality. "People often see what they want to see in rock art, and I think it safe to say that few of Guthrie's interpretations would be readily accepted by most specialists in ice age art," wrote one critic in the journal *Nature*, even as he described the book as "enlightening and valuable." Not readily accepting a theory is a far cry from rejecting it, and Guthrie's theories continue to spark debate.

Some cave art inarguably deals with sexuality. Even the bison on the cave walls have penises, and some images show animals copulating. The controversy surrounds only what these images *were for*. Such drawings may have been nothing more than a realistic depiction of day-to-day experience. Then again, some exaggerations of size and shape suggest that many of these images were making some sort of statement beyond "I paint what I see."

Plenty of evidence backs up the idea that cave drawing was practised by many people other than spiritual leaders. Many of the images—generally ones that don't make it into art books—are clearly the work of unskilled, unrefined artists. Furthermore, in addition to the first known drawings and paintings, these caves also exhibit the first examples of printed images—in this case prints made by coating one's hand with pigment and pressing it on the wall, or by laying a clean hand on the wall and darkening the area around it. Not only was this the invention of both negative and positive printing, but the variety of prints also demonstrates how diverse in age and size were the creators of these images. There is also a casual nature to many of the drawings, one that makes them feel more like hastily scrawled graffiti than profound works of art. It just happened that, unlike your average bathroom scrawl, these images remained intact for tens of thousands of years. By the sheer weight of their age, they garnered more mystique and profundity than their creators likely ever intended.

Unlike many of his contemporaries, Guthrie entertains the idea that a drawing of a caveman with a penis the size of his leg, or a crack in a cave wall that a few quick lines have transformed into a vagina, might be less part of a shamanic fertility rite and more a forty-thousand-year-old dirty joke. Guthrie points to a "universal human behaviour that can explain these patterns."

More than anything else, it was this phrase that made me want to pursue his ideas beyond what appeared in his published work. Though he is supposedly retired, he had just returned to Alaska after visiting several archaeological digs in North Africa when I contacted him. He is still deeply committed to pushing his interpretations of cave drawings.

While some scholars engaged in the debate, many of Guthrie's colleagues have greeted his thesis with silence. I asked him why so many scholars tend toward the spiritual aspects of these images and resist acknowledging the bawdy. He said it has more to do with discomfort than disagreement. "We have a lot of very odd aspects to our morality," he said. "Those that revolve around sex are especially potent. It's just a delicate subject." A delicate subject that seems to wield as great a clout in the ancient world of artistic expression as it does in the modern media business.

There are other scholars who are willing to discuss the universality of sexual depiction. Many tie the phenomenon back to the

basics of survival. Sex, along with breathing, eating and drinking, are the fundamental actions necessary to ensure the continued existence of both individual human beings and humanity as
a whole. Classic arguments from evolutionary biology explain
why activities vital to survival are so pleasurable—organisms
that did not enjoy food or sex would not live long enough to
reproduce, and therefore would be filtered out of the gene pool
in short order. There are also sound, simple reasons why watching other people eat or looking at food can foster hunger, or why
viewing depictions of sex and sexuality can spark erotic desire.
Human beings, though, have a tendency to take the basics and
complicate them.

"I really equate sex and food," erotologist C. J. Scheiner
told me over lunch near his home in Manhattan. (An erotologist is an expert in the depictions of sex and lovemaking, as
opposed to a sexologist, who studies sex itself.) "You need
food to stay alive, but you need the barest plainest food to stay
alive. Yet what we have in front of us here"—we were at a
Szechuan restaurant—"is nicely prepared, it looks pleasant and
it tastes good. It's way more than we need to just give us the
calories to keep us going to tomorrow. And if you go to a five-
star restaurant, it is just way beyond anything that you need
for pure survival."

His point was that humans experiment and test, try out new
recipes and techniques, seek out exotic alternatives, acquire
new tools and equipment, and generally push the limits of tastes
and appetites.

Sex runs the same gamut—from basic survival, to simple
pleasure, to commodified product, to exotic five-star treatment.
And always, extra value is placed on experiencing something
new. This premium people will pay for novelty is key to the
story of innovation. New representations of sexuality don't just

drive consumers of erotica—they also pique the creativity of those who produce it. This is one of the primary reasons why sexual representation goes beyond merely opening up markets for communications innovations. It actually helps make those innovations happen.

"Human beings take the bare necessities, and if we have time, we play with them. We make more out of them," Scheiner said. "Since reproduction is one of the great driving forces to keep the species going, we're going to spend a lot of time on it."

Thus a simple biological impulse becomes a never-ending quest for novelty and experimentation. And because communication is a fundamental part of human sexuality, the *means* of human communication become bound up in a perpetual cycle of reinvention and creativity.

Dale Guthrie does believe that things have changed in the twenty years he has been studying this aspect of human behaviour. He said that an increasing number of academics (including those in fields other than erotology) acknowledge sexuality as an integral part of human expression and as a driver of innovations in communication. And while the means of creating art may have evolved in leaps and bounds, the content hasn't. Today's adolescent boys still draw genitalia in the same crude, exaggerated fashion their ancestors did all those years ago.

Those deep artistic impulses to communicate about sex extended to the other new medium of the day: sculpture. In September 2008, Nicholas J. Conard, an archaeologist at the University of Tübingen, was digging in the Hohle Fels Cave, near the Danube headwaters in southwestern Germany. The floor of the cave is covered in a deep stratum of ruddy sediment. Just twenty metres from the cave entrance, and only about one metre down in the dirt, Conard unearthed six fragments of carved ivory—tiny pieces that fit together to form a sculpture of a woman just a couple of inches high. Broad shoulders, thick torso, large buttocks, huge, exaggerated vulva and giant protruding breasts—Conard said he knew the significance of the discovery as soon as he dusted off the midsection.

The sculpture was about thirty-five thousand years old—about the same age as the cave drawings Dale Guthrie writes about. It is the earliest known sculpted representation of the female body, and one of the first pieces of representational art (though slightly older phallus sculptures have been found in southwestern France). Although the "Venus of Hohle Fels" is the oldest, many other examples in a similar sculptural style have been found, though they were made about five thousand years later.

The journal *Nature*, where Conard published his findings in May 2009, described the tiny statue as a "prehistoric pin-up." *The New York Times* quoted one scholar saying it "could be seen as bordering on the pornographic." (Dale Guthrie got a laugh from this, as the quotation came from one of the researchers who had remained silent about *The Nature of Paleolithic Art*. "I guess he's coming around!" he said.) But, the *Times* went on to say, "Scholars speculate that these Venus Figurines, as they are known, were associated with fertility beliefs or shamanistic rituals."

Pornographic or shamanistic? Here was the same debate that had divided Guthrie from so many others in the academic world. There is something striking about the issue, though. Why does it matter so much whether prehistoric representations of the human sex organs had sexual or religious purposes? Why does this particular aspect of archaeology spark such intense debate? And why is this particular sculpture the one that made headlines in *The New York Times*?

Whatever purpose the Venus of Hohle Fels served, it is now one more example of how overtly sexual subject matter has been part of representational art since the beginning. It also exemplifies how sexual representation, no matter how one interprets it, has the power to get people talking, writing, reading and debating. A thirty-five-thousand-year-old sculpture of a naked woman can still drive people to step up their communication today.

Whether Guthrie is right or not about what those ancient drawings and sculptures were for, his theory about a universal human behaviour stands the test.

The "Hottentot Venus" and the History of Civilization

Jill Cook flinched when I mentioned the Venus of Hohle Fels.
I had sought out Dr. Cook, a curator at the British Museum
in London, for her expertise in prehistoric art, as well as for her
particular interest in representations of men, women and couples.
I met her in her office, which sits at the end of a small maze of
corridors and stairways that are normally off limits to museum
visitors. I wanted to talk with her about the role of sexuality in
those first sculptures and artworks. In particular, I wanted to
speak to her about a number of ancient sculptures of nude women
known as Venuses, and which include the 2008 discovery in
Hohle Fels. I did not know that my education would begin with
a lesson on the far from benign nature of this nomenclature.

"This term"—Venus—"is a piece of the history of sex if you
like, which it is high time we dropped," she said. "The term was
not applied to these female figures because people were thinking
of the classical Venus figures. It was applied because the heavy
breasts and buttocks of these figurines reminded anthropologists

of the day about what we now recognize as the terrible story of Saartjie Baartman."

I did not know the story of Saartjie Baartman, also known as the Hottentot Venus, until Jill Cook told it to me. Baartman was born in 1789 in South Africa. She was an orphan and a slave on a Dutch farm near Cape Town until 1810, when the farm owner's brother, Hendrick Cezar, and a Brit named Alexander Dunlop decided that she should serve a different purpose. Cezar and Dunlop took her to Europe to "exhibit" her.

Saartjie's "exotic" body shape, and the view in white society—perpetuated by her captors—that sex with such a woman was an out-of-this-world animalistic experience, made her fascinating to crowds from all social classes. She was paraded naked in a cage for the elite of Georgian England for a number of years. She was then sold to a Frenchman, who put her on display in Paris—if possible, under even worse conditions. Ultimately Saartjie Baartman died of pneumonia at the age of twenty-five, at which time the French anatomist Georges Cuvier pickled her brain and genitals to keep as novelty research items. So she remained until 2002, when, after nearly a decade of pressure from Nelson Mandela and the African National Congress, her remains were returned to the region of her birth for burial.

Thus it was, as Cook laid out on the table before me half a dozen meticulous replicas of prehistoric carvings, that the term "Venus" was dropped forever from our discussion and from my vocabulary. Saartjie Baartman's story was a reminder that the "universal human behaviour" that Dale Guthrie speaks of—the fascination with representations of sex—is a complex phenomenon that can be greatly liberating for some and equally oppressive for others.

The half-dozen sculptures Cook went on to show me were two or three inches high and represented a wide variety of carving styles and body types. Old, young, fat, thin, pregnant. What did the makers of these tiny works intend? Why naked women? All we know is that these sculptures exist. We can't call these artists pornographers, but we can say that the early adopters of the first known media immediately turned their talents to human nudity.

Cook emphasized that we cannot know what these statuettes were for. She used Guthrie's own argument about universality to suggest that perhaps there wasn't anything pornographic about them at all. "Unlike a girl that you might look at in a sexy magazine, who is gazing out at you, gesturing with her eyes, mouth and hands, and being very physical in putting her body forward to you, these little figures do quite the opposite," she said. "They tend to look down upon themselves. They are not gesturing towards their sexual characteristics. Indeed their hands are generally tucked in or tucked away. And in each instance these figures show women of all ages, and at all times of life."

She had a point. Even though they are explicit representations of naked women, these sculptures did not seem very sexy to the modern eye. Given that forty millennia ago humans had basically the same endocrine system and would have responded to the same sorts of visual stimuli, these figures, Cook said, do not appear to have been a very effective form of erotica. "If these figures don't appear to us to be pornographic," she said, "I think it's reasonable to assume that that wasn't the primary intent."

"Most art historians," Cook said, "have been men, and most artists in historic times have been men, and so the representation of women has had a sexual element. I think one has to come nearer to our own era to make a comparison to this distant period. One needs to look at the work of women artists and how they think about their own bodies and other women's bodies and how they represent them. And that's not always sexual. There is an element of these figures that might suggest that they are by women for women." She points out that in the shape of the breasts and the curves of the hips, the figures seem to present the view a person would see looking down at herself rather than looking at another person.

If the sculptures weren't pornographic in intent, the obvious counterargument—that humans will never cease to astound other humans with the unlikely things that arouse them, and so how your average author or museum curator reacts to a particular artifact does not necessarily speak to the question of whether prehistoric Europeans had a thing for tiny, rough-carved statuettes—only takes you so far. The few artifacts that have survived from that time simply do not provide enough information for us to determine what these figures were for. The very best interpretations are still just (highly) educated guesses.

Interpretation is also complicated by the differences in how men and women were represented: most depictions of men from the time have erections, which seems to tip the balance toward some sort of erotic end, but men are also the only ones represented as part human and part beast, suggesting that prehistoric art truly was tied up with shamanism and communication with the animal spirit world.

One other fact lends credence to a non-pornographic interpretation of prehistoric art: for all the nakedness and sex organs, the protruding bums and boobs, there is no known depiction of people having sex in the first twenty thousand years of recorded human expression (though the Chauvet cave in southern France contains thirty-three-thousand-year-old images of animal coupling). There was no limitation in the media that would prevent such depictions, but somehow (as far as we know) millennia went by during which nobody chose to create the staple of modern pornography: people engaged in the act of sex.

"So that is a problem for Dale," Jill Cook said with a laugh.

Most of the first images of human coitus date from about eleven thousand years ago, with one earlier exception: a small carving that dates from about three thousand years earlier. It was found in the Judean Desert near Bethlehem, and it depicts one partner nestled in the lap of another, their arms wrapped around each other in an intimate and surprisingly tender sexual embrace. This tenderness is not diminished by the fact that from almost every angle, the silhouette of the carving looks like a penis.

Cook explained, "It's made at a time when people are just beginning to domesticate animals and they are beginning to settle down and think about agriculture, at which point the male role in reproduction becomes extremely important. To domesticate animals, you really need to know that two and two makes four." It is possible that pre-agricultural societies were less aware of the relationship between sex and pregnancy—the first signs of the latter, after all, don't appear until weeks after completion of the former. It is possible that breeding animals provided a greater understanding of the role of sex in reproduction, and was thus the catalyst for the shift from standalone nudity to depictions of actual sex.

Art, erotica, documentation, religious totem, how-to guide, medical record, dirty joke, lucky charm—the few surviving representations of sexuality could have been used for any or all of these. We will likely never know the conclusive truth: not only is there a dearth of context but there is also the question of how many drawings, carvings and who knows what other human expression have not survived through the ages that might have given a very different and more complex picture of what was driving the communicators and artists of the day.

"I think we have to be a wee bit careful," Cook said. "On one hand we have human sexuality, and of course it's a normal and natural thing that gets our endorphins going and makes us excited and makes us a bit high and creative. Of course sex is something that inspires creativity. But we forget other social elements at our peril. We forget things like social norms and taboos that exist in all societies in many different ways, and to look back on this as if it were some great heyday of free love is probably a mistake. For people who can paint and draw and do so without any shyness, the fact that they don't represent intercourse all the time suggests that there is some reason that they don't."

Ultimately, there is no reason to cleave to a single interpretation of prehistoric art. Male shamans, hormone-frazzled teenaged boys, self-portraitists in the early stages of pregnancy and a panoply of other sculptors and painters could have coexisted in society then, just as such variety exists in modern life. More important, it does not actually matter what the statues and pictures were for. Even if in their own time and place these representations had no erotic merit or intent, sexual representation was still an inherent and influential application of the very first means of recording human expression. Even if we can never know what all those phalluses, labia, breasts and buttocks meant, we know they were a powerful driving force of creativity.

In 2010, the British Museum began broadcasting a series of radio documentaries called "The History of the World in 100 Objects." The small carving of the embracing couple has already been selected as one of the hundred. That in itself suggests that, no matter how many questions remain unanswered about this little stone carving, we don't need to define its purpose in order to be assured of its significance.

Of course, you don't have rely on an august research institution like the British Museum to find sexually explicit material. A family hotel can sometimes serve just as well.

With 1,590 rooms, the Delta Chelsea is the largest hotel in downtown Toronto. The Delta makes a particular effort to be family friendly, with a childcare centre, video arcade, dedicated family suites and an indoor waterslide. Which made it all the stranger to find the hotel's Churchill ballroom hung with dozens of oversized images of couples coupling, threesomes and five-somes, faces of the male and female participants glazed over with glee and passion. The floor of the cavernous ballroom was filled with display cases, highlighting phalluses of every size, shape and form, along with statuettes of copulating newlyweds, faces with penises in place of noses, and pottery covered with a panoply of erotic imagery.

One assumes it was the antiquity of these objects that made them an acceptable display for a family hotel. These artifacts of Chinese sex traditions dated back as much as five millennia. I had come to hear James Miller, an associate professor of Chinese religions at Queen's University, give a lecture on ancient Chinese sex legends, rituals, tips and tricks.

The hundreds of artifacts that created the backdrop for his talk are the opposite of exceptional; they are typical across cultures and throughout history. The British Museum, Paris's Bibliothèque Nationale and other mainstream museums have renowned collections, but most people's introduction to the real ubiquity of sexual expression comes at specialty museums such as New York's Museum of Sex, Barcelona's Museum of Erotica and Las Vegas's Erotic Heritage Museum. (The Chinese sex relics at the Delta were a promotional show for an upcoming similar institution in Toronto.)

At such museums, one finds no shortage of examples of drawn, painted, printed, etched, written, carved, photographed, filmed and computer-generated representations of human sexuality drawn from every known culture and depicting every theme and variation of the subject matter itself. The *Kama Sutra*, a classic Indian book that contains advice on life goals, prosperity and mate selection, is almost exclusively known as a sexual instruction manual. The *Kama Sutra* has become a metaphor for sexual variety, but it doesn't come close to representing the truly astounding variety of multicultural sexual representation. So many art forms, so many modes of communication shaped by their intimate relationship with sexuality.

The most striking thing about the display at the Delta was the level of craftsmanship and artistry so evident in the work. The fine detail in the pottery illustrations, the delicate brush strokes in the paintings. These were not the work of amateurs or hacks. Here was a room full of sexual artworks created with the highest-quality techniques and technologies of the day. It made me wonder whether those who attained such skill then chose to apply it to erotic ends, or whether it was the desire to create erotic work that drove them to master the techniques. Either way, the ballroom had become a warehouse of examples of the nexus between creativity and sexual imagery.

In many earlier cultures, the modern Western taxonomy that divides art, literature and entertainment into erotic and non-erotic forms did not exist. This both complicates and simplifies the process of winnowing out examples where sexual representation drove the technologies and techniques of communications tools. The argument is more complicated in that there is simply no way to isolate sexual content as a discrete force of innovation. The task is made much simpler, though, as the very ubiquity of sexual themes speaks to a near-universal motivation not only to depict sexuality but also to find as many different ways as possible to do so.

China has an unbroken tradition of erotica dating back more than five thousand years. They are in good company: South Asia is dotted with ancient erotic paintings, sculptures and entire temples covered with images of Hindus frozen in the act. Africans, Native Americans, Europeans and Middle Easterners all have millennia-old artistic and literary traditions centred around sexual representation. Despite such ubiquity, even those like James Miller who work in the field never seem to quite get used to it. Miller began his talk at the Chinese Sex Relics show by saying just how difficult it was to give his presentation when a two-and-a-half-foot stone penis loomed at him just a few feet away.

His lecture, titled "Chinese Sexual Yoga and the Way of Immortality," placed sex in the context of Chinese religion. In ancient China, he said, sex was seen as a form of energy exchange between partners. If you had enough of the right kind of sex, it could take you beyond good health and reverse aging. Do it right—and often—and legend says you can live forever (often at the expense of your sexual partners, who would be sapped of their energy and age proportionately quickly). Miller spoke for nearly an hour about the myths and rituals that surrounded these artifacts, ancient instructions on how to attain immortality through sex, and the spiritual energy men could gain by climaxing without ejaculating. When I asked him about it later, he acknowledged that many of these artifacts would have been used as aphrodisiacs. But in his lecture he didn't once mention a possible straightforward erotic or pornographic purpose for the materials in the room. He wasn't dogmatic about it, but his natural tendency was to focus on the non-hormonal aspects of these ancient Chinese sex secrets, even while he was speaking in a room filled with artifacts bearing a striking resemblance to the contents of a modern erotic novelty catalogue.

Many people—scholars and not—who are willing to discuss sacred or culturally significant objects will not deign to apply the same analysis to common bawdy gewgaws. It is an issue that has dogged such analysis for many decades and in the context of many ancient societies. And it affects how authoritative, comprehensive and meaningful such discussions are. It's an issue that many academics have only begun to address in the past few decades.

British academic Catherine Johns, in her groundbreaking 1982 book *Sex or Symbol*, writes, "In the recent past, particularly in the nineteenth century, all objects from ancient cultures which were shaped or decorated in a way that was considered improper by the very severe standards of the time were relegated to the category 'obscene': if they were of sufficient artistic merit or archaeological importance to be housed in a museum, they were locked away in special collections which were made as difficult to access as possible." Her book sifts through the panoply of sexual images from Ancient Rome and Greece, untangling threads of fertility, power, worship and eroticism that run through this vast body of sculpture, pottery and painting.

Recent decades have seen a shift toward more open acknowledgement of the obvious—that representations of human sexuality are a widespread and integral part of the development of countless art forms and communications media, and that, while they may well have religious or high-art significance, they also were made to arouse, stimulate and inflame the passions. The British Museum's decision to publicly display that sculpture of a prehistoric embrace and the exhibit of Chinese sex relics at a family hotel are both testaments to an increased recognition of the significance of sexual representation in the myriad means of human expression. At the same time, though, there is still great resistance from many corners toward explicit talk about explicit subject matter. In order to fully understand how important this type of content has been to so many communications advances, it is vital to recognize the full extent to which sexual depiction has permeated the history of human expression. There was never a time when sexuality was not a part of the evolution of communication.

The Virgin and the Naughty Monkey

R oger S. Wieck is the curator of medieval and Renaissance manuscripts at the Morgan Library and Museum in New York City. He has also held curatorial positions at the Walters Art Museum and the Houghton Library at Harvard. He has published many books and articles on medieval manuscripts and is one of North America's most respected experts in the field. He is the author of *The Hours of Henry VIII: A Renaissance Masterpiece by Jean Poyet* (2000), *Painted Prayers: The Book of Hours in Medieval and Renaissance Art* (1997), *Time Sanctified: The Book of Hours in Medieval Art and Life* (1988) and many other well-respected books and articles on medieval manuscripts.

We met in the reading room at the Morgan, a sumptuous space designed by the architect Renzo Piano, part of an addition to the museum that was completed in 2006. A combination of artificial and heavily filtered natural light illuminated floor-to-ceiling shelves lined with ancient books and manuscripts. On the table in front of us was a Book of Hours—a prayer book for non-ordained Christians—that originally belonged to a woman who lived in northern France in the fourteenth century. The hand-printed manuscript was full of ornaments in ink and gold, the Latin prayers to the Virgin Mary framed and delineated by tiny detailed drawings in the margins and filling in short lines of text. It was one of the most beautiful works of art I had ever seen firsthand. Wieck had graciously agreed to share his expert analysis of some of the bookmakers' marginalia.

"The monkey looks like he's making bread, but he's actually poking a naked behind with a pole," Wieck pointed out. The accompanying Latin text, from I Corinthians, translates as "The Lord Jesus, the same night on which he was betrayed, took bread and giving thanks, broke it and said, Take you and eat: This is my body which shall be delivered for you." Elsewhere in the manuscript, a soldier with a bare bottom has a spear jutting out from between his legs, while nearby a half-man, half-beast is fellating a gold phallus. "Forty years long I was offended with that generation," the text reads here, from Psalm 95. Both passages are from the Hours of the Blessed Sacrament, a set of prayers based on the Catholic rite of imbibing holy wine and eating wafers in the belief that they turn into the body and blood of Jesus Christ.

"I counted all the naked behinds in this book and there are a lot," Wieck told me. These naughty drawings were literally marginalized—they were so tiny that Wieck and I had to peer through magnifying glasses at the edges and corners of the pages—a bird with human buttocks, a nearly naked soldier, a man about to be goosed by a thistle, another monkey that seems to be pooping. (This last image sat next to the text "Bless the Lord, thanks to God.") Wherever bums were shown, Wieck pointed out, the anus was highlighted. And always there was the poking—poking with poles, bird beaks, swords, arrows, plants. The illustrations had little or nothing to do with the prayers they accompanied. Wieck saw no need to pretend they had some non-titillating purpose. "What does it mean?" he asked. "It doesn't mean anything, but there are allusions to anal sex and oral sex throughout."

In a follow-up email, Wieck did put forward a theory for one particular image. "I was struck that so much scatological imagery is to be found in the Hours of the Blessed Sacrament section. I think some of these might be meant to be parodies on the consumption of the body and blood of Christ and what happens to the consumption of food and drink. I was struck by the monkey drinking wine (presumably) from a chalice-shaped vessel while seated on an oven. We thus arrive at wine and bread in the image and blood and body of Christ via the text.

"Or perhaps," he added, "I've been staring at this stuff too long."

Given the modern tradition of separation of church and humour (not to mention sex, bottoms, poop and monkeys), it seemed impossible that such a manuscript could even exist. Yet, while these kinds of pictures were not the norm for a Book of Hours, they were far from rare. Mind-boggling as it might seem today, in their own time they were neither subversive nor scandalous. In fact, the main reason I had tracked down Wieck was so that he could talk me through the ways these tiny sexual drawings had affected the rise and fall of illuminated manuscripts. It turned out that nearly seven hundred years ago, monkeys' bums and tiny sex scenes were altering the arc of media evolution.

Until about 1250, only ordained members of the church—monks, priests and nuns—owned and read books; lay people simply were not taught to read. In the mid-thirteenth century, there began to emerge in Europe a middle class, and with them came the spread of literacy, libraries and universities. The lay literate class was still very much upper crust—shopkeepers and fieldworkers remained illiterate—but a growing number of families could afford to learn their letters and to own a book. They developed what Wieck calls a "bibliophilic jealousy" of the church leaders. The demand created by this jealousy was met by the production of prayer books for lay people. Complex protocols required the owners to recite certain psalms on specific days, to cycle through all 150 such prayers each week, to use the other prayers in the book appropriately for special situations. People discovered that these books demanded a formidable commitment.

The laity wanted something simpler—reading and prayer were all very fine, but if they wanted to read and pray for a living, they wouldn't be laity. Eventually, the complicated parts, including the psalms, were taken out, leaving a much simpler set of prayers, highlighted by the Hours of the Virgin. In those pre–printing press days, each book was individually hand-crafted, and customized for the commissioning patron. The buyer made the call about what kind of illustrations would grace the pages, meaning that the fourteenth-century French woman would have asked for all that naughty marginalia.

And consistent with many other media, people were often willing to pay a premium for that (sex) appeal. "You have to pay for all this stuff," Wieck said. "Before she paid her bill they would count all these line fillers and marginalia, and you would pay two pennies per item or whatever the price was. So she would have specified the number of decorations she wanted, and I suspect have had input into the nature. The artist couldn't on his own freedom put in these kinds of naughty bits, especially like ass-kissing, and know that it would be acceptable to the patron, especially a female patron."

The sexuality of these images is more humorous than erotic. But that doesn't make their presence in a prayer book any less surprising. Another prayer manuscript portrays a man and woman having sex in the corner of a page. Another shows two men linked at the genitals in a tiny box bordering six lines of Latin holy text. To the modern eye, nothing could be more incongruous.

One item in the Morgan's collection, a Book of Hours from fifteenth-century Italy, commissioned by a woman named Cecilia Gonzaga, is a rare exception that takes this saucy humour out of the margins and into the main illustrations. In what looks like a traditional depiction of Baby Jesus being bathed, the infant saviour appears to be sporting a porn-star-grade erection. But wait—it's only his mother's hand protruding from between his legs. Just an honest mistake? A few pages later, the endowment is back in another picture, only this time it turns out to be the knife of the High Priest who is circumcising Christ. Other than the visual penis joke, these illustrations look exactly like any other depiction of these scenes from that century.

There was no scandal when this book was made. "This was a private commission," Wieck said. "Now whether she asked for those images, who knows? But clearly her personality must have been known enough by either the bookseller or the artist or both that they knew they could get away with this sort of little in-joke."

Such a "little in-joke" could well be a source of major apoplexy today. Six hundred years of cultural change make these images simply unbelievable to the modern eye. They existed in the first place only because of a unique combination of social values and technological circumstances. These sexual images exist only in books that were commissioned by, and customized for, individuals: the book-making process of the day created one-offs rather than multiple copies. That allowed the elite few who could acquire such documents to have them customized however they wanted, without fear of upsetting anyone. When the printing press came along, Books of Hours started to become more standardized. It wasn't quite mass production, but the market broadened just enough to cause the idiosyncrasies and jokes to disappear.

"They occur in a small percentage, but consistently, in these manuscripts," Wieck said. "The humour and the erotic element played a small role in people's desire to own these books and enjoy them. If we only had this in one book here and another a hundred years later, you could say it had nothing to do with it. From the middle of the thirteenth century on, there's an explosion of manuscript production. Humour and erotic imagery were a factor in why these books were popular, why they were consumed and why they were commissioned. Clearly there was always a percentage of society—a small one—for whom these images had great appeal."

A Book of Hours could serve multiple purposes, from prayer to prurience. A certain sector of the market was willing to pay extra to mix a little sex in with their prayers to the Virgin. But it does not stop there. The economic influence of sexual marginalia on the medium goes even further. In some cases, these images played a role in whether customers were willing to pay for an illuminated manuscript at all. Interestingly, this influence was most evident near the end of this medium's life. (This goes contrary to the more common pattern, in which sexual representation wields its greatest influence during the early stages of a mode of communication.)

Illuminated manuscripts entered their waning years in the fifteenth century, with the advent of moveable type. Unique books were on their way out; print runs were on their way in. But it took a long time for the manuscripts to die out, thanks to the fact that they could still cater to those who desired content that was not suitable for mass production.

People continued to commission manuscripts for about a hundred years after the invention of the printing press, until the middle of the sixteenth century, in no small part because it was a means of keeping sex in the pictures. The printing press brought into existence the concept of mainstream or mass markets. Mass-market publications were necessarily less risky, which inevitably meant less risqué. Because some customers would be offended by sexual content, the entire print run needed to be expunged of bawdiness. That left those with the desire and means with no choice but to cleave to the old technology of handcrafted manuscripts, despite the inevitable higher price of buying a one-off product. With this new divide between mainstream printing and the increasingly marginal medium, manuscripts became even more explicitly sexual. By the start of the Renaissance, manuscripts were solely in the domain of the ultra-elite and were populated with images that were too hot for mainstream. Manuscript makers had found a way to keep their product viable: sell to the very rich, who were immune both to the higher costs and to the stigma that was starting to be attached to the possession of erotica.

This market existed at the very top echelons of society. When Louis XII became king in 1498, he celebrated by commissioning a lavish Book of Hours with what Wieck calls "the most salacious Bathsheba that was ever painted in a manuscript."

The story of Bathsheba, from the Book of Samuel in the Old Testament, recounts how King David spied on Bathsheba as she bathed, had an affair with her and then had her husband killed. The Hours of Louis XII illustrates this tale with a level of sensuality and graphic detail that would never have been acceptable in a mass-produced book (at least not until the twentieth century). Thanks to customers like King Louis, erotica prolonged the demand for manuscripts and demonstrated how niche markets can be highly profitable, if you have the right product.

Fleshing the Press

In the 1400s, people began to associate sexual material more closely with riff-raff and the lower classes than with dukes and kings. The growth of mass-produced erotica meant that salacious products became more broadly affordable. Pornography, and literature in general, was becoming more democratized. But as more people gained access to erotica, it began to garner negative stigma. The same types of images that had long been the acceptable purview of elite connoisseurs became socially objectionable when placed in the hands of hoi polloi. New kinds of outrage were increasing the divide between the prim mainstream and the low folk so enamoured with tawdry matters: modern-day divisions had begun to take shape. And the technology at the heart of this incipient conflict was the moveable-type printing press.

Very little is known about the man behind this most influential of inventions. Johannes Gutenberg was a fifteenth-century German entrepreneur who combined and refined existing technologies of metalsmithing, etching and wine pressing, who experimented with inks, alloys and machinery, and who ultimately developed a system of moveable-type printing that was faster, cheaper and more flexible than anything Europe had ever seen before. The new press made it possible to produce hundreds of copies of the same book in the time it would take a manuscript maker to produce a single edition. It changed everything about who could afford books, and therefore who would learn to read. Though this massive change is often referred to as "the Gutenberg Revolution," the little that is known of the man himself suggests he was more interested in growing wealthy than he was in enfranchising and enriching the masses via the printed word.

In 1440, the quickest and safest way to make money with a printing press was not pornography. The first major profit-making book to roll off the Gutenberg press has become indelibly associated with the inventor's name: the Gutenberg Bible. Gutenberg's version contained no salacious marginalia or images of bathing beauties. It was a masterpiece of artistry and technological know-how, but with nothing that might offend the pope.

The moveable-type printing press—and literacy itself—spread quickly across Europe. Though one has to be careful with such analogies, the Gutenberg press was in some ways the Internet of its time: a powerful democratizer of information, opening up the world of books, pamphlets and other printed material to much broader segments of society. In the fifteenth and sixteenth centuries, literature and literacy were still far from universal, but they did start to become more attainable for middle-class Europeans. Book libraries became more popular (outpacing old-media libraries of hand-printed manuscripts), and book fairs selling classical texts alongside contemporary ballads, travelogues, prayer books and poetry proliferated. It was not long before there were many markets other than the Catholic Church—markets for very different kinds of publications.

When it came to smut, this time of great change was, at least on the face of it, a story with causality moving in the reverse direction—it was technology affecting erotica rather than the other way around. But the effects were complex. As the printing press gained popularity, it changed the relationship between media innovators, pornographers and anti-pornographers. This was the start of the clash between freedom-of-speech advocates and protectors of societal and religious values that frames much of the debate around pornography today.

Erotic books were not a part of the printing-press revolution on anywhere near the same level that adult content would be in the Internet revolution four hundred years later. The biggest sellers in the early stages were prayer books and other religious texts. Next on the list were self-help books—though they were focused less on self-esteem or the power of positive thinking than on when to plant crops or how to build a really strong fence.

Lascivious material was certainly in production, but it accounted for only a small part of the market—estimates put it at 10 per cent or less of the total book market. But the numbers do not tell the whole story. This time of change brought with it the first hints of an industry specifically devoted to pornography as a distinct product and an increasingly organized effort to condemn and censor this material.

Before the printing press, and for some time after it was in common use, sexual words and images were very present, but there was no special classification for erotica. "Certainly in periods before the nineteenth century, the understanding of how eroticism fits into life was very different than how we now understand it," said Ian Moulton, a professor at Arizona

State University and the author of *Before Pornography: Erotic Writing in Early Modern England*. "I often feel that there wasn't even a separate category for erotic. There was sexual stuff, but if someone said, 'Show me your erotic books,' people would have looked at them like, 'Well what do you mean? I can show you all my drama, I can show you my collections of poetry, I can show you my satire, but I don't know what you mean by erotic books.'"

Whereas the Books of Hours at the Morgan Museum had sexual content that was completely extraneous to the subject matter at hand, secular books had sexual material woven into the actual stories and ideas. There was no divide as there is today. This lack of partitioning did not reflect some freewheeling progressive utopian value system. Far from it. In fact, it was a result of a different kind of stark divide, between upper and lower socioeconomic classes. Literacy had spread more widely since the days of the Virgin and the naughty monkey, but sexual imagery was still acceptable precisely because the very wealthy and educated had exclusive access to it. The rich could handle it, so it was thought. And as long as these images didn't fall into the hands of the unwashed masses, the church was also not bothered.

The interplay between sexuality and elitism was as evident in the world of fine art as it was in the early stages of the printed word—a legacy that lives on in modern art galleries and museums. Just as ancient stone phalluses can now find their way into a family hotel, material that would otherwise be considered X-rated is proudly displayed for busloads of schoolchildren.

Take, for example, Agnolo Bronzino's famous 1545 oil painting, *Venus, Cupid, Folly and Time*, which today hangs in London's National Gallery. "Here we have a female nude, Venus, who is about to be French kissed by an adolescent, who is in fact, if you know the legend, her son," says art historian Edward Lucie-Smith in the documentary *Pornography: The Secret History of Civilisation*, almost gleeful in his description of the taboo sexual elements that are the essence of the painting. "So they are in the process of committing a little incest. Cupid's bottom is stuck out in a most provocative way as if he is offering himself for a sexual act. But this is a picture that everybody is quite cool about. Nobody is bothered. They lead their five-year-old kids, or worse still their twelve- and thirteen-year-old kids in front of it, and [say,] 'It's a masterpiece, dear.'"

It is almost as though people can stare at such a painting and see only the brush strokes, the textures and the technique, and filter out what is actually happening in the picture. This type of blindness is relevant to the later relationship between pornography and technology because people seem to draw on the same ability to compartmentalize, allowing themselves to remain ignorant, for instance, of how pornography drove the explosive growth of the early Internet.

In the sixteenth century, of course, these sexual themes didn't have to be ignored by the masses, simply because the masses had no access to them. The rich and powerful people who commissioned such artworks felt well qualified to handle mature subject matter and strong themes. The Gutenberg press spelled trouble for this status quo.

The starkest illustration of how the printing press changed taboos around erotica happened in the 1520s in Italy. There are four main characters in this story: the painter, the engraver, the author and the pope.

The painter, Giulio Romano, was one of Italy's most esteemed—at the time of this story, he was in the process of taking over the workshop of Raphael, who had died at the start of the decade. Giulio had a big smock to fill: Raphael was considered one of the three great masters of the Italian High Renaissance (along with Michelangelo and Leonardo). Giulio needed to maintain the reputation Raphael had built for his workshop, while making a name for himself through his own talents and ideas.

One of these ideas was a series of sixteen drawings that came to be known as *I Modi*, which can translate as "The Positions" or "The Ways." In Italian the word is more nuanced, somewhere between "positions" and "postures." Each illustration featured a man and a woman having sex. This was nothing new in and of itself: such explicitness was already common in fine art. Traditionally, though, even the most naked figures were dressed up as Greek or Roman gods, goddesses or other legendary figures, providing a cloak of cultural legitimacy to their nakedness. Giulio Romano departed from this tradition, instead using as subjects ordinary, if exceptionally athletic and flexible, human beings. Still, this was not a huge problem—after all, it was all in the name of fine art.

Raphael had established a professional relationship with a well-known engraver named Marcantonio Raimondi. Giulio had continued this relationship, and in 1524, he passed the sixteen drawings on to Marcantonio, and then immediately left Rome to design a palace for a duke in Mantua (a palace, by the way, in which Giulio was directed to create many heavily erotic frescoes).

Marcantonio's possession of the sixteen positions put him in a rather nice position of his own. This set of erotic drawings from one of Italy's greatest artists represented a potentially huge business opportunity. He turned the drawings into engravings, mounted them on a printing press and began producing large quantities of *I Modi* for sale. This was an early attempt at catering to a mass market for erotica. Although no records remain that can suggest how profitable this venture might have been, it had explosive results for the engraver.

While Giulio painted lascivious goat-gods and bare-breasted women on the luxurious walls of the Palazzo del Te for Duke Federico Gonzaga (no relation to Cecilia), Marcantonio was swiftly arrested and jailed by the forces of Pope Clement VII for selling filth. So effective was the papacy's campaign to confiscate and destroy the images that almost nothing remains of them today.

What happened? Why did these two men meet such different fates? Some accounts suggest that Giulio was also in hot holy water, and that he had in fact fled Rome to avoid similar scandal and persecution. This theory, though, doesn't hold up to scrutiny. "Not only was Giulio untouched by the calamity that befell Marcantonio, but his Roman departure was serene," writes scholar Bette Talvacchia in *Taking Positions*, the definitive modern account of the matter. The papacy came after Marcantonio because he took these images beyond their normal sophisticated and genteel audience into the public realm, a feat she says was "made possible by the print medium. The intrusion of imagery considered obscene into the public realm was an ingredient of Marcantonio's transgression, and perhaps one of the most consequential."

This incident was the start of many centuries of war between censors and the censored. It was also the start of a proud tradition of using sexual text and imagery as a means of demonstrating the hypocrisy and impotence (literal and figurative) of the political and religious leaders of the day.

Enter the writer. Pietro Aretino was a satirist, playwright and poet who kicked off his literary career with a satirical pamphlet that purported to be the last will and testament of Pope Leo

X's recently deceased pet elephant, Hanno. (The elephant was real; the will was not.) Pietro then went on to, among other things, invent modern pornography. He was already famous and controversial by the time this particular scandal broke.

Pietro intervened on Marcantonio's behalf and had him freed from prison. Incensed by the incident, he proceeded to write sixteen companion sonnets for *I Modi*. The images and poems were republished together (possibly some years later). Talvacchia quotes an acidic letter of Pietro's explaining his motivations: "When I obtained from Pope Clement the liberty of Marcantonio Bolognese, who was in prison for having engraved on copper plates the *Sixteen Positions* et cetera, I felt a desire to see the figures that were the cause of [Cardinal Gian Matteo] Giberti's complaints, who demanded that such a fine virtuoso should be crucified. And having seen them, I was touched by the spirit that moved Giulio Romano to design them. And because the ancient, as well as modern poets and sculptors, sometimes engaged in writing and sculpting lascivious works as a pastime for their genius—as attested by the marble satyr in the Chigi Palace who attempts to violate a young boy—I exhibit them above the *Sonnets* that stand below, whose lewd memory I dedicate to you, *pace* all hypocrites. I despair of the bad judgment and damnable habits that forbid the eyes what delights them most." (That same anger can be seen in the words of many modern pornographers.)

Pietro's sonnets should also dispense with the idea that modern pornographers invented anything truly new or shocking. Here is a translation of part of the accompaniment to the third position:

My legs are wrapped around you neck,
Your cazzo's in my cul, in pushes and thrashes!

I was in bed, but now I'm on this chest.
What extreme pleasure you're giving me!
But lift me onto the bed again: down here,
My head hung low, you'll do me in.
The pain's worse than birth-pangs or shitting.
Cruel love, what have you reduced me to?

The printing press brought an unholy mix of sexual content and political criticism to a broad public—an intolerable situation for the Catholic Church. Though Pietro and Marcantonio's collaborative reworking of *I Modi* was a hot item across Europe, the battle had only just begun.

The papacy struck back with the *Index Librorum Prohibitorum*—a list of prohibited books. The Netherlands published such an index in 1529. Venice and Paris followed suit, and Rome got in the game in 1559, under the leadership of Pope Paul IV. (This Index remained in effect until 1966.) In the sixteenth century, as now, the censorious officials, in this case religious higher-ups, combed through any potentially salacious (or irreligious, politically uncomfortable or on occasion scientifically accurate) material to ensure the protection of those less well equipped than they to deal with such representations.

The medium here is as important as the message: the papacy fought books with books, using the same tool to facilitate their censorship as that which they were trying to censor. This pattern repeats itself right up to the computer age, with both sides of a moral battle adopting the latest technology to further their own ends.

The push and pull between prurience and primness began in the West, but over time it spread around the world, on the coattails of other conservative attitudes toward sex-related issues such as homosexuality and prostitution. (The explanatory materials for the Chinese sex relics show included the statement, "The first law against male prostitutes went into effect during the Song dynasty [960–1279]. However, the law was not effectively enforced. The more devastating event for Chinese homosexuals was, ironically, the enlightenment that came after the Self-Strengthening Movement, when homophobia was imported to China along with Western science and philosophy.") Nowhere was this shift more pronounced than in Japan, which evolved from a culture in which sexual representation was an integral part of creative and artistic expression to one where these erotic traditions and influences are systematically glossed over and ignored.

The eighteenth century in Japan, an era known as the mid-Edo period, was a time of great social and technological change. At the start of the previous century, a shogun named Tokugawa Ieyasu had established a de facto capital in the small fishing village of Edo, on the coast of Japan's largest island, Honshu. (Edo would be renamed Tokyo in 1868.) Edo grew at breakneck pace, part of a pan-Japanese trend toward rapid urbanization and modernization. Tokugawa rule was built on a class system, which divided the populace into four main strata: warriors, peasants, artisans and merchants (plus the inevitable fifth category of social outcasts). These rigid divisions did little to allow for upward social mobility, but they did allow Japan to experience nearly three centuries of growth, peace and prosperity. Though merchants were near the bottom of the class system, meaning they had little in the way of political power, many grew wealthy beyond their low social standing. All in all, this was an exciting time to be Japanese.

That is, unless you were one of thousands of farm girls kidnapped from your home and taken to a walled city within the capital where you were forced into a life of prostitution, serving Edo's vastly male-dominated population. These girls were allowed out of the Yoshiwara brothel district exactly once a year (to see the cherry blossoms), unless a parent died, in which case they could visit their family. When they turned twenty-five, they were kicked out into a city and a world that was completely unfamiliar to them.

Wealthy merchants, many of whom had more money than they knew what to do with, would compete with each other to determine who could pay the most for a night with the most desirable of these sex workers—some paying the equivalent of tens of thousands of dollars for a single visit (all fees going to the brothel owners, of course, not the women). For those who lost in these battles of financial machismo, consolation came in the form of pornography—if you couldn't buy the girl, you could buy the fantasy. And so sprang up an ancillary industry based on erotic images known as *shunga*, highly stylized depictions of men engaged in various sex acts with prostitutes. The vast preponderance of these images portrayed the very highest ranking prostitutes. *Shunga* allowed men to enjoy the fantasy not just of sex but also of the affluence that would give them access to the most expensive sex available.

The primary imaging technology of that time and place was multi-coloured woodblock prints. Woodblock printing is a demanding technology, requiring great skill and training. The artist had to carve a relief image on a block, so that only the raised areas would come in contact with the ink and then the paper. Images with more than one colour required the meticulous alignment of imprints from multiple blocks, each dipped in a different ink. The demand for this technology was driven by not-quite-wealthy-enough merchants and their fantasies of spending a fortune for a night of sex.

The competition among men was reflected in these images in other ways, too. One of the most glaringly obvious is in the *shunga* depiction of men's genitalia. The penises are not just porn-star big—they are caricature/physical deformity big.

"I actually did a blood flow study and found out how much blood it would take," said Elizabeth Semmelhack. "And no man could sustain consciousness *and* an erection in a Japanese print." Semmelhack studied Japanese woodblock printing in graduate school and curated a 2006 show at Manhattan's Museum of Sex titled "Peeping, Probing and Porn: Four Centuries of Graphic Sex in Japan." "Not only do you have this man with all of his glory showing; you often will have the sex workers in the images [looking as though they're thinking] 'I can't take all that. Oh my goodness, I've never seen anything like it. Oh, it's just too much.' Part of the fantasy is that this man is impressing a woman who has seen many, many, many, many, many other men. This one man may not know if he is big or small because maybe he doesn't see that many men with erections. But here he has the perfect judge—somebody who has ten people a day—and she's never seen anything like that before."

Thus men's fantasy about the size of their reproductive organs drove the very real technology and techniques of image reproduction.

Somehow, though, human-head-sized penises and high-end prostitution seem to have dropped off the radar in many histories and analyses of the art of Japanese woodblock printing. This happened about the time that Westerners began to take an interest in collecting the prints in the late 1800s.

"Japanese prints were collected by Westerners with a connoisseurship eye," said Semmelhack. "Let's not deal with the fact that these were mass-produced popular culture items. Let's find out who the geniuses were who made these works. Let's talk about the individual art maker. And let's not talk about content at all. Let's talk about form rather than function." Filtering out the pornographic images took some doing, not least because the Japanese geniuses whose art Westerners collected might create an illustration from a sacred Buddhist text one day and a scene from a brothel the next. So at the exact same time they were purportedly focusing exclusively on form over content, collectors necessarily had to sort images according to the very content they were trying to pretend did not exist.

There was an even greater irony to all of this. Collectors, academics and historians believed they were scrubbing clean the medium's pornographic past by omitting the obvious images of sex and sexuality from exhibits, books and collections. But in so doing, they eliminated the very references that revealed rampant sexuality endemic to the entire gamut of woodblock images.

One of the great eighteenth-century woodblock masters was Utamaro, who did a lot of prints of women's vaginas. But those were not the prints people collected, Semmelhack said. The Utamaros that found their way into the art world depicted people considerably more clothed. "If you don't look at that [erotic] work, then you don't understand that all the sleeves that he made of women are basically representations of women's vaginas."

In fact, all Japanese art from that time, not just the overtly sexual material, is rife with libidinous and pornographic meaning. British art historian Timon Screech argues this case with barely contained impatience in his book *Sex and the Floating World*. He also finds it necessary to systematically refute denials from the academic community that the overtly sexual *shunga* images were used for masturbatory purposes. Semmelhack waged similarly frustrating battles when she was doing her doctoral work in the 1990s, fighting to prove the merit of studying (or at least acknowledging) the pornographic aspects of the form.

In fairness, highly stylized images of consciousness-robbing erections and sex workers from a bygone culture might simply seem unsexy to the modern Western eye. Though the general subject matter is the same, *shunga* images don't much resemble in style most twenty-first-century pornography—not even the *hentai*, or modern Japanese pornographic comic books and animation that are their direct intellectual and artistic descendants. The influence is clear, but as with much erotica from distant times and places, *shunga* doesn't seem to speak to a present-day audience on the same kind of visceral erotic level. While pornography seems universal, what specifically works in one culture does not appear to transfer easily to another.

This very phenomenon explains why people like Elizabeth Semmelhack fight to bring pornography back into mainstream study. Pornography is a constant force of business and culture, yet response to it is so different from one time and place to another that it can provide geographically and temporally specific information that could not come from any other source.

"If you're somebody who's interested in what was actually happening and what was actually meaningful within a culture at any given period, study pornography," Semmelhack said. "It has to be sexy and work *in that moment*. These ephemeral things that are constantly changing are the way that you can actually take the pulse of the culture."

PART TWO

Mechanical Reproduction

Exposure Time

T he advent of photography was arguably the biggest shakeup
the visual arts world has ever seen. Every visual art form
that preceded it—drawing, etching, painting, block printing and
so on—relied on the dexterity and nuance of the artist's hand.
Before photography, every portrait, still life, landscape and
incestuous mythological sex scene was filtered through the creator's interpretation, memory and imagination. What appeared
on canvases and cave walls might never actually have existed or
been witnessed by the artist.

Photography was a different kind of visual medium.
Photography captured reality. However much creativity he
brought to the subject, a photographer could not create a photographic image simply by realizing an idea in his head—whatever
he wanted in a picture had to exist in the real world. Unlike a
painting, a photograph of people having sex required people to
be having sex. A person buying such a photograph was paying
for the opportunity to see real people in real situations—a kind

of voyeurism that had never before been possible. Erotic photography was based on the same sexual fantasies that had fuelled previous media, but now these fantasies were rooted in reality, which gave them a special kind of power—a power that vastly increased the influence of erotica and pornography over the development of this new technology.

This was the start of the modern pornography industry, and that industry drove the development of photography from its very first moments. "The history of erotic and pornographic photography begins with the invention of the camera itself, a circumstance that reinforces the thesis that the urge to represent sexuality helps drive the evolution of communications technologies," writes Joseph W. Slade in his three-volume extravaganza, *Pornography and Representation: A Reference Guide.*

The invention of the camera cannot be pinned down to a single moment in time. Its precursor, the camera obscura—literally a "dark room" and essentially a vestibule-sized pinhole camera— had been in existence since at least the eleventh century. Ancient Greeks and Romans had knowledge of how to refract light through a lens—the Roman Emperor Nero was reported to have watched gladiatorial matches with the aid of a corrective lens made of emerald. In 1614, a Dutch scientist named Angelo Sala discovered that silver nitrate darkens when exposed to sunlight. Painters had been using proto-photographic tools to project images onto canvases to aid their artistry since at least the 1700s, and arguably for much longer. Thomas Wedgwood of Wedgwood china fame was the first to articulate the concept of using such technology to create permanent images. Joseph Nicéphore Niépce took the first long-lasting images in the 1820s, using a different process that never caught on widely. These and other optical and chemical discoveries circled around one another, fuelling the imaginations of many inventors independently pursuing parallel goals of creating images by machine rather than by hand.

On January 7, 1839, the French artist and chemist Louis-Jacques-Mandé Daguerre announced that he had achieved a practical method of producing images mechanically. Centuries of experimentation had created a glow on the horizon, but the daguerreotype was the dawn of the photographic age. Portraiture, landscapes, still lifes and everything that had previously been exclusively the purview of painters came to be seen in a very different light. Out of this technology, a massive new industry developed. Pornography had a part to play from the very beginning.

Photographic technology did not begin with Daguerre, nor did it end with him. His process had limitations, and advances and improvements came fast and furious. Daguerreotypes were one-offs—there was no negative from which to make multiple copies of a single image. William Fox Talbot developed the first photographic process, called calotype, that used a negative-positive process. Although it never really caught on, thanks to Talbot's zealous patenting and some technological and quality limitations, calotype was the precursor to the celluloid photographic film that had become the industry standard at the beginning of the twentieth century and which remained so until the advent of digital photography. (The physical flexibility of celluloid also made moving pictures possible.)

Initially, daguerreotypes required very long exposure times, often up to ten minutes, meaning that landscapes and still lifes were the only practical subject matter. It would take a few years for the process to be improved with chemical accelerators to the point where it became possible to get a clear image of a person. That is why the oldest known hard-core photograph dates from a full seven years after Daguerre's announcement.

The image, which depicted a middle-aged heterosexual couple in the act of coupling, was not necessarily (or even likely) the first such image—just the oldest one still in existence. The advent of nude, erotic and pornographic photography so closely coincided with the advent of photography itself that it is reasonable to say they were concurrent.

Photo-realism added a shocking element to sexual representation. Wrote one critic in 1851, "The Daguerrian nude was painfully accurate, with none of the stylized musculature that characterized Raimondi's engravings or plaster casts of Roman sculpture—or the idealized figures combining the perfections of various living models advocated for centuries by the French fine arts academy." Also described as "un-artful," photography revealed something more "real" than painting ever had. Nudity in this new medium had a different and more powerful nature than anything that had come before. It was the exact kind of sexual potency you could take to the bank.

In the second half of the nineteenth century, it cost more to buy an erotic photograph than it did to hire a prostitute. Partly this was because you get to keep a photograph for repeated viewing, while an actual sexual encounter is more fleeting. Unlike a prostitute, a picture could be stared at by its purchaser indefinitely, or put aside for another time. But there was an even greater draw. The products of this new technology, these images of real naked human beings, unmediated and raw, were like nothing that had ever existed before. They commanded a kind of fascination that fetched very generous fees.

The technology improved, with daguerreotypes swiftly being replaced by negative-positive processes that allowed for the mass production that could meet what seemed to be an insatiable market. Paris quickly became a global hub of photography in general, and erotic photography in particular. Pragmatically, it would have been impossible for it to be one without being the other.

In 1848, there were thirteen photography studios in Paris. Twenty years later, there were more than 350. Most survived by selling erotic images, though they were not officially labelled as such. Photographers took advantage of the cultural divide that had sprung up by that point, which separated nudity into either the acceptable category of art or the tawdry and taboo category of erotica. Tens of thousands of dirty pictures were sold as "art studies," supposedly meant to be the basis for the great paintings of aspiring artists. (The practice extended into the twentieth century in forms such as gay erotica thinly disguised as athletic photography, and "documentary" portrayals of nudists.)

"In 1852, when only seventeen photographic titles were registered for public sale in Paris, over half were studies for artists," writes Elizabeth Anne McCauley in *Industrial Madness*, her study of early commercial photography in Paris. "Of the 417 images registered for public sale in 1853, 40.5 per cent were artists' studies, which consisted primarily of female nudes and occasional genre scenes."

Take Bruno Braquehais, a deaf and mute photographic portraitist who plied his trade in mid-nineteenth-century Paris. Braquehais began as a lithographer, graduated to daguerreotypist, and finally ended up practising print photography. He came from a reasonably wealthy family and married a woman of similar socioeconomic class. He won prizes as a draftsman and critical acclaim for his photographs and daguerreotypes. One of the most influential critics of the day was particularly taken with Braquehais's "artistic studies of the nude female model." Though Ernest Lacan criticized Braquehais for overuse of a (busty) plaster bust of Venus as a photographic prop, he was highly admiring of the photographer's ability to capture these women in a style akin to that of the great neoclassical painters.

Modern critics have a little more trouble discerning the high-minded artistic merits of Braquehais's nudes. McCauley notes, "Lacan's willingness to transform what many viewers today would consider awkwardly staged tableaux featuring plain undressed girls into Greek heroines reflects a polite blindness to the images' erotic content and an acceptance of the stereotypical poses and props that bespoke 'art' rather than 'pornography.'"

"Polite blindness" allowed Braquehais and hundreds of other photographers to grow wealthy selling pictures of naked women, while eluding the condemnation and legal ramifications of dealing in pornography.

In later years, many technologies would exploit pornography as their initial commercial market and then scrub this erotic history from the record when it came time to go mainstream. Early photographers, though, seemed to have an astounding capacity to look society in the eye and say that the stacks of nude pictures they were selling had nothing to do with erotica. Lawmakers were so confused by this new technology, and by the trickery of those who called it art rather than pornography, that this segment of the photographic market burgeoned for years before there was any sort of coherent crackdown. As long as nobody called it what it was, any condemnation was limited enough to allow trade to prosper.

"The remarkable number of photographic nudes registered by companies specializing in their production," writes McCauley, "along with their peculiar descriptions, which were more detailed and narrative than the bare titles of other types of prints and photographs, is a clue to the true nature of this segment of the burgeoning photographic market. Under the guise of artistic studies, photographers were in fact selling soft-core pornography to an audience that was much wider than the self-contained group of practicing artists and art students."

Which helps explain the distribution networks for these "nude studies." Rather than being sold in the halls of academe, these images were found under the counters and in the back rooms at photography studios, as well as at public dance halls, brothels and other places of ill repute. They were sold alongside condoms, dildos, naked dolls and other sex-related material. (Enterprising photographers also increased their profit margin by selling ancillary products such as magnifying glasses and the addresses of the models.) It was common for Parisian photography studios to operate on both fronts at once—the "legitimately artistic and scurrilously erotic," as McCauley puts it. The pervasiveness of this dual role became apparent when obscenity laws did start to be enforced, and the heads of many of the major commercial studios were sent to jail, sometimes for possession, production and distribution of hundreds of thousands of obscene images. These images ranged from dancing girls in skimpy outfits to what would today be called hard-core sex scenes.

Aside from the sale of photographs themselves, pornography drove a huge underground trade in private custom shoots, repackaging and reproduction of existing images, and other activity that contributed to the flood of obscene photographs that flowed through and out of Paris. Press reports at the time indicate that genteel society was aghast at the pandemic of obscene pictures as early as 1851, though most of the major busts did not happen until the next decade.

Most of our information about the prevalence of pornographic photography in the 1850s and 1860s comes from police records of arrests and seizures. As such, it speaks to massive quantities of porn, but says less about what percentage of an average studio's revenue came from the sale of erotica. Given how common it was for even the most reputable studios to have a significant sideline in pornography, though, it is clear how essential the material was to the bottom line.

Photography fits an often repeated motif whereby pornography plays its most influential role early in the life of a new technology. Early adopters gravitate toward producing erotic content to generate a major portion of their revenue. Business expands, and ultimately mainstream applications account for a larger part of revenue generation. The demand for pornography never goes away—more photographic images are sold today than in 1860—but it becomes a smaller percentage of a larger business sector.

The path of technological development is rarely linear. A medium such as photography often splits off in many directions. And in this case, erotica held particular sway over the markets for some specific offshoots. There were daguerreotype nudes. There was erotica shot to negative film. There was stereoscopic hard-core pornography, which combined two nearly identical images that, when looked at through a special viewer, created the illusion of a three-dimensional scene. Each theme and variation on mechanical image reproduction was instantaneously adapted, adopted and co-opted for the purpose of photographing people—mainly women—without their clothes.

One small technological development marked the start of an unexpected offshoot from the growing cluster of photographic technologies. "A [police] seizure in 1863 involved a type of photograph that was particularly adaptable to pornography—microphotography," writes Elizabeth Anne McCauley in *Industrial Madness*. "These tiny images, sold as transparencies, were impossible to read with the naked eye and were packaged with special magnifying viewers (called Stanhopes)."

The Stanhope lens was named after Charles Stanhope, an eighteenth-century British nobleman and inventor whose contributions to the media world also included a vastly improved printing press and a device for tuning musical instruments. (By strange coincidence, Jill Cook, the British Museum curator, had a bust of Charles Stanhope stored on a high shelf in her office, stuck in the Prehistory Department because there was no room for it anywhere else.) The lens that bears his name was essentially a one-piece microscopic viewer. Such lenses were embedded in jewellery, knife hilts, watch fobs and so on. The viewer would hold the item up to his eye, revealing the tiny picture hiding within.

Elizabeth McCauley's casual reference to Stanhopes opened up a whole new avenue of research for me. There is something compelling about these strange little devices that can secrete a picture just about anywhere—it's easy to see why they were such a marketable novelty. As I learned more about them, though, I discovered two things. First, these funny little photographs, whose primary purpose was to pander to porn peepers, ended up transforming the way librarians and archivists preserve documents. Second, Stanhopes are still being produced to this day. The story of this technology followed some unexpected turns over the span of more than a century. It's a history that might never have begun were it not for the demand from the pornography market that originally propelled Stanhopes forward.

There were actually two markets for Stanhopes in the early days: politics and pornography. This is not surprising, given the historically close relationship between the two: from *I Modi* on, pornography became a commonly used tool among political agitators, advocates of free speech and critics of government and religious leaders. In the United States around the beginning of the twentieth century, Stanhope-equipped watch fobs appeared in the shape of a pig. Some, called "learned pigs," came with a message inviting people to look inside to see the next president of the United States. This was not flattering—viewing a portrait of, say, Grover Cleveland involved peering into the pig's behind. (Even more devastating were fobs with pictures of Mrs. Cleveland—sending the horrifying message that a woman might be running the show behind the scenes in Washington.) But presidential elections only came along every four years. In other years, the devices were repackaged as what some people today call "male chauvinist pigs"—same fobs, but with naked women inside instead of politicians. Politics and porn each commanded a healthy premium over Stanhopes with more innocuous microphotographs, leading some to speculate on how profitable it would have been to sell Stanhopes with a picture of Grover Cleveland's naked wife.

Stanhopes also came to be known as peep-holes, peep-eye viewers or just peeps. (Very similar terms would be resurrected almost exactly a century later to describe coin-operated booths in which the customer watched blue movies. While the two technologies had very little else in common, their shared nomenclature speaks to a common feature of using mechanical devices to create a thrill for voyeurs.) As a technology, the Stanhope had two major appeals: the image was essentially hidden from the rest of the world, and viewing the image was akin to peering through a keyhole—it gave a viewer who desired it the illicit thrill of feeling as though he were spying.

Until the 1920s, the only real money to be made in peep technology was in erotica. Without sexy pictures, Stanhopes might have become a forgotten form of never-profitable technology. Instead, they survived for decades, and so were still around when people started finding new reasons to create and view images too small for the naked eye.

A New York banker named George McCarthy registered a patent in 1925 for a "Checkograph machine," which kept permanent microfilm records of bank transactions. The Kodak company bought his technology three years later. In the 1930s, Kodak's Recordak division began creating microfilm editions of *The New York Times*. More periodicals and many rare books would follow. Microphotography meant that delicate or vulnerable works could be protected while people accessed photographic copies of them on microfilm. By World War II, the technology had improved to the point that a page of text could be reduced to a piece of film the size of the period at the end of this sentence. These microdots were virtually undetectable, making them an ideal way to hide and transport secret military documents.

In the post-war years, the technology (along with its cousins microfiche and microcards) became a prime means for libraries and other institutions to save space and preserve documents, and today back issues of everything from local newspapers and rare texts to *Playboy* magazine have been archived in miniature. A technology that Thomas Sutton, in his 1858 *Dictionary of Photography*, described as "of little or no practical utility" had survived, thanks to a small but dedicated market of voyeurs, long enough to fundamentally change our ability to archive and document material that might otherwise have been lost to deterioration, fire or plain old lack of room. Without the Stanhope and the erotic material that kept it alive in its early years, our cultural archive would be greatly impoverished.

Today, Stanhopes have returned to their original role of novelty item, with naughtier versions still selling at a premium.

Pennsylvania tinkerer Michael Sheibley keeps the microphotography flame alive through his business, Stanhope Microworks. He stumbled across the technology decades after it had all but disappeared into antiquity. "I'm a violinmaker by profession," he told me. "I make forgeries of authentic instruments that are worth a lot of money. I had a virtuoso here one night. She was playing a $4.5-million violin and it broke. She didn't know what to do. She shows up at my place about one o'clock in the morning, and I fix her violin through the night so she could play it again the next day. As she was leaving she said, 'Have you ever seen a bow like this?' She told me it was a Vuillaume bow."

Jean-Baptiste Vuillaume was one of the most famous French violin and bow makers. In the 1850s, he partnered with a Parisian jeweller to insert Stanhopes into the frog of a bow—the part at the held end that keeps the bow's hair in place. "When I looked inside, there was a picture of Niccolò Paganini, the most famous violinist of all time. It blew me away."

An entrepreneur and experimenter at heart, Sheibley reverse-engineered this lost technology and made it the basis of a modern business. As had happened the first time around, erotic images drove the early market, paving the way for Sheibley's expansion into mainstream.

"Earlier on, the majority of what we did was nudes," he said. Once things got rolling, though, he kind of kept that to himself. "We shot porn then, but now, because of the popularity of the Lord's Prayer, crosses and things like that, we shoot mostly religious. We don't push the porn like we used to. I think, though, there's always a corner in every market for porn somewhere: it is such a collectible item. In fact we charge ten dollars more for pornographic pictures, just because they are porn."

Sheibley sells pens, pendants, pocket knives, charm bracelets, compasses, jewellery and violin bows, into any of which he can insert a tiny stock image—you can get the Lord's Prayer in twenty different languages, the Ten Commandments, Corinthians, or Psalm 91, also known as the Soldier's Psalm. Given that God and country have become major sellers, Sheibley no longer advertises the pornographic line the way he once did. Still, the orders for stock images, and for individualized sexual images and items, keep rolling in.

"I get a lot of custom orders. I had a woman send me one from Australia. It wasn't even good porn. It was just a picture of her genitalia maybe from the belly button to the bottom of where her forest grows and she was wearing a thong made out of a string of pearls. And then the picture of the fellow was just him with his equipment schlonged over to the side and you only saw him from the belly button to the knees," he said. "And then they reordered and made them for their friends."

Stag Nation

As pornography pushed early still photography in multiple directions, a similar story had begun for moving pictures. The names of those proto–movie cameras capture the romance and excitement of this phase of invention and development: Phenakistoscope. Zoetrope. Praxinoscope. Zoopraxinoscope. Magic lantern. From the start, there was something miraculous about cinema. The glowing, moving images seemed to have the spark of life. (It's interesting that in its early days, this new medium was referred to as "moving pictures" rather than, say, "recorded drama" or "a play on film." The terminology reflected how cinema descended directly from painting, drawing and photography, rather than from storytelling and stage plays.)

But this wasn't all. From the moment Thomas Edison and W. K. L. Dickson unveiled the Kinetograph (used for recording moving images) and the Kinetoscope (for playing them back) in the late 1800s, movies have had a voyeuristic element that many people have found deeply erotic. More than the text and still images that preceded movies, and in some ways more even than the immersive and interactive technologies that would follow, film (and later video) would have a deep connection to erotica and pornography. In the second half of the twentieth century, the business of making and distributing pornographic movies reached the epic scale that has given the industry its reputation as an unstoppable force. Long before the so-called golden age of porn, though, the development of cinematic technology was closely tied to erotic impulses.

The critic Erwin Panofsky, sometimes called the father of art history, places early film in the context of a folk art tradition that is deeply tied to sexual representation. In his 1936 essay "Style and Medium in the Motion Pictures," he writes: "The stationary works enlivened in the earliest movies were indeed pictures: bad nineteenth-century paintings and postcards (or waxworks à la Madame Tussaud's), supplemented by the comic strips—a most important root of cinematic art—and the subject matter of popular songs, pulp magazines, and dime novels." Early film was folk art, not high art, he said, and the storytelling traditions it drew on included gratifying "a taste for mild pornography."

Given that heritage, and the voyeuristic nature of the medium, it is small wonder that in one of the very early erotic films, *Peeping Tom in the Dressing Room* (1905), the action is framed by a keyhole, through which the title character is peeking, watching a busty female try on a corset. (The tradition of sequels was already becoming entrenched—this short film followed thematically from another from eight years earlier, simply titled *Peeping Tom.*)

How much is there really to be read into the sexuality that drove this new medium? Was it a coincidence that the public unveiling of Edison's Kinetoscope in 1894 took place at a former bawdy house in New York City, and that it featured a film called *The Kiss* that left the audience feeling hot and bothered? (This titillating twenty-second film, with a close-up of a kiss, was denounced as shocking and pornographic by early movie-goers and caused the Roman Catholic Church to call for its censorship.)

"It is virtually impossible to overstate the vulgar origins of the cinema," writes Joseph W. Slade, who is a media historian and professor at Ohio State University, in his article "Eroticism and Technological Regression: The Stag Film." "It was not only that the cheap medium dealt with cheap subject matter; it encouraged voyeurism, the pleasure in looking that itself seemed indecent."

In an interview, Slade suggested that the causal relationship between sexual representation and communication was more nuanced than it might appear on the surface. He thinks the causality is there, but that it has as much to do with how people feel about the technology as it does with how they feel about seeing depictions of sex.

"I do think that the urge to represent sexuality drives communication technologies, but I am a little cautious," he told me. "The belief that this dynamic is at work stems in part, I think, from a widespread conviction that modern eroticism derives in part from human relationships with the artificial and the non-reproductive, and in part from a fear that technology advances sensuality, as in the anxieties over the Internet's potential for sexual predators, or the earlier fantods suffered by early critics of telephones, who worried that vile seducers would call help-less young women in their homes."

In fact, that same kind of nervous fit has dogged many other media—from the fears of vulgarity rolling off the printing press into the hands of the ill-equipped fifteenth-century masses, to the comic-book-related panic induced by the 1954 essay

"Seduction of the Innocent." Each technological innovation in human communications seems to lend itself to night terrors about corruption and seduction of hapless consumers.

That said, the early era of film is one of the few points in modern media history where pornography appears not to have had discernible direct effects on the development of the technology. Though pornography and film were intertwined, there are few clear examples of pornography shaping the development of cameras, projectors or other film equipment. And even though pornography is an inherent part of the content of early film, the producers did little to innovate, either in filming techniques or business practices.

For instance, Edison's Kinetoscope was almost immediately overshadowed by an alternative moving-picture technology created by French brothers Louis and Auguste Lumière. Their cinématographe succeeded not because burgeoning stag-film producers embraced it but for the more mundane reasons that it was smaller and cheaper and allowed films to be shown to larger audiences than the Kinetoscope. Pornographers naturally preferred this technology, but so did every other type of filmmaker.

In the early film era, the use of sexuality was more about remaining competitive than it was about the survival or evolution of the technology. Frederick S. Lane, in *Obscene Profits*, writes, "Within 15 years, filmmakers from around the world . . . were competing vigorously for audiences. As with photographers a half-century before, the idea occurred fairly quickly to filmmakers in a number of different countries (but particularly France) that filming and displaying nudity was a potentially lucrative activity." Women were undressing in films as early as 1896, and by the 1920s, Lane says, hard-core stag films had become a "cultural institution" in the United States.

Pornographers were certainly early adopters of moving pictures. Stags quickly became staples of all-male clubs and parties and remained so for the first half of the twentieth century. But in this case, hard-core material lagged behind the times. Joseph Slade knows of only one case of pornographers making a technological advance during this era.

"The film historian Terry Ramsaye records the story of the development of Kinemacolor, the first two-color process for motion picture stock," he relates in "Eroticism and Technological Regression." "According to Ramsaye, Charles Urban, the inventor of the process, got his idea when he encountered a man selling filthy pictures in the Tuileries in Paris. These pictures were unusual because they came in two parts: one was green, the other red. Separately, they revealed only an innocent man and woman. When the purchaser put one piece of celluloid on top of the other, however, the two people seemed to copulate. Urban rushed to his lab, combined two color filters and voila!—Kinemacolor."

Slade by no means discounts the connection between pornography and mass communication. "Early adopters of new communication technologies do seem to be motivated in part by sexual uses," he told me. But the pattern of pornographers making the technological and business-model tweaks necessary to make a new medium take off doesn't hold in this situation.

Dirty films of this era were primitive. Few had sound or colour. They were short—generally twelve minutes, the length of one spool of film—and formulaic in their technique and content. If a mike appeared in a shot, or somebody knocked a light stand over onto a set, or walked into the frame, the producers didn't edit it out. Quality control and pushing the technological envelope simply were not in the picture. There were no major changes or technological innovations to the stag film from the beginning of the century until the mid-1960s, when

8-mm and 16-mm film "loops"—films designed to play in end-less repetition—came on the scene.

Pornography as an engine of technological innovation appeared to stall in the early days of film, which is strange given the medium's seemingly ideal suitability to the subject matter. A number of factors contributed to this stagnation. First, hard-core films were so condemned at the time, and the legal conse-quences of making and selling them so dire, that producers kept them as simple as possible. Producers often developed porno-graphic film in makeshift tubs in people's homes to avoid being arrested taking such material to commercial labs. In addition, there was not a lot of money to be made from early adult films—stag reels weren't like videocassettes that could be sold and viewed discreetly. The high cost of film equipment meant that you needed a large viewing audience in order to make the venture worthwhile—usually a crowd at a private men's club. As a result, stag films came with inherently low profits on top of the high risks. It was still profitable to make such films, but not to the extent that the pornographers could influence the course of technological development.

In addition, the place of sexuality in American culture was changing. That allowed for directors to put more erotic material in mainstream cinema, even as completely explicit material faced increasingly tough persecution. Hard-core remained the exclusive purview of outlaws, while Hollywood studios were free to experiment with some very steamy sex scenes. The erot-icism that was so inherent in moving pictures found enough of an outlet in regular film to satisfy the more prurient market for this new medium. And although marginalization has sometimes sparked greater technological creativity among pornographers, in this case the oppressive consequences seem to have quashed the desire to innovate.

In the 1960s, stags stopped stagnating. Film technology was changing once again, and this time, pornographers would do more than get by—they would get rich. This was the start of the first golden age of pornography. This was when the industry began its true ascendance as a force of change in the world of communications technology.

There is one technology that it is hard to imagine ever made it big in the mainstream: a stand-alone booth. The patron closes and locks the door, then inserts a quarter into a slot. Two minutes of flickering 8-mm film project onto a small screen. Then the booth goes dark. More play? More pay.

Hardly the sort of thing one would use to watch *Star Wars*. Still, in its day the peep booth was its own kind of blockbuster technology. In the 1960s and '70s, it was a staple of the American pornography business—in fact, peeps marked the real start of the modern pornography industry.

Peeps, not unlike the Stanhopes that had gone by the same name a century earlier, started as novelty items. At carnivals and fairs across North America, they showed cartoons or exotica in brief bursts to paying crowds—at this point the screen was part of a stand-alone kiosk that was open for all to view. And, just as Stanhopes idled along in the erotic margins for decades before the technology found purchase in the mainstream, the pornographic peep booths of the 1960s are now leading the way toward ultramodern media distribution. Today's pornographers use the descendants of peep booths to sell and rent videos in new ways, while mainstream distribution companies play catch-up.

The simple innovation of enclosing a coin-operated film player in a private booth changed the business of pornography forever. The idea came from one of America's most notorious pornography entrepreneurs, an elusive multi-millionaire tax evader named Reuben Sturman. He stocked his peeps with twelve-minute repeating loops. No more did men have to gather with their friends and acquaintances to watch a stag together. It became technologically feasible to watch pornographic films alone. Sturman's innovation transformed the business of showing stag films from a public, barely profitable industry to a major national business built on millions of tiny cash transactions taking place behind thousands of closed doors. And in building his pornography empire, he invented the very concept of a porn mogul.

"The widespread introduction of peep machines in the late 1960s gave porn filmmakers access to a vast new market and created an unprecedented demand for new films," writes journalist Eric Schlosser in *Reefer Madness*, a book that includes a definitive account of the rise and fall of peeps. "Soon there were roughly fifty to seventy-five new peep loops being released every week. What had long been a hobby, or a sideline, or a way to earn a few extra dollars turned into an organized, profit-seeking activity, with investors, processing labs, and full-time employees—an adult film industry."

The profits were staggering: a loop cost about $8. The machinery was simple and reliable, meaning maintenance costs were low. Revenues could be anywhere from $2,000 to $10,000 a week. More than $2 billion worth of coins dropped into peep booths in the 1970s, and most of the profit ended up in Sturman's pockets. Peeps fuelled his enterprises, which expanded into an international empire of skin flicks, porn shops, film production, factories, sex-toy sales and much more. He was not a conscientious tax filer, which makes his earnings difficult to determine. (In 1989, he was convicted for evading $29 million in taxes and died in prison eight years later.) The most reliable estimates, according to Frederick Lane in *Obscene Profits*, suggest Sturman was making at least $1 million a day.

Unlike the Stanhope, which went on to have military and archival applications, the peep booth in its original form never really found purchase beyond its X-rated origins. Peeps would continue to make piles of money (literally, as the revenue was in quarters) for people like Reuben Sturman until the VCR one-upped it in terms of privacy of consumption. Not long after that, all pornographic roads started to lead to the Internet.

Peep booths still abound, usually in large urban centres—the demand for them has never quite gone away. They serve a market of people whose homes do not afford easy privacy, or who enjoy spur-of-the-moment pornography consumption. They also often function as cruising areas for casual gay and straight sex, as well as for prostitution.

And they have entered the digital age. Credit cards and pay-as-you-go passes replaced coin slots. Film loops are long gone, first replaced by banks of VCRs piped into phalanxes of private booths on a closed circuit, then by upgrades to DVD. At the 2009 Adult Entertainment Expo, several dealers were hawking purely digital services with touch-sensitive screens and the capacity for hundreds of films to be accessed from a single hard drive.

Today, not only are the user interfaces high-tech but the back-end software gives booth owners second-by-second data about which films—and even which parts of films—are heavily accessed and which are ignored. The technology allows them to dynamically swap out less popular films for new additions and to give greater prominence to big sellers. Today's peep booth effectively allows owners to do real-time market research and adjust their product lineup accordingly.

Peeps have evolved even further, going beyond a pay-by-the-minute model to feature new means of buying and renting entire films. A booth at the 2009 Adult Entertainment Expo featured a video-distribution and sex-toy vending booth called the FlashNGo. This next-generation kiosk allows you to preview and buy adult DVDs on the spot. The FlashNGo is an advanced version of the Redbox kiosks and similar devices that populate grocery and convenience stores across North America. The Redbox is a vending machine that takes credit cards or coins and dispenses DVDs for rent or sale. The FlashNGo does this as well, but it also has ports that allow users to rent or buy movies using USB flash drives. This is the "flash" in FlashNGo (or so I hope). The booth also dispenses dildos, condoms, lubricants and so forth.

Lance Ablin, the man behind the FlashNGo, is tall and lean, and not particularly flashy. He has an angular face framed by a goatee and a ball cap in the same shade of grey. Dressed in a black cloth jacket and dark jeans, he looked tougher and more guarded than your average tech entrepreneur.

As soon as I mentioned the word "technology" to him, though, it became clear that I was speaking to a man who had thought a great deal about the relationship between pornography and communications. He said he had missed the boat on previous innovations and did not intend to let it happen again.

In the mid-nineties, he said, "I was told, 'This coming Christmas the biggest gift will be a DVD player.' And I said 'bullshit.' Well, they were right." As an entrepreneur, and as a consumer, he arrived late to this new technology. But he also saw another important shift coming down the pipe. DVDs were an optical medium—information was stored on discs in a form that could be read via laser light. Ablin foresaw that digital media like computer hard drives and flash drives would surpass optical. This time he would not be left behind. For him, being on the cutting edge meant dealing in pornography.

Ablin was aware that the mainstream, non-adult market does not allow digital downloads because they are worried about losing control of the digital rights management, or DRM— they're afraid of copyright infringement and computer piracy. He recognized, though, that mainstream software and enter- tainment companies would ultimately find solutions to DRM issues. In fact, he was counting on it. He aimed the FlashNGo at the pornography market not just to make money quickly but also to stake out the territory for when the rest of the world came calling.

"As we pioneer this in the adult sector, we hope in the near future that the major mainstream studios will get involved— that they'll see this shift and want to get in on it and we'll be at the forefront. We're out there. We're testing and proving up, we're KISS"—keep it simple, stupid—"compliant, we're safe with a credit card, all those sorts of things. So they will hope- fully embrace us with both arms.

"In the meantime, we're doing adult industry. Adult has been reaching out to us to have this Flash format because they get it. They get it quick."

The FlashNGo is very slick, but not seamless. Although it is easy to transfer a movie file to a flash drive, you still have to go online with the device you'll be watching it on, in order to get an access code. When you buy a film, the code unlocks the file completely. When you rent it, you specify the number of days you want it, and the code will disable the film at the end of the allotted time. That means you do not have to return a disc to the store. In addition to extolling this as green technology—one fewer trip to the movie kiosk, no money or carbon fuels wasted manufacturing and distributing DVDs across the country, no packaging—Ablin says it's also a more honest business model than standard rentals, which he firmly believes rely on revenue from people who forget to return their discs.

The back end is equally sophisticated, tracking movie downloads along with sales from the vending-machine section. Digital downloads also allow for a greater number of available titles—the physical size of the kiosk itself would limit the number of DVDs on board.

Other conveniences are of special importance to porn consumers, Ablin says. "What's unique about this is that it's a very discreet viewing method. More people watch adult than would like to admit, so this can play easily on a laptop, your cellphone or any other USB devices. You can buy any kind of flash drive, and you've got your movies on here and you can go watch it on your lunch break on your laptop. And if you're taking a trip, you've got it right there."

In fifty years, the peep-show booth evolved from a niche technology with precisely one economically viable purpose to a media-distribution system that is, at least for a short while, occupying the space that mainstream distribution outlets are slower to reach.

"We've answered a lot of questions by doing this," Ablin said. "And as this gets proven in the adult industry, it's very important for mainstream. The mainstream Hollywood studios will say, 'Well, it works there, so we better embrace it.'"

I contacted a Redbox representative to find out whether the company had plans to offer Flash-based videos at their kiosks. The response reminded me of Larry Kasanoff's line about pornographers already making money while the mainstream is still musing. "Redbox cannot speculate on the future," said spokesperson Christopher Goodrich, "but the company continues to monitor the industry and evaluate consumer behavior to make informed decisions moving forward."

This makes entirely good sense. One of the laments I repeatedly heard at the Adult Expo concerned the dearth of market research in the adult industry. The only way the industry has to "evaluate consumer behaviour" is to put a product like the FlashNGo on the market and see what happens. A more mainstream company like Redbox (which does not stock X-rated movies) has the luxury of being able to do market research, and thus avoid unnecessary risk. But this luxury comes at the expense of being the last out the door with a new content-delivery system. In some ways, Lance Ablin is conducting the focus groups that will help Redbox determine how to proceed.

The Format War

P eep booths and Stanhope lenses exemplify one major way that pornography can help shape communications. Pornography created the primary market for each of these specialized technologies, then maintained those markets and kept them viable for decades until unforeseen mainstream applications ultimately emerged.

Yet porn has had a much more pronounced impact on many other innovations in communications, especially beginning in the second half of the twentieth century. One of the most famous stories has to do with the VCR. A myth has grown up around this technology that is often cited as the quintessential example of the power of porn. Unfortunately, the story that's usually told is untrue.

The format war, as it came to be called, began three years after the release of the quasi-mainstream X-rated film *Deep Throat* and three years before the first multi-player online role-playing game would create a medium for cybersex. In 1975, a battle began that would be waged over a matter of years. It would pit mediocrity against greatness, quality against marketing, and elite electronics enthusiasts against oblivious consumers. This was the battle of VHS vs. Betamax.

Mediocrity won.

This long-ago, far-away contest between two videotape formats still provokes passion and has relevance to this day even though videotape technology itself is already six kinds of obsolete.

The old legend still gets told: that the pornography industry settled the Format War; that porn producers chose VHS over Beta—mediocrity over quality—and that mainstream media companies had no choice but to follow suit. According to this story, the adult industry liked the VHS tape's longer playing time and didn't care that Beta had better sound and picture quality. Since porn accounted for the vast majority of the early video sales and rental market, porn consumers set VHS on a course toward dominance and sent Betamax the way of the Kinetoscope.

References to this myth can be found in every subsequent account of porn's technological influence, from the first commercial ventures on the Internet to more recent format wars (HD DVD vs. Blu-ray, for example). The format war made the porn industry's reputation as a driver of communications technology. A genuine phenomenon was given credibility by a false claim. The format war was a real battle, but it was not decided climactically.

Paul Saffo was for two decades a professor at the Institute for the Future in Palo Alto, and is currently at Stanford University. He has been writing about communications technology for all that time, and is one of the most respected and quoted forecasters in Silicon Valley. He can readily rhyme off his own favourite examples of pornographers as early adopters—the first thing he mentioned to me was a (now defunct) museum in Cincinnati with an excellent collection of old pornographic playing cards.

The VHS format is not on his list of porn-driven media. "One of the problems with the format war story is that it didn't really emerge until a good fifteen years after the fact," he told me. "That's a reasonable indicator that it is more myth than fact."

Saffo is not alone. Whereas his expertise comes from studying media history, technophile Ray Glasser's comes from living it. Glasser was deep in the trenches during the format war. He bought his first Betamax machine in 1976, for $1,260. Today, he still has an entire room devoted to his collection of more than 2,500 Beta tapes and players from many eras and in varying states of repair.

I first saw Ray's name on the Ultimate Betamax Information Guide! website, which he runs. A notice in big red letters on the page said, "We are on YouTube!! . . . With various Betamax commercials, camera videos of Betamax VCRs, etc. Since my username is constantly changing (I've had 6 accounts already, and some of them have been suspended!), do a Search for 'Betamax' and 'Ray Glasser' together in the YouTube Search box, and you'll be able to view the videos!" (I found out later that Ray gets banned for posting copyrighted material to the site—mostly digitized versions of stuff from his Beta collection. His disregard for copyright goes back to the early days of Beta. In the 1970s and '80s, he used to go to "conventions" where he and other Beta enthusiasts would hole up at a hotel and spend the weekend dubbing each other's tapes to round out their collections.)

Ray clearly remembers those crucial early days. "In the beginning, about 50 per cent of the first Beta rentals—and we're talking 1978–79 when video stores came on the scene—were pornos. That was a huge part of the market, and Beta had a big part of that market because they were still the dominant format," he said. In fact, he contends that in those early days, *more* porn, not less, was available on Beta.

If facts and anecdotes are not convincing enough, the truth of the format war is deducible from pure logic. One of the demonstrable qualities of pornography is that it will find an outlet wherever, whenever and in whatever medium it is humanly possible to put it. If people are willing to put naked women on ball caps, balloons and ballpoint pens, if for forty thousand years people have been drawing naughty pictures on cave walls and in bathroom stalls, if you can buy penis-shaped pasta at a premium price, does it really make sense that the adult moviemakers would shy away from Betamax simply because they could initially put only an hour of material onto a tape?

It doesn't. And they didn't.

Another equally false version of the legend has it that Sony scuppered its own Beta format by banning adult content from its tapes. True, Sony didn't produce pornographic titles itself, but it had no control over what third parties might do with its tapes.

An early ad in *Videography* magazine reveals the truth about the format war, touting "The largest selection of Adult rated video cassettes in New York . . . Sweetheart's Video Centers . . . we stock Quality X in both Betamax and VHS formats!!"

In the early days of the war, porn was widely available in both formats. The success of VHS had little to do with porn, and much to do with marketing and timing of upgrades.

One of the odd things about the passions inflamed by the format war is that they continue to this day, even though the VCR is by any modern standard a lacklustre medium. Technologically speaking, the videocassette is nothing more than a wound strip of iron-oxide-coated Mylar, stored on a pair of spindles inside a plastic box. Even in its own day, it hardly marked a major leap forward, given its close antecedents, reel-to-reel tapes and audiocassettes.

In fact, videotape recorders had been in use commercially since 1956, when inventors Charles Ginsburg and Ray Milton Dolby (later of Surround Sound fame) developed them. They shook up the world of broadcasters then as they would the consumer market twenty years later. Before this watershed moment, all television was broadcast live. With the new technology, recorded television, which could be edited, quickly took over.

The technology came with a hefty cost: the Mark IV, the first recorder good enough to sell, went for $45,000. It was unveiled at a meeting of about two hundred CBS affiliates in Chicago in 1956. Despite the price tag, eighty-two of them sold in the first year.

Twenty years later, Betamax did for the home viewer what the Mark IV had done for the networks: it brought newfound freedom and flexibility (but still for a hefty price). In 1975, it became possible to record live television and play it back whenever you wanted.

Old-school as it might now seem, time-shifting marked a fundamental change in how people consumed television and movies. It was the first major crack in the monolithic mass medium of broadcast TV. It swiped the Play button out from underneath the corporate thumb of the broadcasters and repositioned it where individual media consumers could hit it whenever they wanted. In so doing, it set us on a direct trajectory toward the fractured media universe we live in today. Time-shifting was one of three major revolutions sparked by the VCR.

It wasn't just about time-shifting, though. It was also about choice.

Sony introduced the Betamax VCR in May 1975. The early advertisements made up for a lack of concision with an abundance of enthusiasm. "Now you don't have to miss *Kojak* because you're watching *Columbo* (or vice versa)!" one ad exclaimed. In his book *From Betamax to Blockbuster*, Joshua M. Greenberg, the director of digital strategy and scholarship at the New York Public Library, recounts how this slogan led to a twelve-year legal battle between Sony and Universal Pictures, the latter of which happened to produce both TV shows. Sony's Betamax represented a new kind of consumer choice and power. The studios were unhappy both because they were losing control over who watched what when and because with taped shows, people could fast-forward through the ads.

Soon, though, consumers faced a choice even more difficult than Telly Savalas vs. Peter Falk. Sony was the first to market with a videocassette recorder, but it didn't have much of a lead. Japan Victor Company quickly entered the scene with its competing product, known as the Video Home System. The JVC VHS VCR hit stores in Europe and Asia in 1976 and came to America in 1977. The war had begun. Consumers faced a major risk: here was a new technology that was expensive, unfamiliar and full of strange new three-letter acronyms. With expensive equipment and no clearly dominant format, investing in the wrong technology meant consumers might have spent a lot of time and money on dead-end equipment.

All of this meant that the VCR was far from a shoo-in for commercial success. Even the initial marketers of the VCR weren't sure what they had on their hands. Sony pitched its device strictly as a time-shifting tool—a solution to the *Kojak–Columbo* tug-of-war.

Time-shifting, though, would not be the primary driver of early VCR adoption. People were used to watching TV when their show was on. A tech-savvy guy like Ray Glasser might use the technology that way, but for most people, the iconic symbol of early VCR usage was the flashing "12:00" on the front of the box, a glowing reminder of the near-universal inability to so much as set the clock, let alone program the machine to record a television show.

The real draw of the VCR would turn out to be the rental and purchase of factory-produced videotapes. But even this was not an immediate mainstream success. People liked going out to the movies. A select group of cineastes, though, were interested in a very specific type of movie that they could only fully enjoy with a solo viewing. So it was that pornographic movies led the VCR revolution. They were not quite the first out the door, but they were the ones that threw it open wide and changed forever the nature of media consumption. They proved the market.

In 1976, a bright light named Andre Blay approached the major Hollywood studios with a proposal to release their movies on prepackaged videotapes for home consumption. His initial mail-order business did not deal in adult films, though it did offer the advantage of supplying uncut, unedited versions of Hollywood films that were unavailable on television. His business demonstrated sufficient demand for prepackaged videos— within a year, videos were driving VCR sales rather than the other way around—that retailers were willing to buy in. "Arthur Morowitz, a New York video distributor . . . took the next logical step," writes Greenberg. "In May 1978, Morowitz opened his first Video Shack store at 49th and Broadway with an inventory of 600 titles (the majority X-rated) and no VCRs."

While mainstream movie theatres saw the VCR as a threat to their trade, porn cinemas became early adopters, savvily expanding their business into the home market to compensate for their declining cinema revenues. Porn consumers exploded the demand for videotape and machine rentals. They were a ready-made market comprising individuals who wanted to watch adult movies in the privacy of their own home.

In 1979, less than one per cent of American households owned a videocassette recorder. How could VCR companies survive with such dismal market penetration? It was thanks to pornography consumers, who were willing to pay top dollar for both the machines and the tapes. That premium helped offset the small size of the market, and keep it viable for everyone from VCR manufacturers to local rental stores.

"Every independent video store—this was before Blockbuster got the whole thing for themselves—they had a back room full of porn," said Glasser. "I remember in the early seventies, I saw people with their 16-mm or 8-mm films of porn they showed in their apartments. So obviously, if you get a nice videocassette format for the masses, hey, there's the porn. It's a much easier way to watch it and to get it."

It was a tremendous boon to the VCR market to have this ready-made audience of (mostly) men who were willing to pay a premium for a new technology that allowed them to watch stag films at home. Pornographers had even more going for them, though. With six decades' worth of stags, loops and peeps at their disposal, plus many recent big-budget adult features, the porn industry had a huge stock of product that was easily transferred to videotape and could sell at an astounding price—as much as $300 per cassette. This was enough for investors to take the plunge and build the infrastructure that would be used by pornography and non-pornography con-sumers alike. Those kinds of prices were enough to keep the business and the technology moving forward—even while

99 per cent of American homes were not yet part of the VCR market.

Texas A & M University history professor Jonathan Coopersmith has done much research on the nexus of pornography and communications technology. He backs up with academic rigour what Ray Glasser knows from experience. "The VCR," he writes in "Sex, Vibes and Videotape," "is an excellent example of how a niche market can accelerate the diffusion of an expensive new technology. Pornography played a major role in the initial years of VCRs by providing customers with a product, and, at the same time, justification for acquiring costly equipment. VCR buyers in the late 1970s and early 1980s comprised a challenging market. Not only was the equipment very costly, but two incompatible formats . . . were jousting for market superiority so users had to risk buying a format that might soon disappear."

There was another reason pornographers were quick to adopt VCRs. At the same time this new technology was coming on market, community and legal backlash against porn cinemas was on the rise. They were easy targets, vulnerable to zoning ordinances and licensing restrictions that could not touch the VCR markets. Precisely as a result of their marginality, porn producers embraced the risks inherent in adopting a new technology.

Meanwhile, mainstream cinema couldn't yet wrap their heads around this new format. They had a business model built on the major studios, distribution networks and movie houses— that's how Hollywood worked. Mainstream theatres remained wedded to the traditional cinema-based movie experience and refused to evolve with the technology. The signs of change all had glowing triple Xs on them.

As Joshua Greenberg writes, "The one sort of theater that did embrace the new medium with open arms was the adult movie theater, in whose lobbies or adjacent storefronts video became a prominent fixture." Whatever else you say about the pornography industry, it has the ability to change with the times.

Not only was it quicker in with the new, it was also quicker out with the old. In a time of rapid adaptation, some species die out. So it went with porn cinemas. Today, mainstream cinema has adapted much more successfully to the video revolution than have adult movie houses. When home video went mainstream, cinemas started bleeding money. But they fought back with new sound systems, stadium seating, fancier food and other innovations that are tough to replicate in the average home theatre. Hollywood was slow to adapt, but it has so far managed to keep its hand in the game.

Porn cinemas, on the other hand, could offer little that would draw in customers who sought a solitary, or at least private, experience. The VCR killed the porn movie theatre. The technology had come back to bite the hand that pushed it forward.

Of course, the video market did broaden. Thanks in great part to Morowitz and thousands of other X-rated cassette hawkers, VCRs survived long enough for their quality to improve, for prices to drop and for mainstream audiences to familiarize themselves with the new medium. By 1985, the adult video market was approaching $1 billion a year. Prices of players and tapes were both dropping, and by 1988, 60 per cent of Americans owned a VCR. By 1998, it was up to 87 per cent.

As the video rental market grew, it became possible to make a go in the business without relying on pornography. The first Blockbuster video store opened in 1985, in Dallas, Texas. It grew into a massive international chain of "family friendly" video stores, which did not carry hard-core pornographic films (though even Blockbuster relied on soft-core series such as *The Red Shoe*

Diaries for its revenue). Pornography was not entirely scrubbed from the video rental scene, though. Independent mom-and-pop video stores across North America found that the only way they could compete against Blockbuster was by stocking more adult flicks for sale or rental.

Independent video retailers in the United States reported in 1999 that, while adult titles might make up a third or less of their stock, they accounted for as much as two-thirds of their revenue. That same year, the National Association of Video Distributors reported that 1,400 independent video stores went out of business, the vast majority of which had opted not to stock adult titles. (This number was only for non-adult or mixed stores. Thousands of other retail outlets dealt exclusively with the sale and rental of adult films.)

Once pornography had created the market for VCRs, once families got into the habit of renting wholesome features, then and only then did the mainstream start to discern how it too could profit from a device that had at first seemed like a terrible threat.

Porn sparked one other video revolution, but this one had to do with media production rather than consumption. Traditional filmmaking was—and is—an expensive and highly specialized field. Along with the video players, though, came video cameras, which recorded to tape cassette rather than film. Suddenly, you needed neither Steven Spielberg's talent nor his money to make your own movies. Sony introduced a home-market camcorder in 1983, and by 1990 it was selling three million of them every year.

Not only were camcorders relatively cheap and portable but they also came with automated features that simplified some of the trickier aspects of a shoot. The two most important of these improvements were an autofocus and the ability to adjust for low-light situations—both useful to those who wanted to shoot sex scenes. Porn makers were very adaptable to new and cheaper ways of creating product. Professional pornographers started churning out exponentially more movies for far less money than had been possible with any previous technology. And they were joined by a new force in porn: the amateur. The camcorder meant that couples could record themselves in the privacy of their own bedroom, and never have to worry about the prying eyes at a film processing studio. Conversely, if someone, as many did, *wanted* other people to see the video, distribution was also easily accomplished with this new technology.

One need only look at the number of adult films created in the United States to see how ever-decreasing technological impediments drew in new producers, directors and performers. About a hundred porn features were made in 1976. In 1996, about eight thousand new titles were released. (For 2008, estimates vary, but gravitate toward thirteen thousand. This figure, though, is complicated by the massive repackaging business in which scenes from different movies are mixed and matched, or re-edited for a different hardness of core and released as a new title.)

One way and another, the VCR was a technology quite literally made for pornography. All those amateur porn tapes helped foster a shift in the public consciousness as well—it dawned on people that anybody could make a movie. The great democratization that began with amateur pornographic videotapes would reach its zenith (and some would argue its nadir) with websites like YouTube, where neither technology nor talent poses any barrier to moviemaking.

So, while porn didn't determine the winner of the Format War, it did create the initial market without which there might have been nothing to fight over. Porn was responsible for the early adoption of the VCR itself, regardless of whether consumers went with VHS or Beta. This was a power shift. Pornography had always been influential, but with the VCR it came into its own as an economic and technological powerhouse.

People who worked in the adult industry at the time were just starting to get a sense of the influence they now wielded.

"There was an awareness. I think we all knew," said former porn actress turned iconic erotica producer Candida Royalle. "Wholesalers and retailers needed product. And so we were aware that it was our industry that was really fostering the development and expansion of the VCR."

Royalle performed in about twenty-five porn movies in the 1970s, before going on to create her own company, Femme Productions. She was paying particular attention to the advances in video technology, as they helped her carve out a niche in the adult market: erotic movies aimed at women and couples. The porn industry at the time doubted the potential for such films, yet today many producers and distributors cite "women and couples" as the demographic with the biggest growth potential. In a phone conversation, Royalle recounted to me how she realized that with this new technology, erotica no longer had to follow the same old patterns.

"I had grown up in art schools. Nude modelling was not a big deal, even though I was actually very bashful, which one wouldn't expect in this industry. I went looking for nude modelling and the agent asked me if I would consider being in an adult movie. I guess he probably called it a porno movie. I was horrified and insulted and I stormed out. But my boyfriend at the time, who was a musician, said, 'Well gee, interesting. I think

I'll try it.' He got a lead role in a very high-end Anthony Spinelli film called *Cry for Cindy.*

"I went and watched what it was like and I was really surprised by the level of professionalism and the respect shown on the set. It wasn't some little sleazy home job. It was a pretty decent shoot at the time when they used to spend money on them. So I was impressed. I was very much for free love and experimental sexuality and I thought, 'Well you know this isn't so bad. I don't think sex is dirty or bad. The money is great. Why not? I'm going to try it.' And that's what I did.

"But over time I became put off because I felt the majority of the films really were not creative. They weren't sensual. They weren't lovely. They didn't reflect female desires at all or what sex really could be between people. And I began to get uncomfortable with being part of it."

The pornography-driven demand for new content opened up the possibility of greater variety in the product. Both with pornography and mainstream, media markets were fragmenting, giving people like Royalle a chance to find a niche and scratch it. The stag films, peeps and porn features that had preceded video all relied on an almost exclusively male market. New technology changed all that.

"The VCR allowed you to watch it in the safety and comfort of your own home," Royalle said. "It gave people a private place rather than having to go sit in a grimy public place. That privacy was the only way women were going to start exploring this type of movie."

Her then father-in-law, a Swede named Store Sjöstedt who had made his fortune producing spaghetti westerns for Paramount Pictures, had gone on to finance a few big-budget X-rated features, including *Roommates* and *Games Women Play.* Both films were released in 1981 and were part of a wave of such movies made with the aim of integrating pornography into mainstream culture. This trend began with *Deep Throat* (1972), *Behind the Green Door* (1972), *The Devil in Miss Jones* (1973) and a handful of other hard-core movies that played in regular cinemas. Despite the proliferation of pornographic businesses in the Internet age, the *Deep Throat* era is still known as the golden age of porn. With terms like "porno chic" finding a place in *The New York Times* and other reputable publications, the golden age reflected a sense of acceptance that was even more important than how much money these films were making. This trend did not last long. The inevitable backlash drove these films back into the porn cinemas, and increasingly onto videocassette.

Royalle's father-in-law gave her her first VCR—a huge, clunky machine that was state-of-the-art at the time. "I got my idea for Femme just a couple of years after that. I recognized that women are curious. I was a feminist back in college and we were very pro-sex. And that combined with the advent of the VCR and cable TV gave me a safe place to look. That's really what motivated me."

Though she got out of performing, the experience remained with her. "It didn't go away. On a couple of different levels I was bothered by the fact that even though I thought I was perfectly fine to do it—I wasn't hurting anyone—there was a little voice in me that was feeling some amount of embarrassment and shame over it. I didn't want to drag that around with me. I've always been very analytical by nature. I thought, I have to explore this and find out why this is an issue for me. Why do I have two voices here? I went into therapy with a very bright woman and worked through all of this stuff and I realized that I had to try to separate myself from societal norms and try to judge myself.

"I don't want to feel this way because society tells me to feel this way. I want to judge for myself whether I did something that I should feel bad about. And so I really tried to look at it from a historical perspective. From the cave etchings and drawings and the history of erotic expression and art. Is it bad? And what about modern-day pornography? Is this something bad? Have I done something really terrible? Did I harm my sisters in the movement?

"I did come to the conclusion that there really is nothing wrong with performing sexually for other people to enjoy viewing, that it has been done historically, that humans have always been very curious to look at each other and look at sexual, erotic situations. Whether it's art or just clumsy drawings, I think it's just human nature."

That didn't mean that she was going to continue the pornographic tradition of portraying women as insatiable objects who can never get enough penetration. She had seen which way the wind was blowing, and the same demand that drove the successful launch of the VCR allowed her to continue to make erotic films, and to find a market for products that did not make her feel ashamed.

This was the third revolution that pornography sparked: it helped drive a new technology that allowed people, first within the adult industry and then beyond, gain greater control and freedom over the media they produced and consumed. This revolution happened independent of the format war, which was settled for reasons that are far from the stuff of legends.

"In the early 1980s, Beta's format began to dwindle as far as market share," Ray Glasser told me. "The rest of the world got VHS because the machines were cheaper, the tapes were cheaper, they ran longer than Beta, and all their friends got VHS."

Both camps improved their product—longer tapes, better picture and sound, more features, lower prices. But JVC's VHS simply hit the right technological notes at the right time. And once the balance started to tip toward VHS, there was no turning back. Video stores had every interest in settling the matter quickly so that they would no longer have to stock copies of every movie and TV show in both formats, and stock two kinds of players for rental. "The video stores started carrying fewer and fewer titles in Beta and more and more in VHS," said Glasser. "There was a time when video stores had a small Beta room, and the rest of the store was VHS. Then a couple of shelves were devoted to Beta, then Beta vanished from the video stores entirely." It was as simple as that. No conspiracy of pornographers, no debilitating prohibition from Sony. Just the right features at the right time to have the format war go JVC's way.

For some, the debate will never truly be over. Reports from *Macworld* to *Forbes* still repeat the mantra that when it came to home movie formats, as went the porn industry, so went the rest of us. But the reality is that porn was not the determining factor in the format war. VHS won because of better timing and better marketing.

It is strange that so many people still cling to this myth when pornography's actual claim to fame is even greater: it was instrumental in the successful launch of the VCR itself, irrespective of the format war.

"U" Tube

Throughout the second half of the twentieth century, pornography's reputation as a driver of technology grew. It was only a matter of time before mainstream entrepreneurs also began to factor it into their business models. Erotic material was not the only way to draw people into a new medium—exclusive coverage of a moon landing or royal wedding might just garner enough eyeballs to get a technology off the ground—but few new-media pioneers had the start-up funds to launch a new service with this kind of "killer event."

The ascension of the VCR had proven that pornography could make the difference between success and failure for a new technology. Porn was one of the most effective and least expensive ways of persuading people to try something new. In the 1970s, there was plenty of competition for the attention of early adopters of various technologies. In the United States, a branch of the military called the Advanced Research Projects Agency was using a proto-Internet technology called ARPAnet. In 1970,

Germany demonstrated the first videodisc (another contender for home movie viewing). That same year, Pittsburgh began offering picturephone service, and the large-format IMAX film technology was invented.

In 1972, Home Box Office launched the first pay-TV service, and satellites were first used to transmit television signals; in England, the BBC launched a two-way cable information service called Ceefax; and Xerox created the first graphical user interface for computers. In 1973, computer terminals began popping up on the desks of newspaper editors and reporters. In 1974, the first ROM chips were installed, in the arcade video game Tank. Microsoft was founded in 1975 by Bill Gates and Paul Allen. In 1976, Apple started selling its first home computer (though the first Macintosh was still eight years away). Japan launched the world's first cellphone network in 1979, which was also the year Sony launched the Walkman portable tape player.

The explosion of communications technology was both exciting and chaotic. With so many new media and competing applications emerging at once, there was no way all could survive. For budget-strapped mavericks and entrepreneurs trying to innovate in the mainstream, pornography could sometimes be a means to an end. It could give the boost needed to move a new medium from unknown to phenomenon.

Concurrent with this technological maelstrom was an upheaval in social values—not just a revolution in sexuality but also urbanization, new ideas about cultural and ethnic diversity, and the growing influence of younger voices in the media. One of the people who was at the global forefront in this time of great change was a young player on the Canadian television scene named Moses Znaimer. In the early 1970s, he had bold ideas about how television might better reflect a modern, sophisticated, multicultural city like Toronto. He felt that urban audiences were ready for smart, playful news and entertainment that reflected and respected their intelligence, diversity and sophistication.

Unfortunately, there was no place in the traditional television world where he could develop these ideas. To realize his vision, he had to break away from standard channels and persuade people to use a new television technology. Znaimer was working with a limited budget, but he had a low-cost idea that he believed would entice people to try this new medium: pornography.

Znaimer first tried to develop his brand of modern urban programming at the country's national public broadcaster, the Canadian Broadcasting Corporation. The CBC, a massive, bureaucratic organization, could not or would not push into new territory quickly enough for Znaimer. He departed for the private sector and launched his own television station, called Citytv. One of the first challenges he faced was to find an unoccupied spot on the frequency band for City to broadcast. At the time, Toronto was the world's most competitive television market, with local, regional and national channels from both Canada and the United States crowding the dial. All the spots on the traditional VHF (very high frequency) dial were occupied by the major networks and other established channels. The only broadcast real estate Znaimer could find was in a barely known bandwidth range known as UHF, for ultra-high frequency. Televisions had only recently begun shipping with UHF tuners, and most viewers had no idea what this extra dial on the front of their set was for—and no interest in finding out.

"It was the first commercial U," said Znaimer. We were talking in a boardroom at the head office of his current media empire (which is built around active baby boomers, whom Znaimer dubs Zoomers). "People had to be educated, they had to be convinced."

Znaimer needed to draw people away from the VHF channels 1 through 13 up into the exotic territory of UHF channel 79. This involved more than just changing the channel. UHF technology was fussy: while the VHF selector clicked definitively from station to station, UHF required fine tuning just like a poor-quality radio. It may not sound like much of a hardship, but it's notoriously difficult to jolt people out of a familiar, simple means of media consumption to take a chance on something new. Znaimer required a "killer event" to get people over the hump: something like a Super Bowl game, the Stanley Cup playoffs, the Summer Olympics, a presidential inauguration. Such mega-events, though, cost millions, and even if he had had the resources, no organization in its right mind would award the rights to such an event to an unknown television channel. Znaimer was left with only one solution.

"Sex was the thing that motivated people to think, 'What's a UHF station?'"

Znaimer's Citytv was the first local, urban, ethnically diverse TV station in North America—it was a shift in concept as well as technology. Because the idea was brand new, Znaimer drew in viewers by airing, every Friday night, erotic films on a program known as "Baby Blue Movies." Soft-core pornography was Znaimer's killer event. And it was far more effective than a Super Bowl.

"Today's perspective is that porn is a legitimate marketplace," Znaimer told me. "Vast billions are at stake and so major investments can be made, sometimes even for tasteful, beautiful, sort of glossy or erotic things. In 1972, material was quite grotty and fairly difficult to come by. I was determined to do it, and I knew

I needed provocative marketing, so I thought I'd call it 'The Blue Movie' just flat outright. Then with a week to go, Marilyn Lightstone, my gal [and now wife], said to me, 'Now c'mon. You're not really planning to show hard X, right?' And I said, 'Of course not,' and she said, 'Well, truth in advertising, it's not blue, maybe it's baby blue.' She used the words Baby Blue, and I grabbed that."

Overall, Citytv's early viewership was so low that the ratings books didn't even assign a figure—just a hash mark to say that the numbers were not statistically significant. But all over Toronto—Canada's largest city—during the two-hour period starting at midnight Friday, fully two-thirds of the television viewing public were tuned to the soft-core films showing on channel 79. (Znaimer suspects the real number was even higher, given people's propensity to under-report porn consumption.) Success was instant and overwhelming, though it would take a little while for profit to follow.

"There was undoubtedly demand," Znaimer said. "I'm just saying that it wasn't the financial basis for an empire."

Despite stellar ratings, erotica repelled rather than attracted national sponsors. That was fine, though; Znaimer was not interested in becoming a porn mogul. He just needed these early UHF adopters to overcome the technological barrier and get used to tuning in on Friday nights. Baby Blue viewers therefore formed the initial market for everything else Citytv had to offer. When significant numbers of people then started watching Citytv during some of the other 166 hours of the week, advertising revenue started to roll in.

Pornography was the draw that allowed Znaimer to make money from other sources, and empowered Citytv to change how broadcasters around the world viewed programming, especially for urban audiences. Znaimer broke down the divide between the station and the community it served—the faces on screen were younger, more diverse, and more connected to the lifeblood of the city than anything that had been seen on TV before. He put female journalists into non-traditional roles. News was reported by lone videographers rather than camera crews. This was a major money saver, but it also made the news feel more fresh and raw. He started something called "Speakers' Corner," a coin-operated television booth where ordinary citizens could speak their mind for a minute or two. This was a democratization of broadcast television, allowing the video-taped rants, love letters and deep thoughts of any Torontonian to find their way on air.

The Citytv model has been imitated and emulated in many parts of the world, with the station's own brand licensed in Colombia and Spain. Znaimer became a millionaire. He never earned much from erotica, but without it, he never could have made his mainstream fortune.

When I asked Znaimer why he thought pornography had this special power to push people toward new media, he looked at me as though I must be a little bit simple.

"The 'why' is it's built into our creation, it's God's Great Gift, it's the world's most interesting subject, it's fucking," he said. "Fucking is fun and fucking is forbidden in many cultures, lots of religions seek to control it, and so the social strictures can sometimes be extremely grievous for long periods of time. So, at every stage, as soon as people can make symbols, create pictures, they make pictures of fucking. So, it's the abiding, fabulous thing. Think of where human life would be if we didn't eat and we didn't fuck. The answer is, there is so much cultural confinement of this natural impulse, it has to find expression in art or in some kind of media reproduction. And then, since the history of media is about getting closer and closer to the real thing, the interest in sex and the utility of sex in leading that charge will never be exhausted."

Today, tuning in to channel 79 does not sound particularly extravagant. With hundreds of channels available via cable and satellite television, anything in the double digits is pretty small potatoes. In its early days, though, cable television faced even greater hurdles than UHF. It required more than fiddling with an extra dial—users had to acquire an entirely separate device: a cable box. Cable television had actually been sputtering along since 1948, having begun as a means of bringing TV signals to places that broadcast could not reach. In the 1970s it was still a medium of questionable potential. Many people said it made no sense to pay a fee for cable programming when broadcast television was free. That changed only when pornography entered the frame, swiftly overcoming decades of technological inertia.

In 1972, the Federal Communications Commission decreed that all Americans should and would have the right to produce their own cable television programs. (Or at least, all Americans in the 100 largest cable TV markets.) Access to the means of production and airtime would henceforth be provided to the public, to ensure that this relatively new medium, which the FCC called an "electronic soapbox," would be accessible to all, regardless of economic status, political bent or skill.

The FCC had recognized that cable TV was different from broadcast TV. The fact that its signals went through wires, rather than through the air, made it a fundamentally different kind of medium.

First, cable TV provided new choice. That choice came in part because cable vastly increased the number of available channels. For the first time, programs that had aired in other geographic regions could be piped through cables into new markets, meaning that New Yorkers could watch shows that had previously been available only to Angelenos (and vice versa). It also vastly increased the number of potential channels, which led to great demand for new content—shows created expressly for cable.

Increased variety was one thing, but the real choice people had, the one that made a qualitative rather than just a quantitative difference, was this: they could decide whether to subscribe to a cable service at all. Because of the nature of traditional broadcast television, you couldn't own a TV without having NBC, CBS and ABC enter your home. With great ubiquity comes great responsibility—thanks to combined pressure from the public, the government and the advertisers, broadcast networks kept the airwaves clean and pure. No sex, no swearing, no controversial content that might cause viewers (or worse, their televisions) to get turned off.

Cable television worked differently. If you chose not to subscribe, the signal did not enter your home. This meant that standards for cable shows could be more relaxed than those for broadcast. Couple that with the FCC's requirement that any member of the public could step up to the camera and put a show on air, essentially on a first-come, first-serve basis, and the results were entirely predictable. Pornographers, swingers and exhibitionists all started doing their thing on public-access TV.

The 1970s were an experimental time for both sex and technology. This was not coincidence. It's easy to see how faster, broader and more specialized communications technologies affected pornography consumption. There was a steady trend toward cheaper and easier means of making, duplicating, distributing, selling and buying the material. But the influence went both ways. Cable television was another example of a technology that exists today in its current form thanks to the early draw of nudity and sex.

Enter Manhattanite "Ugly" George Urban. In the late 1970s, Ugly George created, produced and hosted a show called "The Ugly George Hour of Truth, Sex and Violence" on Manhattan Public Access Television (part of Manhattan Cable, which was owned by Time Life, which is now Time Warner). On the show, he dressed up in a silver suit, with a video camera strapped to one shoulder and a parabolic reflector (to improve the sound picked up by the camera's mike) on the other. Then, he walked the streets of New York trying to persuade women to duck into an alleyway or dark hall with him and take off their clothes for the camera.

A mutual acquaintance offered to put me in touch with Ugly George, assuming I had "a few hours" to talk. I wasn't sure exactly what I was getting into, but one day Ugly George phoned me from New York's Times Square, where he still prowls the streets. He delivered a series of monologues that did indeed speak to the relationship between pornography and technology. Ugly George, though, had more to say. He ranged over subjects as diverse as women, sex, reluctant early cable adopters, reality TV and religion, his thoughts united by a common theme: his own massive contributions to them all.

Wedged in among his overblown (but not completely false) claims are important pieces of information about how erotic content drew viewers into a new medium at a time when it appeared to be sputtering. I present George the way he presented himself to me: in his own unvarnished words. The story of pornography and technology is not always pretty.

Cable TV in late '76 was nothing. [Manhattan Cable] had about eighty thousand subscribers, which is nothing in New York

City, it was nothing. There had been sex shows on already, but they were very poor sex shows, I mean ugly girls. I have one clip of one of the girls who was on around the time. She is so bad you would probably throw up. But her attitude was, "Look at me, I'm nude, you have a chance to see my wonderful cellulite-ridden nude body." So basically it was low-lifes or anyone desperate enough to look at very ugly women taking their clothes off, so it did not make a great impact on the technology. They looked at the girls, rolled over and went to bed and they never thought about it.

What I had to do was, now again this is hard for you to understand because you're in a normal place, New York women are incredibly beautiful, incredibly successful and incredibly cold, all right? They're not friendly at all. Probably because so many jerky guys approach them. So I found I needed both hands. No girl ever willingly took her bra off for me. That never happened, so I had to do it. All the while the girl was protesting, "I don't want to do this," "It's not what I want to do," "Hey, take your hands off my bra," "Hey, you're pulling my panties down" and all this.

How could you hold the video camera at the same time you got a reluctant girl in a hallway for fifteen minutes who's probably never going to come back, but you gotta do what you gotta do for fifteen minutes? So, at that time, as you know, cameras were cumbersome, you had a big camera and a big recorder with a cable, you also had lights that you had to carry, and the sound wasn't very good, so the parabolic, as you probably know, is really for sound.

I had to rig up this backpack so I wouldn't have to hold anything. I could just set the camera to run and the parabolic would just pick up the sound.

And then in a very short time, we have a lot of Hispanics here in New York, and they saw the backpack and they would say, "Hey, jou know jou look like an astronaut, are jou an astronaut?" So I said wait a minute, I gotta make up a silver suit, cause they're calling me astronaut. So I did.

And the whole thing fell into place, as you know. That's where Bill Murray walked up to me on the street and he said, "Where do you think I got the idea for Ghostbusters? Why do you think they wear silver suits and backpacks? You helped us make $200 million. Thanks a lot, George, see you around." I haven't seen him since then.

I was using a film camera, a format that is largely forgotten today called Super 16. With Super 16, you can't record the sound on the film. So, it was too cumbersome to carry a recorder, a camera, a big battery pack and an inverter and also you ran out of money very quickly, because most of them were misses, not hits. I ended up using up a lot of film on a girl who wouldn't do anything after wasting a ten-minute roll of film. And of course you had to have it developed and printed. So, this became very expensive.

When video came along, I checked with the station and it just so happened that a camera like that was available for cash, very quickly and quietly. It was black-and-white, it was reel-to-reel and it was mono-sound, in other words, the lowest technology of video. But it was better than nothing and I quickly found out that it was the opposite of film technology, you spent a lot of money on the video equipment but the tape was very cheap. Whereas with film, the cameras were relatively cheap but you went broke buying film and getting it developed.

I never threw out a tape, because I got to tell you this with no conceit: I became so colourful that even the misses were funny. They didn't just say, "No, I'm not going to do it." They had all sorts of agonizing, tortured, New York liberal reasons why they couldn't do it.

I am the inventor of modern reality television. I'll tell you a dirty word: tripod. I never used a tripod, because that wasn't what I was doing. I would be walking down the street. I would see a celebrity, the celebrity would see me, you know? I had about twelve seconds to get the camera up and running. I never had a chance to set up anything. No tripods, no script, just open the iris to the correct thing, try to look in the viewfinder to make sure you had the right exposure, pull the trigger, and that was the technical end of it.

When I would pick up girls, about 50 per cent of the time you'd get a crowd of idiots in the background going, "Don't do it, girl, he's a pig, he's a pervert, stay away from him, girlie, I wouldn't let him touch me if I were you." You'd hear this in the background, sometimes they'd jump into the picture and yell and scream because they were nobodies and they wanted to be on TV. So, this was really street theatre, not always a good street theatre either.

I was surprised at this myself since this was liberal New York, but you'd very rarely get a nice response on the street. People were nasty, they were insulting, very insulting. Girls would sometimes flip me the finger or say four-letter words to me, they were not very nice when they were misses. When a girl I sensed would do it, she never ever said yes. I don't think I ever once got a yes in my life. You know, "Yeah, sure. Let's go into a hallway and take my clothes off, I've been dreaming about this." I never got that. It was always, "I can't do this," "I won't do this," but I would sense something about her "no" that really meant, "Hmmm, I might be interested if you handle it in the right way."

I was on both local TV stations. They had teasers. "Do you know what's coming up on channel J at 12 o'clock? Oh, it's disgusting. Let us give you a little preview of the disgusting filth you are going to see, with the naked women, at 12 o'clock on cable TV." Their ratings went through the roof and I found out the next day the cable station's phones lit up like never before.

What happened was—this is only in New York. In normal places this probably wouldn't happen—hundreds and thousands of people suddenly called the cable station and said, "I just saw a news report about filth and smut and degrading women on cable TV. What channel is that so I can be sure not to watch it?"

At that time the cable stations had letters, not numbers, so the letter was J and people called up and said, "I'm tuning my TV so I can be sure not to catch that guy Ugly George on channel J, but I can't find channel J. All I have is 2, 4, 6, 8, 10. Where is channel J so I can be offended?"

The next day Manhattan Cable's phones lit up and everybody suddenly wanted cable who had never wanted it before. It wasn't Time Warner yet, it was just Time, had about eighty thousand subscribers. My contract was thirteen weeks, by the time thirteen weeks came along and I had to sign my second contract, mysteriously they were up to a hundred thousand. In two years they hadn't had a surge like this. Never. So, within thirteen weeks, I sold an additional twenty thousand subscribers for them. That had never happened before. It was a huge impact.

ABC, NBC and CBS would constantly have all kinds of propaganda going out, usually not identified as propaganda, and they would say, "We are quality. We have the biggest stars in the country and fine filming and this and that. And there's that pay-TV, that they want you to pay for."

It was about ten to twelve dollars per month. That was of course very low and the cable company was not making a lot of money from that. What they wanted to do was for you to start paying for premium channels, and the biggest premium channel was Home Box Office. They said, "Spend five dollars alone on Home Box Office," but it didn't work. That's where I come in, because certain staffers would quietly tell me that I became the biggest threat to Home Box Office. People said, "Look, I'm paying my twelve dollars a month, I've got Ugly George three times a week, what the hell do I need HBO for?"

So there I am with nudity and I'm being accused of, "Well, see, you run nudity, of course people are going to watch it." And I would point out over and over that they'd done nudity for two years before I got on. I didn't invent nudity—it was there before. It was just crummy nudity.

Then, they did something they had never done before. Time had an unwritten rule, which they made up themselves, no nudity before twelve midnight. That's not in any city rule, that's their own rule. They were terribly afraid that the Roman Catholic Church would mount an organized campaign against cable TV. In fact, a phrase had already been used—a phrase that I hate, by the way. The phrase was "purveyors of pornography."

They were very afraid of that. So one of their ways around it was to say no nudity before twelve. So when I first premiered I was twelve midnight, they quietly called me and said, "Would you like to go on at 11:30?" and I said, "Sure." I was the only one they did that for, because my show was basically not pornography, it was not girls spreading their legs, saying, "Look at me, I spread my legs." It was how to pick up girls.

By the time I signed my second thirteen-week contract and was on again, [subscribership] was going to about 150,000. Within a short time it hit about 300,000.

It isn't the technology. It isn't the box, whatever the box is. It's whatever they want to see or hear. If they really want to see or hear something, they will buy that box, whether it's a cable box or this or that or the other thing. Without something they really want to see, the box is doomed for failure.

In the mid-seventies do you remember how much a VCR cost? It was $1,600. And do you know how much the blank was? Seventeen dollars. And it was a lousy-quality one-hour blank. They were not making a lot of sales, people were not buying the VCRs— either Beta or VHS—and they were not buying the blanks in any great number. And then I came along and sales in New York City of VCRs and blanks went up substantially.

It was very interesting. People would tape it off the air and then send a copy to their friend in Dubuque, Iowa, or Toronto or Kitchener in Canada. And suddenly this show, which was, remember, only on the island of Manhattan in New York, suddenly began to become famous all over the country and in some sense, Canada. Literally thousands of tapes were made each night I was on. I was on three times a week, and they were all duped and sent to people there who would of course have two VCRs and they would run them together and make a dupe of a dupe. So there were literally hundreds of thousands of copies of Ugly George shows in circulation. As you can guess, I never made a nickel, but Sony and Panasonic and JVC, they did okay.

Erotica Online

E ven as the VCR, UHF and cable television were riding
pornographic coattails into new realms of profitability and
technological progress, the medium that would ultimately make
them all irrelevant was starting to take shape. Pornography was
beginning to draw a generation of tech-savvy enthusiasts into
the brave new world of computers and cyberspace. Porn exerted
more influence on the development of the online world than on
any previous medium.

American science-fiction television producer Rick Berman
once said, "Without porn and *Star Trek*, there would be no
Internet." For a medium that originated in the American military and found its way to the wider world via some of the
world's most prestigious research universities, the Internet
would appear to have some major non-pornographic drivers.
But the thing that gave the online world its widespread appeal,
the draw that transformed this technology from an esoteric,
complicated mess into an essential facet of modern life, and

the feature that led to the commercialization of the Internet, was the trading and selling of sexual pictures, stories and videos. The online traffic in pornography predated the Internet, was the driving force in its early popularity and still accounts for a major part of Internet use. According to Internet traffic-ranking service Alexa.com, at least five of the top 100 websites are pornography based. A 2006 study by Hitwise suggests that nearly 20 per cent of all Internet traffic comprises visits to porn sites—second only to the catch-all category of "computers and the Internet." And while estimates vary, most people agree that pornography represents an even bigger percentage of commercial Internet traffic.

Today, cyberspace is a vast and diverse place, big enough that many surfers spend their entire time in "clean, well-lit areas" where there is no risk of running into pornography. But this was not always the case. Sexuality was such a dominant presence in early online experiences that it was almost unavoidable.

Today it is pretty much a given that using a computer means going online, and that going online means surfing the Internet. Yet in the early days, it was uncommon for computer users to own a modulator-demodulator (or modem, as it came to be called). Those who did have modems used them to dial up other specific computers that existed in single locations somewhere out there in the world. That was it, though—you connected to just one other computer through a phone line. No domain names, no network of networks, no worldwide anything. Such computer-to-computer connections were the first digital footpaths of what would later grow into the information superhighway. In the late 1970s right through the early 1990s, it often still mattered where an online service was located. If you were not fortunate enough to have such a service in your area (or if you lived somewhere were local calls were not free), you could go broke just dialing in.

Because these early online services centred around local communities, and because one of the things they offered was the ability for one person to upload a computer file so that others could download it, they were known as bulletin board systems, or BBSs. Bulletin board systems would become another dead-end technology, ultimately subsumed by the Internet, but while they thrived, they were many people's introduction to the online world. And thanks to a robust trade in pornographic images, they also drove the market for home computers and modems, creating the user base for subsequent online services, including the Internet.

In fact, if the VCR was the machine that allowed the pornography industry to fully awaken to its own power over technology, the computing world was where it flexed its muscles. Online and off, personal computers became hubs of a sprawling mess of interrelated technologies that transformed news, entertainment, correspondence and research more quickly and more radically than anything the world had ever seen. At every stage, in dozens of ways large and small, pornography pushed computing technology past hurdle after hurdle, creating new markets, acclimatizing people to the vocabulary of computers and the Internet, demonstrating how to make new media profitable, and sometimes directly creating and refining communications technologies that went on to shape mainstream media consumption.

Nobody would have guessed all that in 1978. That year, the first BBS was launched, three years before Hayes Microcomputer Products released the first home modem. (Before that, modems were most commonly used by large companies and organizations to transmit messages via teletype.) The Hayes Smartmodem transferred data at a maximum of 300 bits per second—about one ten-thousandth the speed of a good high-speed connection today.

It is virtually inconceivable to us today how slow, unreliable and expensive it was to go online, how much patience it took to make a cantankerous modem do what it was supposed to, how much tweaking and troubleshooting it took for a process that never seemed to go smoothly. It is astounding that anyone ever followed through. Moses Znaimer had to jump through hoops just to get people to fiddle with a second dial on their TVs. What would it take for people to adopt this vastly more difficult device? What "killer event" would reward those who put in the hours to make this new technology a go?

"It was for bonding and hanging out and exchanging porn," recalled Annalee Newitz, on the phone from her home in Berkeley, California. Newitz, a journalist and author, writes about science, technology, science fiction and all things nerdy. She and the online world came of age at essentially the same time.

"Hanging out" was a cumbersome process in those early days. Technological limitations allowed only a few people to log on simultaneously to a BBS, which meant that most communication happened asynchronously. The system allowed users to leave messages either publicly or privately, meaning that getting to know someone bore more resemblance to having a pen pal than attending a mixer. It was an intersection of intense geekery and old-fashioned courtship.

"It's like courtly love, because courtly love was based on love letters, on the exchange of text," Newitz said. "I mean, there was also fucking and that's great, but it was a very strong model of romantic love. I met one of my boyfriends in high school online through the courtly love method. It was romantic."

Romance and online erotica might seem mutually incompatible. But one of the most surprising things about the sexuality that drove people into cyberspace is that much of it was deeply personal, passionate and intimate. Investigating the power of pornography and erotica to transform how we communicate requires examining one most unexpected aspect of sexuality: passionate love.

This idea was first suggested to me in a very different context. I was trading emails with Gaetan Brulotte, a professor of erotic literature who studied in France and now teaches at the University of South Florida in Tampa. "I am already convinced that erotica and also passionate love had a progressive influence on communication means throughout history," he wrote. He was referring to a recurring motif whereby artists and writers were perpetually driven to find new ways to express love and sexual desire, to seduce and to tantalize. Time and time and time again, passionate love appears where you would least expect it in the story of technological development. BBSs and the Internet were without a doubt breeding grounds for the most perverted, skanky and cheap trade in pornography, but they were also places where people found new kinds of emotional connections and sexual liberation.

The creative power of sexual depiction isn't rooted entirely in a craven desire to acquire filth, or even just in a desire for erotic stimulation—it also draws energy from a deep and powerful desire to find new ways to connect with other people on an intimate, passionate and sensual level.

As a driving force, passionate love might seem a bit archaic—more appropriate to pre-Victorian erotic literature than today's cutthroat, anything-goes digital society. But this is a misconception on two fronts. First, plenty of centuries-old material is every bit as hard-core as anything that exists today—today's swingers and fetishists have nothing on those of past centuries. And second, the erotic material that drives even the latest technological developments is often based on emotional intimacy and passionate love.

Not that it was all romantic. Huge quantities of pornography were changing hands on BBSs. Making money from such exchanges quickly became both an opportunity and a necessity. Images took up bandwidth, and pornographic pictures were being uploaded and downloaded by the millions. System operators had to keep upgrading their equipment and installing new lines as demand grew. And fans of pornography were more than willing to foot the bill via access charges.

There were two money-making models at work on BBSs, both of which would be replicated many times over as the Internet took over the world. First, phone companies, modem makers, computer manufacturers and others (vendors of image scanners, for instance) benefited directly from the BBS porn trade. Porn was not the only reason people sunk their money into these things, but it was a big one.

Second, BBS operators made money selling content itself. Forty years later, mainstream media companies are still trying to find viable ways to get people to pay for online content. Pornography distributors figured out how to do it almost immediately.

According to Frederick Lane in *Obscene Profits*, by 1992, there were forty-five thousand BBSs in the United States alone, servicing twelve million computer users. BBS subscribers paid $100 million in fees, and required nearly five million new phone lines, which generated more than $850 million in revenues for local phone companies. Pornography was paying for the infrastructure of the information age.

Soon those same phone lines also began to connect people with the Internet itself. Rather than connecting to a single remote computer running a BBS, people could now connect to a "network of networks" that gave them access to thousands of servers all over the world. Digital file exchanges and online communities very quickly became global operations, with files and messages circulating around the globe virtually instantaneously.

Pornography was such a massive force on the early Internet for several reasons. Anonymity and convenience were part of it—you could get porn piped directly into your living room without ever having another person see your face, hear your voice or even know your name. The global scope of the Net meant that people who lived in places where pornography in traditional media was illegal or unavailable could now acquire it. And at the same time, people were no longer limited by geography when it came to connecting with others. The Internet opened up entirely new possibilities for friendship, romance and passion.

People talk about the Internet today as though it were a single medium, but it isn't, and it never was. The one-medium perception is enhanced by the way the majority of modern online experiences—email, web surfing, database searching, social networking—tend to filter through a single application: a browser. Some people might use a separate email program, and gamers, pirates and computing professionals still experience parts of the Internet via other software, but for many people, the Internet, the World Wide Web and their browser are essentially the same thing.

By 1980, users of online services needed a fluency in the technology itself, including terms from "telnet" and "FTP" to "baud" and "data packet." Users forced themselves to learn dozens if not hundreds of alien terms to describe various software and hardware features. (In fact, many people started by learning the terms "software" and "hardware.") Neophytes faced a sprawling mess of protocols, applications, devices and arcane terminology that reflected the diversity of innovation and creativity spurred on by an increasingly networked world. And within that maelstrom of change, pornography remained a constant, guiding beacon, keeping people focused, and motivating them to find the time and patience to master the Internet.

Early cyberspace was a testament to the true power of pornography to draw people to a new technology. It's one thing to use sex to get people to fiddle with an extra dial on their television or install a new cable box. Learning how to get online, though, involved investing hours and hours of time in return for only the most grudging cooperation from the technology.

One particular early application, called Usenet, was key to both pornography and to the development of the Internet. Although it is still in use today, it never really gained the same kind of prominence in the public mind as the World Wide Web or email. Usenet was a global variation on those early BBSs. It was also a direct technological and intellectual precursor to both modern peer-to-peer file sharing and social networking sites such as Facebook and MySpace.

Usenet is a combination of email and public discussion area. Sending a message to a Usenet "newsgroup" is very similar to sending an email—you can start a thread, and reply to and quote from previous messages. Usenet messages, though, reside on a server or servers that are connected to the Internet, which means the postings are accessible to anyone, anywhere. Threaded discussions can involve dozens or even hundreds of people, with thousands more reading the conversations but not contributing (a practice known as "lurking"). As with email, users could also send computer files—word-processing documents, images and eventually videos—to a Usenet newsgroup. The means of doing so, though, were every bit as difficult as anything else related to twentieth-century Internet technology.

Usenet protocol could not have been more off-putting had it been specifically designed to alienate new users. A history of Usenet from a modern-day provider of the service, UsenetMonster, demonstrates how even the simplest actions were more than enough to befuddle a neophyte:

Usenet was originally designed for sharing text articles among computer networks, organized by subject. The standard for the text articles is that they would consist of 7-bit ASCII characters, no more. This means that only the first 128 characters of the ASCII set could be used, the "English Printable Characters." Almost all systems will now allow 8-bit characters. This allows use of characters with accents or other special characters for most European languages, but still does not allow the characters used in binary files. Because of this limitation, in order to include a binary file [i.e., a picture] in a text transmission, it must be encoded—all of the bytes of data in the binary file must be represented in a text file by printable characters.

In the very early days of Bulletin Boards and UUNet (later Usenet), I saw a number of schemes tried out to do this. One of the earliest that I recall in the DOS era (CP/M had by that time gone the way of the Beta VCR—lamented, but overwhelmed by the more ubiquitous DOS) was to encode a binary file into ASCII characters with a simple "Substitution cipher" using a DOS utility called Debug—and transmitting the file as a script or batch job that the debug program could run to write the binary file back to the disk. It *usually* worked—and made it possible to trade all sorts of utilities, pictures, etc. Mostly, these types of techniques were used to transfer (incredibly crude by today's standards) pictures of nude models from gentlemen's magazines. From the very beginning, it was transferring Thunderscanned centerfolds, much more than sharing scientific data or culturally important art or anything else, that drove the development and capability to transfer binary files over the cumbersome text systems. While not very tasteful, there it is, the immense capabilities for sharing great things is largely there because the engineers and technicians that largely drove the development of the capabilities wanted to trade nudie pics.

To be fair, Usenet wasn't used exclusively for trading sexual pictures. It was also used for trading sexual text. Usenet, like all early Internet applications, was text-based. This limitation was a simple reflection of the state of the technology, but it had a remarkable effect on early users, creating an outpouring of verbal creativity that was unlike anything the world had seen before. It was as though an entire cohort of computing enthusiasts were just waiting for a medium that could serve as an outlet for their pent-up passions. Usenet was that medium. It opened the floodgates for a torrent of textual, sexual output that sprang forth from seemingly everywhere at once. Wherever the Internet became available, people scrambled to get access to this interactive world where they could read about other people's fantasies and share their own.

"In university, one of the first things I discovered were newsgroups where you could share dirty stories," said a man I will call Mo. "It was all in text. I was eighteen. I had come from a Middle Eastern country. I wasn't conservative, but I had been raised in a conservative environment, so I was very hungry for information and experience. I discovered that as part of my tuition fees, I had access to this massive sea of filth."

Mo studied computer science and now works as a programmer and designer. He agreed to meet me for lunch to talk about both his pornographic and technological experiences. Though he spoke frankly and with ease, he requested that I not include information that could identify him. For Mo, the proto-Internet was both a source of erotica and also a place where he could educate himself about sexuality in a safe environment.

He talked about the sheltered environment he experienced in the Middle East. "One of the things that I had had almost no exposure to was homosexuality," he recalled. "I knew that homosexuality was somehow related to AIDS, but I wasn't clear on much more. Browsing the Usenet groups, I would do little searches—I'd find people who were out and gay and talking about gay sexual issues. I'm completely heterosexual, but I was like, 'I don't understand this stuff and maybe I need to talk to people.' I didn't know it at the time, but I was relatively homophobic. So it was great to get into conversations and get into the mind of a gay person."

Mo's story highlights one of the major elements of the early Internet that made it such a draw: anonymity. He did not feel comfortable talking to other men about potentially taboo subjects like homosexuality. When he went online and became anonymous, he had nothing to fear. "Being able to talk to somebody in text form was liberating because I could be as frank as I wanted to," he said.

It didn't stop there, though. Sex in Usenet was more than educational. Mo described these text-based conversations as "the gateway to all the newsgroups which weren't discussion: they were just posting stories and fantasies."

Throughout history, community has been shaped by geography; common culture and values tended to be a product of common location. If you didn't fit in where you lived, you pretty much had to move elsewhere to seek a community where you could belong. Usenet eliminated these geographical barriers. The basis of Usenet communities was common interest, rather than place. Hobbyists and aficionados of even the most obscure subject areas could find each other and get to know one another, regardless of where in the world they lived, no matter how far they were from the mainstream. This was especially true in the realm of sex, for which there were newsgroups to suit every theme and variation. (A colleague once told me: "If you can imagine it, someone online is into it.")

The tens of thousands of Usenet newsgroups were divided into a hierarchy to aid with searching and navigation. All of humanity's impulses and desires were sorted into nine top-level categories. The "comp" groups were for talking about computers. "Sci" and "humanities" reflected the academic origins of the early Internet. "Rec" was for discussions about games and other forms of recreation, "soc" was for socializing, "talk" was where political debates and arguments happened, and "news" was for, well, news topics. "Misc" was the catch-all for newsgroups that didn't fit anywhere else. Each major category had thousands of subcategories. Under the rec groups, you would find rec.sports, rec.games, rec.music and so on. Dig down deeper, and you could find rec.sports.hockey and eventually rec.sports.hockey.field. Somewhere in there, you were likely to find someone who shared your passion, no matter how unusual it was.

The ninth major hierarchy was "alt"—or alternative. Using the "information superhighway" metaphor of the day, the alt groups were an isolated community living at the end of a dirt path in the middle of a desert so far from civilization that the rules of law and general propriety did not apply. Which was odd, given that the vast majority of people who accessed Usenet were either in university or working for technology companies, and were in general educated urbanites. The Wild West feel of the alt groups reflected not a physical isolation so much as an intellectual disassociation.

Alt was for everything that didn't fit into the other eight groups (including the misc hierarchy, which you'd think would about cover it), and individuals had pretty close to complete freedom to create whatever newsgroups they wished and fill them with whatever they wanted. In particular, the alt hierarchy is where discussions and other writing related to drugs and sex found a home.

By 1993, a single group in the alt hierarchy had garnered 3.3 million subscribers—8 per cent of the total Usenet readership. That group was alt.sex. This might not seem like much of the market share, but given that there were tens of thousands of groups, it's significant. And that does not include the hundreds of alt.sex subcategories—alt.sex.stories, alt.sex.spanking, alt.sex.erotica.market, alt.sex.pictures.men, alt.sex.fetish.sailor-moon and so on. It was here that people like Mo and millions of others explored their own and other's sexuality. They shared information and fantasies. There were few rules and no taboos. This was a paradise for those like Mo, who were seeking healthy liberation, but also for others whose motivations were somewhat darker. Precisely because this electronic outpost of anything goes was so far removed, some of those communities included the kind of stuff that isn't legal or accepted anywhere: pedophilia, bestiality, incest, rape and on and on and on and on. All imaginable forms of sexual material were heavily in demand.

The good, the strange and the disgusting all played a part in pushing Internet technology forward. There was a perpetual demand for more. Not just for more of the same, but for new and improved media, and better ways to access them. The desire to get higher-quality pornographic pictures and video was nothing more or less than a desire for improved Internet technology. Faster servers, higher bandwidth, simpler file formats, easier interfaces—these were the keys to improving users' pornographic experiences, and subsequently the foundation for the mainstreaming of the Internet.

———

It is interesting to note that none of this Usenet-based trade in pornography had anything directly to do with money. The suppliers of pornography were posting stories, pictures and videos for free, motivated either by a sense of generosity or (more likely) by an expectation that others would share their collections as well. There was no premium for downloading material, other than the time and work it took to acquire it. People were spending money on hardware, software and services in order to access Usenet porn, but once connected, it was all available for free. The by-products of this massive trading in pornography were demand for more powerful computers, faster modems and especially greater bandwidth.

The demand for pornography—and the technology to deliver it—was so extraordinary, so seemingly limitless, that it took on the trappings of a highly addictive drug. For the first time in history, pornography was so readily available that its out-of-control consumption could begin to be discussed as a mental disorder.

There are no entries for "pornography addiction" or "sex addiction" in the *Diagnostic and Statistical Manual of Mental Disorders*, the bible of the American Psychiatric Association. The *DSM* does cite a number of sexual disorders, including aversion to sex, inability to have or control orgasms, and erectile disorder. Nevertheless, many psychologists believe that people whose porn consumption is out of control, causing them to lose sleep, time, relationships and money that they cannot afford, exhibit all the signs of a psychological addiction.

Even if porn is addictive only in certain instances, that offers one more explanation for why this industry seems to have such a disproportionately powerful effect on the development of new media: one of the key aspects of an addiction is that the addict develops a tolerance for the substance, and requires a bigger hit to get the same pleasure. For pornography, that can mean seeking out more extreme subject matter—making the progression from soft-core to hard-core to increasingly extreme fetishes and taboos. It can also mean employing new technologies to enhance the experience—higher resolution, better-quality video, more secure privacy, quicker delivery, a more immersive environment.

Internet historian Harley Hahn, who has written more than thirty books on technology and culture, has researched the addictive qualities of online porn. He accepts that pornography was one of the driving forces of the Internet, but that fact does little to impress him. "When you are successfully selling an addictive product, you're always going to find yourself a pioneer in certain areas of the marketplace," he told me. "It's not so much that it allows you the freedom, but it pushes you into a market faster than other products."

Hahn is a long-time netizen who lived through the evolution from Usenet through the cluster of user-generated-content applications known as Web 2.0. For him, the power of mixing pornography with technology is real, but far from benign. In a proposal for a book about technology-driven isolation and addiction, he writes, "What happens when a susceptible individual uses technology to engage in a behavior that would otherwise be impossible, when such behavior stimulates his or her pleasure center unnaturally? If you guessed that such people risk depleting their dopamine levels, thereby creating inner cravings that may lead to addictive behavior with serious long-term consequences, you are correct." His thesis is that the ready access to pornography on the Internet can overstimulate a vulnerable person's pleasure centres, throwing off their body's chemistry and sending them on a downward addictive spiral. It's natural, Hahn says, for people—and men in particular—to be turned on by an image of a naked, attractive human being. It becomes a problem only with the sensory overload of the onslaught of image after image after image.

Once the body's neurotransmitters go on the fritz, addicts are left with a constant craving for more. And access to more pornography means more bandwidth, processor power, resolution, storage space and so forth.

Another odd facet of pornography speaks to the same perpetual desire for more: some consumers of pornography have always seemed to have a penchant for collecting thousands upon thousands of images, magazines or videos. You see this from the start of modern photography, when dealers and collectors were busted in possession of hundreds of thousands of images. In modern times, people fill hard drives with millions of pornographic files. This phenomenon also manifests elsewhere: at that exhibit of ancient Chinese sex relics, the explanatory banners said, "The display has a whole span of five thousand years, showing jade, bronzeware, woodcarving, brick, ceramics and other artifacts of more than 500 pieces and 100 pieces of erotic painting." There was little information about the individual pieces—their merit seemed to rest in sheer quantity and variety. As though having thirty nearly identical stone phalluses lined up in a display case was somehow superior to exhibiting just one or two examples.

Psychoanalyst Norman Doidge, in *The Brain That Changes Itself*, an examination of a relatively new area of study known as neuroplasticity, recounts having seen many examples of men with porn addictions. "The addictiveness of Internet pornography is not a metaphor. Not all addictions are to drugs or alcohol. People can be seriously addicted to gambling, even to running. All addicts show a loss of control of the activity, compulsively seek it out despite negative consequences, develop tolerance so that they need higher and higher levels of stimulation for satisfaction, and experience withdrawal if they can't consummate the addictive act."

Pornography addiction is most commonly discussed in the context of the Internet, but that it not the only place it manifests. "I hate what this place has done to me" were the haunting words written on the wall inside a Montreal peep-show booth, and later quoted on a peer support website for young gay men and lesbians by someone who couldn't seem to stay away.

"I've been returning to that peep show quite often. I feel as though I'm addicted to it and the free sex. I can't stand it," he wrote. "I just hope that soon enough I will gain the courage to come out, to find someone to love, and give up that dreadful peep show."

One characteristic of the addictive nature of pornography sets it apart from other habit-forming products. If an addiction to porn stems from biochemical reactions that demand a steady stream of more and different stimuli in order to satisfy the craving, it creates a demand for innovation. Smokers do not require different flavours, shapes and sizes of cigarettes to satisfy their urges. Cocaine addicts have no need for a "new coke" to keep them interested. Pornography addicts, though, get bored with the existing product easily, which creates a special demand for creativity, both in content and in the means of delivering that content.

This helps explain why pornography so often plays such a key role in the early stages of a new technology. Photography brought a kind of realism to erotica that had not existed before—and this fed the hunger for something new. The most powerful example, of course, is the modern Internet. No technology in the history of the world has been capable of such dynamic innovation. The Internet is better capable of satisfying a porn addict's constantly changing appetites than anything that has ever come before. And of course, those ever-evolving tastes create the markets that make those early innovations feasible.

Statistics on pornography addiction tend to come from organizations that sell adult-content filters or from rehabilitation programs that are therefore suspect. According to one such organization, safefamilies.org, 10 per cent of all adults admit to a pornography addiction; almost a third of them are women. Even if the real numbers are lower, it still lends credibility to Hahn's analysis, particularly if you view addiction as part of a continuum—people who might not meet all the criteria for being an addict may still consume pornography compulsively. Or they might just really like it and use it a lot. Overall, consumers of pornography—whether genuinely addicted, borderline cases or occasional users—create a powerful demand for better, faster technologies to deliver the goods.

Usenet was just part of this demand. At about the same time that newsgroups were growing exponentially, another Internet-based technology came along that offered a different way of experiencing sex, sexuality and sexual representation. Virtual worlds, as they were called, were part computer game, part database and part social scene. They were such a new and foreign concept that nobody was even sure how to talk about them. Sexuality permeated these virtual worlds, but a debate continues to this day about whether such content constitutes a form of pornography or a version of actual sex. Virtual worlds are unlike any other medium. They are far removed from most people's experience of communications technology. The nature of the erotica that drives them is so unusual that newbies frequently need to ask a great number of questions just to get a vague sense of exactly what it is that happens in these virtual worlds. Enter the Frequently Asked Questions document, or FAQ.

Virtual World FAQ

Q. *What is a virtual world?*

A. A virtual world is a computer-generated environment in which a user can explore, interact with computer-generated objects and talk to other characters. These other characters might be computer-generated "bots," or the digital personas of other characters. The user interacts with the world through the usual means of giving input to a computer—typing commands, pushing buttons, hitting key combinations on a keyboard, moving a mouse and so on.

Q. *How is a virtual world different from a video game?*

A. It's not quite fair to say that a video game is a type of virtual world or vice versa. (Minesweeper is a video game but not a virtual world. Second Life is a virtual world but is arguably not a game—there is no way to win or lose.) There is much overlap between the two concepts, though. Many video games, from Grand Theft Auto to Super Mario Brothers, can reasonably be called virtual worlds: they have their own internal laws and logic, players can move around in them and interact with objects and characters, and there are goals and stories that get told through gameplay.

Q. *What does this have to do with the relationship between pornography and technology?*

A. Where things tend to get interesting is in a particular genre called "massively multi-player online role-playing games." These games involve virtual worlds that live on the Internet. People from all over the real world log in to interact in real time. But unlike in a single-player game, a MMORPG (pronounced "more-peg") allows you to interact not only with the game itself but also with other players. So, with a few notable exceptions, the sexuality in these games tends to be generated by the players rather than the developers.

Q. *I find pressing the function keys on my computer distinctly unsexy. Am I missing something?*

A. Not necessarily, though many people who have participated in cybersex would say yes. Whether it's typing dirty to someone in a text-based virtual world or sending your fully rendered Second Life avatar off to a virtual orgy, many people find online sex to be highly erotic and emotionally intense. Participants also talk about the way it fires their imagination or gives them the freedom to act out fantasies that they couldn't, wouldn't or shouldn't do in the real world.

Q. *Yuck.*

A. If netsex grosses you out, that is unlikely to change. I'm not asking you to condone netsex, let alone experiment with it. The only thing that matters is that it is a widespread phenomenon that has played an important role in driving key technologies.

Q. *Tell me more about the relationship between real people and their avatars. For instance, Keanu Reeves's haircut got a lot better whenever he entered the Matrix. Is that what this is really about?*

A. How people present themselves online is a fascinating business. In the days of text-based games, players would write their own descriptions of themselves, creating their own online persona. So, yes, people sometimes created idealized or enhanced versions of themselves. Just as often, though, they remade their identity into that of their favourite movie star, pop idol, or *Lord of the Rings* character, often in ways that had nothing to do with who they were in real life.

Today, graphics-based worlds take virtual identity a step further, allowing participants to create a visual representation of their online persona. Players adjust the height, weight, musculature, clothes, skin colour, nose shape and, yes, hair, along with dozens of other characteristics to create a character that walks, dances, swashbuckles and otherwise performs for all the virtual world to see.

Many avatars look nothing like their owners, while others are close enough that you might recognize the person on the street from their image in the game.

Q. *Now you're going to start talking about netsex again, aren't you?*
A. No choice. From a sexual perspective, virtual personas have allowed many people to try out new identities or explore parts of themselves online that they don't have the freedom or confidence to deal with in the real world. Men experiment with being women. People who live straight real lives explore homosexuality in the virtual world. On a crasser level, players can provide themselves with physical endowments and abilities very different from their real-life limitations.

Q. *How liberating, I guess. What's the down side?*
A. As with so many Internet-based phenomena, this kind of euphoric freedom to explore has a sinister side as well. Online, people can play out pedophiliac and rape fantasies, and other equally horrifying activities. Even if you accept that virtual

worlds can allow some people the freedom for healthy sexual expression, some of what happens is truly awful.

Q. *I'm not convinced that the world of Internet-based sex has anything to do with my own, decidedly non-prurient media consumption. Is there anything I can Google to get more information? Is there a podcast I can download from iTunes? Does CNN.com have anything on this? What books could I order from Amazon or Alibris?*

A. You've just answered this one yourself.

eleven

The Games People Play

As with Usenet, virtual worlds began as a purely text-based phenomenon—the technology simply could not handle anything more advanced. Thus the creation story of the first virtual world has a familiar ring to it:

In the beginning was the word.

This word was put together with other words to make sentences. They described a pine forest. A sundial. A graveyard. An ancient yew tree. A rather nasty giant spider. A flying horse. A bathroom with a medicine cabinet.

In the very beginning were these particular words:

ELIZABETHAN TEAROOM

This cosy Tudor room is where all British Legends adventures start. Its exposed oak beams and soft, velvet-covered furnishings provide it with the ideal atmosphere in which to relax before venturing out into that strange, timeless realm. A sense of decency and decorum prevails, and a feeling of kinship with those who, like

you, seek their destiny in The Land. There are exits in all directions, each of which leads into a wisping, magical mist of obvious
teleportative properties . . .

In 1978, these and thousands of other words coalesced into
the first virtual world in human history. No images. No sounds.
No holograms. Just a collection of sentences stored on a mainframe computer at the University of Essex in England.

This world was known as MUD1.

Admittedly, this is not the most spectacular name one could
choose for what amounts to a new kind of reality. And those
first sentences might not exactly seem to match "I have a
dream" or "We shall fight on the beaches" in terms of firing the
imagination or sparking revolution. Those words also might not
suggest the start of a hotbed of sexual exploration and experimentation, but they were exactly that.

That simple description of a tearoom was the start of many
things. It was the entry point not just into the world's first
multi-player online computer game but also into a revolution in
technology, business, entertainment and human interaction.
Modern phenomena including Second Life, World of Warcraft
and a slew of other Web 2.0 Internet applications all emerged
from that primal MUD. And if Web 2.0 is just as foreign to you
as is MUD1, just wait a little while—the virtual-world revolution
has been going on for thirty years, but it is just getting started.

Video games in 1978 were as different financially as they
were technologically from those of the modern era. MUD1 cost
nothing to play. In contrast, worldwide video-game sales in
2008 topped $32 billion (in the same year, combined sales of
DVDs and Blu-ray discs only hit $29 billion) and featured near
photorealistic graphics, multi-track audio, and voicing by
Hollywood celebrities.

Some things have remained constant. Games then and now involve Internet-based multi-player modes. Today's "massively multi-player online role-playing games" and virtual communities like Second Life are the direct descendants of MUD1 and other early virtual worlds. These games have played a key role in an epic story of technological growth and change. They also reveal a unique aspect of the relationship between pornography and communications. The erotica that drove this technology was overwhelmingly user-created. Rather than professional pornographers making money selling to the masses, individuals were creating erotic material for and with other individuals. Because this medium was so personalized, its journey into the mainstream world has been slow. Even today's multi-billion-dollar online video-game industry is more notable for its potential than for its track record to date. In many ways, virtual worlds are now at a stage that email and the World Wide Web were in the 1990s—no longer marginal, but not yet mainstream.

Today, the mainstreaming of video games and virtual worlds seems as though it was always inevitable, but in 1978, it was highly doubtful. Like so many other technologies, early text-based worlds were never guaranteed widespread success. They faced many technological challenges that many people bothered to overcome only so they could create and consume erotica.

At first, there was no money to be made in text-based games. The technology was slow, expensive and unreliable. It required still more arcane knowledge, of the type possessed only by an emerging social class of computer nerds. The chain reaction that led to today's multimedia-rich virtual worlds could easily have fizzled out like a bad science fair project were it not for the fact that users found ways to turn these fantasy games into sex-fantasy games.

The power of sexuality in these games was different than and in some ways greater than that of photography, cinema, literature and almost every other medium. That power, appropriately enough, comes from a word—a specific word that all virtual worlds, implicitly or explicitly, depend on. A word that not coincidentally appears in the opening scene of MUD1. A word that fundamentally changes how a player experiences the medium.

That word is "you."

"You" leave the Elizabethan Tearoom. "You" travel across the land. "You" battle monsters and collect treasure. By typing (more) words into a command-line prompt, "You go north," "You pick up a stick," "You hit spider with stick," and so on. Primitive and banal as this "adventure" might sound, the power of "you" made all the difference.

In most media, the story happens to someone else. The media consumer watches, listens to or reads about the actions of others. This is as true for pornography as anything else: porn involves other people taking off their clothes or having sex. The pornography consumer watches. At most, porn consumers' participation parallels the content, but there is a clear divide between reality and fantasy, and the role of the consumer is that of voyeur rather than agent. This line gets blurry, though, when the story happens to "you" rather than "them."

The erotic content in early virtual worlds was not created by game designers. Game makers filled the first virtual dungeons with swords and sorcery, not whips and leather. Role-playing was oriented toward battles and quests rather than submission and domination. But fantasies are fantasies. The original virtual games became environments in which players lived out all kinds of scenarios, especially sexual ones. The story of virtual worlds and that of online sex soon became inseparable.

There was more. The opening of MUD1 describes the "feeling of kinship with those who, like you, seek their destiny in The Land." Not only was the story happening to you but the other characters were also real people. The sex that emerged in these games went beyond people using a new medium to view porn, and beyond a mere prefabricated story written in the second-person singular point of view, to a world where real people interacted with other real human beings *through* the media. It was a revolutionary distinction.

In 1978, Richard Bartle and Roy Trubshaw were graduate students at the University of Essex in England when they created MUD1. "We always knew what we had," said Bartle. "Roy was always a little embarrassed by all the fuss, but we knew we had something special." (MUD stood for "multi-user dungeon." Four years before the launch of MUD1, Gary Gygax and Dave Arneson had published a new paper-and-pencil role-playing game called Dungeons and Dragons. MUD1 drew inspiration from that game, and the moniker reflects the early dominance of fantasy and science fiction scenarios.)

Within the game, Richard and Roy were omnipotent and omniscient. They could create, destroy and control the fate of all those who entered the world. They could see who did and said what—nothing that happened in that world was beyond their influence. They were the gods of MUD1.

There had been other text-based computer adventure games before MUD1. Titles like STARTREK (1971), Hunt the Wumpus (1972) and especially Colossal Cave Adventure (a 1977 text simulation that blended descriptions of an actual Kentucky cave system with elements of fantasy and magic) had already demonstrated just how much fun one person could have typing compass directions into a computer. The thing Richard Bartle knew he had was the capacity to allow many players to log on to the system remotely and concurrently. When Roy and Richard typed the words "RUN MUD" into the operating system shell of a mainframe computer on the Essex campus, they opened a virtual door through which many people could crowd at once.

Because these events happened so recently, it is breathtaking to consider exactly how different the lie of the technological land was in 1978. Just four years before MUD1, aficionados first started uttering the word "Internet." Also in 1974, the first WYSIWYG applications hinted at emancipation from the command-line interface, though this was still years away for the average computer user.

When Bartle and I first connected via email, I made the mistake of bragging to him, "I am of the age where I remember thinking 2400 baud was pretty fast." "Ha!" he wrote back. "We played MUD1 on 110 baud teletypes!" (Sending information at 110 baud, or bits per second, means it would take about four seconds to send this paragraph from one computer to another.)

How did anyone ever endure the technology of that time? Computer-to-computer links that were so slow they were almost stationary; monochrome screens full of esoteric gobbledygook decipherable only by elite misfits; computer processors tens of thousands of times less powerful than today's bottom-of-the-line models; counterintuitive interfaces; simple tasks that required whacked-out alphanumeric strings and arcane keystrokes. Plus lots and lots of incompatible and undependable technology. Connections were dropped, crashes were routine, recovery was slow, and even when everything worked smoothly, it was, technologically speaking, a monumental pain in the ass.

Repellent as the technology was, its attractive force was even greater. Accounts of these early computer games are always tinged with awe, as though the writers have just discovered fire—or at least how to play with fire. As players moved around MUD1, they discovered puzzles and perils, weapons and tools, magical objects and secret passageways. And they discovered the other players. Simple chat functions allowed them to type short messages to one another. For most people today, instant chat is just the background noise of everyday existence. But in 1978, it was an awesome thing to be sitting alone at a computer terminal and suddenly be connected in a real-time virtual environment with others who could be thousands of miles away.

This balky, clumsy technology had a remarkable effect on users. Perhaps it was all that idle time spent waiting for bits and bytes to creep from one place to another, or perhaps it was the very fact that there were no ready-made pictures or animations, but one way or another, these technologies led to a new form of written erotica that went even beyond what was happening on Usenet. MUD-based erotica was usually created in real time by multiple authors who could be thousands of miles apart. Their connection was via glowing monochrome text in block letters on a black screen enhanced only by the occasional mechanical beep. They were forced to use their imaginations. For many, many people, that primitive interface and the stripped-down, text-only gameplay became addictive. It infiltrated players' dreams, and kept them at their PCs night after night writing and co-writing sexual fantasies in real time.

Addiction was particularly likely to find purchase in the world of multi-player games, which fostered compulsive behaviour just for the games themselves—people could not get enough of the puzzles, the battles, the quests, the tales of adventure and heroism starring "you," the player. Such environments were deeply immersive. They plunged participants into a world that felt on some level real. Strangers met there anonymously, disguised in the trappings of their virtual personas. They had unprecedented freedom to role-play and explore fantasies of all kinds. What is more, MUD1 originally ran on a university computer that was earmarked for research activities during the day. That meant players were permitted to log on only in the wee hours of the night.

Such an environment could not help but become erotically charged. Curiously, though, while MUDS as a genre were full of sex, this was not the case for MUD1 itself. A few more elements would have to fall into place before virtual sex could really take hold in this new medium.

"There's nothing about the chat facilities of MUD1 that made cybersex impossible or even difficult," Bartle said. And yet, he wasn't surprised that there was no initial stampede toward erotica. "Almost all of the early players were male. Furthermore, they were sexually repressed, shy computer types," he said. "In a world where there are few women, and those that there are, are treated as honorary men, you don't want to be reminded of what you're missing out on. The players would no more have tried cybersex than they would have written love letters to one another."

Perhaps even more significant was the fact that if you took your eye off the game, you'd likely be bitten by a poisonous snake, attacked by an evil black rat, consumed by fire or otherwise imperilled, killed and forced to restart the game. So even if these men had decided to indulge in some hot chat, there was too much else to concentrate on to make it practical.

"MUD1 had a very intense gameplay," Bartle recalled. "You were constantly on guard against attack, and there were very few places you could safely stand still for ten minutes. People were there to play a game, and that's what they did. As an analogy, imagine a team of gay soccer players in the middle of a match: are they going to whisper sweet nothings to each other while the game is in progress? Well no, they're not—they're going to try to win. There isn't the time for that kind of thing in soccer, and there wasn't in MUD1."

Even before sex came into the picture, though, MUD1 had already begun to alter the way people related to each other through the technology. The chat function Bartle was talking about had the same surprising potency as the other text-based aspects of the game. People could type short messages to everyone in the game, just the people close to them in virtual space or just to one other individual. Those "shy computer types" started connecting on an emotional level that was purely and astoundingly a product of the medium.

Some people say it was because online, nobody knew you were a shy computer type. It's more likely that the initial bonding was due to a more basic fact—in MUD1, *everybody* was a shy computer type. That was the thing people bonded over. And this was the perfect medium through which to do it. Friendships formed. A community grew. Though many on the outside might dismiss this intimacy as ersatz, cockamamie or worse, it was for many people liberating, empowering and really quite wonderful. And with that kind of personal intensity, online social interactions led inevitably toward online sexual interactions.

Brenda Brathwaite is a titan in the video-game world. She has worked in the industry for more than two decades. She has helped developed some adult-only titles, including Playboy: The Mansion, and also founded the "Sex Special Interest Group" for video-game producers. She uses the term "emergent sex" to describe the erotic activity between players in a game not specifically created for such a purpose. She believes that as soon as emergent sex becomes possible, it becomes inevitable.

"If you give them tools, they will make penises."

———

MUD1 was hardly the last word in online text-based adventure games. The original Essex MUD was licensed to then-burgeoning online provider CompuServe in 1985. Its massive popularity led to many knock-offs, variations and innovations—games with premises and programming as varied as any other form of entertainment, allowing for many kinds of interactivity. MUD went from referring to a specific game to referring to a type of game, and soon there were many subgenres, each of which allowed for different types of play.

One type of MUD that became immensely popular was the TinyMUD, the first of which was written by a Yale computer scientist named James Aspnes. It went online in 1989. TinyMUDS differed from their predecessors in that there was no combat and no peril. They were designed to be social communities, where people could just hang out and chat with one another. (Because of their non-combative nature, the "D" in TinyMUD came to mean "domain" or "dimension" rather than "dungeon.")

Richard Bartle and Brenda Brathwaite both agree that, where there is no peril, there is emergent sex.

"TinyMUDS were MUDS with no gameplay," Bartle told me. The idea was that you used TinyMUDS to construct things out of words. In other words, other words could be added to the game. Players with a modem and a modicum of programming knowledge could create their own objects and spaces within the game.

Given the tools, they set about making penises. And vaginas. And many other body parts. And boudoirs, PVC outfits, bottles of massage oil, whips, paddles, singles bars and subterranean lairs devoted to S&M rather than D&D. All built from words. Players wrote descriptions of their virtual selves, their love nests, their sex toys and whatever else they could imagine.

"We saw this countless times with TinyMUDs and its successors, and so we knew up front it would happen in Second Life and There and all the other 'What do you do here?' places," Bartle said. He draws a clear distinction between game-based virtual worlds and those where there is nothing in particular to do. "In the game worlds, it's only ever been a side activity rather than a driver—the games were always the thing. It's only when the games are boring or the content is low that people start to look for other ways to amuse themselves." (Some users I spoke to didn't fully agree with Bartle, suggesting that sex was equally as strong a force in action-packed questing games as it was in worlds where there was little to do other than hang out.)

The internal logic of a TinyMUD allowed characters, rooms and objects to take on certain properties—rooms could be entered and exited, doors locked, lights dimmed. Objects could be handed to another character or, as the case might be, used on another character. Meanwhile, characters could maintain a steady stream of dialogue through the chat function. "Tinysex" was not passive, like looking at pornographic pictures or watching a movie. It was participatory. The environment, the implements, the descriptions only came to life through the real-time input of the players themselves.

Many accounts talk at great length about Tinysex but fail to include examples. There are three excellent reasons for this.

First, taken out of context, such passages can seem banal and alienating. (Think of any pet names, flirting rituals and other endearments you have shared with a real-life partner. Rarely would they convey intimacy and passion were they recorded and displayed out of context.)

Second, most people naturally wish to keep their private encounters private. TinyMUDs gave people the illusion of perfect privacy—even if the Internet is notorious as a place where the most intimate and secret material becomes massively public.

Third, Tinysex often includes frenetically typed text that goes to the extremes of both hard-core sex and a mangling of the English language. It also tends to include some jarring computer jargon and process commentary that was an inevitable part of the communication. This can make it seem all the more nonsensical.

To illustrate the strangeness of this medium, I tracked down a "Tinysex Log" that someone had posted to an ancient Usenet group. As with the real thing, virtual sex generally involves foreplay and seduction, which allows me to include only the first part of this log, before things gets too explicit. Two people, playing the characters NightWalker and Ami, wrote the following dialogue in real time from separate computers in separate places. This particular transcript looks how it would appear on Ami's screen.

NightWalker stares deeply into your eyes, searching within you, down to your very soul..

Ami smiles

You say, "that feels nice"

Ami gives you a nice hug :)

NightWalker grins..

NightWalker says, "good.. it's supposed to . . . ."

NightWalker embraces you tightly as he slowly rubs your back . . .

You say, "ohhhh . . . *sigh* :)"

You say, "its been a while since ive had my back rubbed"

NightWalker stares deeply into your eyes as he comes closer to your face . . .

You say, "wait . . . want me to set my description so it looks like me?"

NightWalker nods.. yea, that'll be good . . .

Set.

You say, "Ok!"

Ami set her desc

l me

Ami(#28126PNec)

You see a pert young girl (that's me! :) wearing a black, white, yellow, and red sweater that buttons down the front, a cream colored silk shirt, a plaid skirt, black stockings, and black skimmers (those are like pumps but with real short heels :)

Carrying:

Complementary Toaster

NightWalker grins..

NightWalker says, "you look very nice! :)"

You say, "do you like it?"

NightWalker nods..

Ami darn . . . forgot to mention hair, eyes, and height

NightWalker says, "yes, it's rather becoming of you.. however, there is one thing . . ."

You say, "what is it?"

NightWalker says, "well, you are wearing both a sweater and a shirt, that's a bit much.. here..let me help you.."

And so it goes from there, with increasingly sexual actions and descriptions, along with a generous sprinkling of "ummmm"s and "YESSSS!!!"s. The blurry relationship between the actions of two entwined avatars and the reactions of two physically distant real people highlight both the ambiguity over whether this was pornography or sex, and the related ambiguity of how much reality can reasonably be attributed to a virtual environment.

Like Usenet, MUDs were for the most part free of charge for anyone connected to the Internet. MUD creators did not make money from the sexual content that appeared in their games. Emergent sex, though, drew thousands of people into these games, and kept them there for hundreds of hours. They came to experience this new form of social and sexual intercourse.

In addition to creating demand for new, faster, better technology, the sex in these games had a second, equally powerful influence over the spread of the Internet. A by-product of so many people spending so many sleepless nights unlocking the technological secrets of virtual intimacy was that users became comfortable with computers and the Internet. These sex-driven early adopters formed the core group of users who would go on to be the market for non-sexual Internet use. When mainstream news and entertainment outlets turned their attention to the Internet, they found a devoted group of users who already were familiar and adept with the technology.

The Internet was only part of the story. Non-Internet-based video games had become big business in the late seventies and early eighties. The personal computer had done for video arcades what the VCR had done for cinema—moved the entertainment from public spaces into people's homes. The two technologies were not completely parallel, though. Videotape created a massive pornographic film industry. Yet no such analogue sprang up for video games. Games with built-in sex were few and far between: whereas the videotape revolution changed both consumption and production, home video-game consoles changed only the consumption. Producing a video game still required skill, expertise and monetary resources—elements that did not lend themselves to massive amounts of low-cost, low-quality pornography.

Sex-based games were rarer than movies, but they certainly existed. In October 1982, a company called Mystique released a title for a popular home gaming console called the Atari 2600.

The game was Custer's Revenge. It was the worst of a number of adult games on the market at the time. The player controlled General George Armstrong Custer, who wore nothing but a hat, boots and a huge erection. Custer had to avoid arrows and other projectiles as he crossed the screen to where a naked Native American woman (named Revenge) waited, tied to a post. The object of the game was to repeatedly rape her.

Naturally, this game outraged feminists, Native American groups and anyone who found racist sex fantasies to be an objectionable form of entertainment. Custer's Revenge also happened to have terrible graphics and gameplay even by 1982 standards. Yet eighty thousand copies were sold. (And that is not including a subsequent and marginally modified re-release under the name Westward Ho, and another variation called General Retreat in which the woman fights a barrage of cannonballs to reach the far side of the screen to have sex with the general.) Mystique's other adult games, such as Bachelor Party and Beat 'Em and Eat 'Em, also sold in the tens of thousands.

For what it's worth, Custer's Revenge tops the list of the ten most shameful video games of all time at the industry-watching website GameSpy.com. The technological developments that sprang from Mystique's short-lived adult video-game venture are equally not worth it.

In his book *Porn and Pong*, Damon Brown recounts the only technological advance engendered by such games. It happened when Mystique collapsed and sold the rights to Custer's Revenge, as well as other equally charming titles, to a company called Game Source. "Under the moniker Playaround, Game Source re-released Custer's Revenge, Beat 'Em and Eat 'Em and Bachelor Party . . . Playaround created what it called the 'double ender,' a two-in-one cartridge that sounded like it was a two-headed dildo. Playaround's long cartridges allowed players to buy two of its games for one low price, a marketing ploy imitated by other companies."

So thanks to this marketing innovation from a seller of adult titles, you can now buy collectible double-enders for the 2600 with such stellar mainstream game pair-ups as Robin Hood/ Super Kung Fu, Artillery Duel/Chuck Norris Superkicks, and Tomarc the Barbarian/Motocross Racer.

Another (moderately) less grotesque sex-based game that pioneered a (much) more useful mainstream technological practice was a 1980s product called Leisure Suit Larry in the Land of the Lounge Lizards. (The premise, which may be self-explanatory, involved the main character trying to seduce women.) This game was based on seedy comedy more than explicit content, although it was raunchy enough to require age verification to buy and play.

The writer of the game, Al Lowe, faced the same challenge as the creators of MUD1—how to create an interactive world that anticipated users' commands and dialogue well enough to give the illusion of complete freedom of movement and action. By this time, games had limited visuals and primitive animation, but Lowe was still relying on text as the means of interaction between player and computer. He had to anticipate the commands and dialogue users would type in. He did his best on his own, and then distributed pre-release versions to volunteers who tested them for bugs and enjoyability.

"It was . . . the first documented time a game company did an official public beta-testing," writes Brown. "Each beta-test copy of Leisure Suit Larry had a special file. The program would make a note whenever the player typed in a command it didn't understand . . . Each typed command, such as 'open door' or 'have sex,' needed to be programmed in. In his sex game, Lowe would have to anticipate everything that the gamer could possibly want to do."

Unlike double-ender game cartridges, beta-testing has changed much about our world. It's not just that software companies from Microsoft to Google use it to improve their applications. The concept of group problem-solving itself has grown into the modern phenomenon of "crowd-sourcing." Today, throwing a problem out to the public to help solve is seen in everything from gold prospecting to urban design. Of course, the modern power of collective problem solving is possible only as the result of modern technology, and the first use of technology for that purpose was in 1987, and it was for a raunchy sex game.

Back online, computer games of all sorts continued to break new technological ground. Fifteen years after MUD1 went live, there were hundreds of such games, with many variant technologies, populated by thousands of users. These worlds were still difficult to use and virtually unknown outside of hard-core computing circles, but that was starting to change. In 1993, Julian Dibbell, a journalist at New York's *Village Voice*, published an essay about an incident that happened in one of these worlds, a popular online hangout known as LambdaMOO. (A MOO is a MUD variant. The acronym stands for "MUD, Object Oriented," which describes in computer terms the way in-game elements are handled by the central server.) LambdaMOO was a rich and active community of experienced MUDders—a mature and sophisticated virtual society. It was the kind of MUD that did not involve battling monsters; it was a "What do you do here?" kind of place. As such, LambdaMOO's society tended to be dominated by players who were au fait both with the technology and with netsex. It was a vibrant place, though it was virtually unknown beyond its own community.

It was only when something terrible happened there that the outside world took notice. Dibbell's essay, "A Rape In Cyberspace," was, for many people, the introduction both to virtual worlds and virtual sex. It was not a pleasant introduction. Dibbell chronicles the story of a LambdaMOO resident who worked out how to hack the game's code in a way that allowed him to attribute actions to other characters within the game. He then proceeded to act out rape fantasies using members of this online community as pawns.

He caused lines of text to appear on people's screens like "Moondreamer jabs a steak knife up her ass, causing immense joy." It's unpleasant enough out of context, but probably just enough to classify the writer as a jackass rather than a psychopath. But for the Pennsylvania woman whose online persona was Moondreamer, and for the many other highly developed player/avatar pairs who were victims and witnesses of such attacks, the effect was profound. Dibbell recounts how one victim had "posttraumatic tears" streaming down her face. He describes a violation far different from merely accidentally reading an offensive passage of text, or even from experiencing a game like Custer's Revenge.

Novelists sometimes talk about how their characters become so real that they weep when their creations face death, hardship or tragedy. MUDders spent years developing and crafting their online personas, giving them such complexity, nuance and humanity that they became as close to real as any fiction could possibly get. The bond between player and avatar goes beyond that of novelist and character. Whatever similarities or differences there are between creator and creation, the avatar on some level *is* the player, or at least is an extension thereof. It's what makes netsex so different from other forms of erotica, and it's what makes virtual sexual violence unlike any other depiction or description.

"Netsex, Tinysex, virtual sex—however you name it, in real-life reality it's nothing more than a 900-line encounter stripped of even the vestigial physicality of the voice," Dibbell told me in an email. "And yet, as many a wide-eyed newbie can tell you, it's possibly the headiest experience the very heady world of MUDS has to offer. What happens inside a MUD-made world is neither exactly real nor exactly make-believe, but nonetheless profoundly, compellingly, and emotionally true."

While this particular incident was disturbing and strange, it also spoke of something fascinating and weirdly compelling—a different way of sharing intimacy born from an emerging technology. This erotic frontier represented something so curious and compelling that it drew in a new round of adopters who sensed there was more available in this medium than disturbed men bent on hurting and repulsing other players. Netsex was pulling people further into this new technology.

"I guess I had been on BBSs and what have you, that was the extent of my forays," said Buffy Childerhose. Childerhose, now a journalist and documentary filmmaker, was in university at the end of the 1980s, when MUDding really exploded. "I had read the classic 'Rape in Cyberspace' and went, 'How the fuck is this even possible? How can you be assaulted? I have to go to these sites.'"

Childerhose learned how to use a modem, how to telnet from one computer to another, how to navigate the uncooperative tools of cyberspace travel, so that she could understand what netsex was. Her journey had nothing to do with the multi-billion-dollar porn industry—it was just one individual exploring a new realm that was available for free.

Childerhose was not alone. Thousands of people, all over North America, Europe and Asia, were logging on for the first time to explore a new kind of sex, passion and intimacy. She was part of a wave of new users who continued to drive demand for bandwidth, computers and peripherals long before they had anything resembling mainstream appeal.

"I felt like the first person with a fax machine. I didn't know anyone else who was online, and everything was so crude," Childerhose said. "It was pre–World Wide Web. Nobody seemed to know what was going on. I certainly didn't know what was going on."

On the MUDs and MOOs, technology and sexual intimacy were deeply entangled. You could not get comfortable with one without being at home with the other. Childerhose grew proficient with both. "I was really more interested in the social interaction and the investment that you would have in your avatar that would allow for you to feel violated. But as soon as you get into those arenas and if you have a female-gendered name, very quickly people are going to turn the conversations to a more sort of salacious kind of thing."

Though the field had begun to open up, the majority of MUDders and MOOers were still men, and many of these men were on their own journey of discovery. Childerhose said, "I swear to God I was probably on for about an hour before someone said something sexy-sexy and I was a bit taken aback by it. I kind of let them—sort of like experimental sex: let them do what they were doing and just kind of observe—which is exactly how it was to come of age, I found, as a teenage girl. Let them do it, observe largely, let them run the show."

Childerhose quickly mastered both the technology and this new form of erotica. She transitioned from ingénue to maven. Soon it was men, skilled with their keyboards, but not exactly masters in the art of love, who were learning from her. "I guess these were all guys in their teens and early twenties," she recalled, laughing at the kinds of things they used to write.

"'You have the biggest vagina I've ever seen,' or whatever elegant phrasing they had. I was just really fascinated by the communication at all and then I realized that it was really easy to delight them because I had some small mastery over the English language and a dirty mind."

She found herself trading off sexual encounters to get to other kinds of intimacy within the games. She likens the connections she made in MOOs to pillow talk—somehow, this strange, clunky medium took players very quickly to that deep form of intimacy, where they could, ironic as it might seem, really be themselves. It wasn't just the speed with which the technology made this happen that was remarkable—it was also the way it allowed so many emotionally clumsy people to open up in ways they never had before.

This aspect of the relationship between pornography and technology often gets forgotten, lost among tales of the millions of pornographic images that circulate. Yes there is a biological imperative that gives human beings a sex drive, and yes, this has sometimes meant that hard-core pornography has been a powerful force for innovation in how we communicate. But both the terms "technology" and "pornography" connote a lack of warmth and an absence of emotion. The truth is that a powerful part of the technology-driving-erotica continuum involves passion, intimacy and love. It involves weeping, and sharing secrets, comfort and connection, and for some, an escape from isolation. And quite apart from any cash changing hands to download pictures or watch pornos, this more personal form of sexuality was—and is—the impetus for many people to find their way onto the Internet.

The relationship between these virtual encounters and the real world was, unsurprisingly, complex. For some people, the only place they could achieve this kind of intimacy was online. For others like Childerhose, netsex enhanced real-world sex. "It was arousing," she said, "but I wasn't like a guy, you know, where I'm going to jerk off while doing it. It was more that you put it somewhere and then you can retrieve it later with images in your head." And it wasn't just mental notes. "I kept logs of the sex that I had and then read it later as pornography, except that it was the best porn that you can have, because you engineered it."

The collision of virtual and real worlds was not always comfortable. There was a MUDder with whom Childerhose had had a stormy relationship. Their connection had been limited to online fighting and fornication, but then he tracked her down one night after they had a major blowout.

"We'd gotten into this big fight. I went 'fuck off' and I logged off. And then my phone rang. I picked it up and it was him, continuing the fight. Except I didn't even know he knew my name, which is really sobering." He was a "God" in the game—a higher up who had access to other people's login details. He could trace her to the university computer she'd been using. Only five people were logged on, and four had male Chinese names. All it took was a call to directory assistance and he had transported their connection out of the virtual world into the real.

"It really freaked me out," she said. "But I remember we'd had this long, larger relationship . . . it's so funny I don't even know what his name is, but he actually played a role in my life at a [later] point when my marriage was in decline. The night that my husband moved out, I was sitting in my double salon in Montreal.

"I'd gone online because I didn't know what else to do. [The guy I knew online] appeared and tried to start something up and I was like 'I'm not in the mood, I have a headache.' I told him what was going on and he was like, 'Oh, that's really sad, can I call you?' So I logged off and he called me and he was like, 'I don't really know what to say because I don't understand this experience. I haven't been there, but I've been working on this piano concerto, can I play it for you?' So I sat there and all the furniture was gone, so it was really echoey, and I just put the phone on speaker and really quietly wept as this stranger in Minnesota or whatever played the piano for me."

As Childerhose grew more familiar with online life, Dibbell's essay, and the question of what, exactly, constitutes virtual rape, became clearer to her. "I understand the sense of being violated, or one's avatar being violated . . . but I don't think it's rape as we understand it. It's more like a violation, like getting spit at in your face, that feeling of disgust you get."

Along with emergent sex, virtual worlds were also a place for emergent social intercourse, emergent community building, emergent politics and even emergent legal and economic systems. But it is impossible to tell the story of the advancement of this medium without telling the story of netsex. Every chronicle, memoir and article about MUDs, contemporaneous and retrospective, gives generous space to cybersex. Sex always seems to emerge, in every form imaginable. Along with the heinousness of virtual rape and the intensity of sexy pillow talk came all kinds of liberating experimentation.

Online, people who lived straight lives in the real world tried out homosexuality. They explored what it was like to be in non-monogamous relationships, or to have sex with several partners at once. Men existed as women and vice versa. (People also experimented with genders beyond the male/female dichotomy—both, neither and other.) This was especially valuable to people who lived in smaller cities, towns or rural areas, where they might not have access to the kinds of diverse communities found in a major metropolis. Even urbane sophisticates found freedom online to explore parts of themselves that they would never have dared to in real life. And along the way, they created a demand for the kinds of technologies that now are fundamental to mainstream existence.

"Honestly, if it weren't for that article, it would have taken me a lot longer to get online," Childerhose said. "I certainly wouldn't have bought a faster computer and modem. Because I didn't really need it for email, but I needed it for that environment."

In some ways, this is the most difficult aspect of the relationship between sex and technology for many people to accept, especially in our modern age where so much pornography is expressly marketed as nasty, dirty and perverted. Equally incomprehensible to some is the idea that filtering sexuality through a machine can actually increase intimacy and allow people to make emotional, sensual and sexual connections that sometimes exceed, enhance or even take the place of real-life interactions.

These kinds of connections are sometimes dismissed as a sort of consolation prize for computer savants who can speak binary but who can't speak the language of love (or if they can, still can't find anyone willing to share in the conversation). Suppose this were an accurate picture of who engages in netsex and why. Does that make the participants pathetic? Childerhose, who made no secret of her fulfilling sex life on- and off-line, doesn't think so.

"If we were to assume that the people who were doing it can't get laid in real life and that's why they are there, because it's their only sexual outlet, well then celebrate it," she said. "Even if we are to go with that conceit, isn't that a lovely, lovely thing that they can find an outlet for their sexuality in a safe environment?"

Regardless what one thinks of netsex, there is no denying its technological impact. All it takes is to accept conceptually that a significant number of people have adopted emerging technologies so as to forge powerful new forms of sexual and emotional intimacy.

Childerhose's story is both telling and typical. The Internet, virtual worlds and sexuality formed a virtuous circle—each fed into the other and spurred development, innovation and creativity.

Bandwidth and processor speed increased. Computer graphics improved. Crashes became less frequent. Tim Berners-Lee and Robert Cailliau developed the World Wide Web in 1990, making it easier for people who weren't computer programmers to make sense of the Internet. The first graphic browsers were developed in the early nineties, though they took some time to spread. The more arcane Internet applications, such as telnet (used to log on to another computer remotely through the Internet), FTP (a means of moving large electronic files from one computer to another) and of course Usenet, donned user-friendly disguises. Point-and-click, plug-and-play and WYSIWYG became household words. You no longer had to do battle with the technology in order to do basic computing and navigation of the Internet. And at every step along the way, sex and pornography were creating a constant demand for faster, cheaper and easier tools, driving us to the age of instantaneous gratification and graphic detail we enjoy today.

One of the other major forces spurring innovation was the games industry itself. When people were not engaging in erotic chat in virtual worlds, they actually were interested in racing, shooting, questing and puzzle solving. Video games make greater demands on computer technology than almost any other medium. They too create demand for better video cards, faster Internet connections and so on. They are a driving force of technological improvement to be sure, but in the early stages, they still paled beside erotica's influence.

Brenda Brathwaite said that the games industry alone, though "would not have been able to push broadband out as fast because there was simply not country-wide demand for it. But pornography, there is country-wide demand for that. I really think that massively multi-player online games are able to use the amount of graphics that we can use, in part because pornography paved the way."

PART THREE

The Modern Pornography Industry

The Commercialization of the Internet

A s more and more people found reasons to go online, the Internet approached a critical juncture. The vast majority of usage was still sexual in nature, but the medium was starting to show signs of making it big in the mainstream.

In 1990, most of the world still questioned whether the Internet was really going to be something major or whether it was just a passing fad for computer geeks and porn enthusiasts. A mere ten years later, on March 10, 2000, the NASDAQ composite— a stock-market index driven by high-tech companies—closed at its all-time peak of 5049 points, more than double its value twelve months earlier. It was driven to that height by huge and irrational market exuberance over the seemingly limitless potential of so-called dot-com companies—Internet businesses set up to mine the electronic gold apparently available to anyone who could register a URL and set up a web page.

"Analysts see the trend continuing," reported *CNN Money* on that record-setting day. Instead the dot-com bubble burst.

Billions of dollars were lost by people who had sunk their money into companies such as Pets.com and WebVan.com.

How did the Internet go from anarchic geek paradise to maker and breaker of billionaires in the space of a decade? Where did the dangerous fantasy come from that it was so easy to make money online? It came from the pornographers. In 1996, estimates of online pornography revenues ranged from $52 million to $100 million. A mere three years later, it was closer to $2 billion—and that at a time when less than a quarter of the American population had Internet access. The adult industry proved there was money—big money—to be made on the Internet. They proved it many times over through a wide variety of business models, including selling bandwidth and access to the Internet itself.

Usenet and MUDS are only two of many areas where pornography and erotica created demand for Internet access. Another sex-driven online application that created a huge market was chat rooms available through services such as America Online.

Wall Street Journal journalist Lewis Perdue undertook a study of these chat rooms in their heyday in the late 1990s. He monitored activity in public rooms, and used a combination of analysis and educated guesses about private rooms, to determine that 82 per cent of the chat activity on AOL had to do with sex—dirty talk, trading pictures or hope-for-future-real-life-interaction flirtation and come-ons. Millions of people bought modems, ran up massive phone bills and paid for Internet access so that they could have private, convenient access to new forms of pornography.

"How is it," Perdue asks in his resulting book, *EroticaBiz*, "that the brightest minds in the world's biggest media companies working with huge investment budgets can't eke out a dime's worth of black ink while some bootstrapped 22-year-old with a ton of dirty pictures can make thousands in profits working part-time from his bedroom and bigger pornographers can easily clear $10 million or more every month?"

Some might point to the "ton of dirty pictures" as the key to the pornographic formula for success. This only takes you so far, though. There was a great irony about selling porn online: a sprawling riot of every imaginable form of pornography was already available for free, as long as you had the technological know-how to find it. "If you pay for porn, you've failed the Internet," Annalee Newitz said to me. The reality is that nobody—then or now—in the technological know would actually pay for pornographic content. Why would they when they could get it all for free?

This is one of the great counterintuitive surprises about the relationship between the Internet and porn: the success and influence of the porn industry was due to more than the material. It was about customer service. It was about making the Internet easier. People who wanted erotic content were more willing to pay for it than they were to learn how to spelunk the depths of Usenet. What people were really paying for was not the product but ease of access. The great accomplishment of the adult industry at this time was to prove that the Internet could deliver that kind of convenience to a paying market.

Consider two examples of early commercial success on the Net: Danni and Jenni.

Seattle born Danni Ashe—her stage name—became a stripper at age seventeen. She first worked in her native Seattle, but cannily exploited a sideline in magazine modelling and soft-core video to build her profile. She toured nationally, and eventually became a headline draw at strip clubs around the country. A self-described "geek with big breasts," she could not have been more predisposed to making money on the Internet had she been genetically engineered.

In 1994, she was already familiar with the nether regions of the information superhighway. "I ventured onto the Internet and quickly got into the Usenet newsgroups, where I was hearing that my pictures were being posted, and started talking to people," she told PBS's *Frontline*. "I spent several really intense months in the newsgroups, and it was out of those conversations that the idea for Danni's Hard Drive was born."

Aside from building a brand on the most obvious double entendre in the computing universe, Danni Ashe's business enterprise became one of the busiest sites on the Internet. When the site launched in 1995, punters paid $19.95 per month for access to soft-core pictures and personal information about Ashe.

In its first week, her site had a million hits. For the first two years of its existence, it was the busiest site on the web. In 1997, Ashe had seventeen thousand paying subscribers; that climbed to twenty-five thousand by 1999. In 2001 she was employing forty-five people and turning an $8-million profit annually. She became a dot-com millionaire, not as a result of irrational hype but by selling content.

These numbers only represent the money people spent directly on Danni Ashe's brand of pornography. Danni herself was aware that her influence extended well beyond her own product. "If it were not for the adult industry, Cisco would never have sold so many routers or Sun as many servers as they have," she told a journalist in 2002.

The impact of Danni's Hard Drive was as much conceptual as it was financial. The mere fact of her success proved that the Internet had genuine profit potential. The most amazing thing, though, was that she got the idea from Usenet, where users could already procure precisely the same material for free.

Thousands and ultimately millions of people "failed the Internet," which made many online adult entrepreneurs very wealthy.

Ashe did not rest on the laurels of her early success. Whether because of her own geeky creativity, or an understanding that her customers were always going to want something new, Ashe continued to innovate. She smoothed the credit card transaction process, which made her customers more comfortable. Her company developed a proprietary streaming video technology called DanniVision, which allowed users to watch movies without needing any cumbersome software add-ons. She and a number of other contemporaneous porn sites developed the conceptual foundation for a marketing scheme that is key to sites like Amazon today: affiliate marketing. Despite Amazon's early claims that it had invented affiliate marketing, several adult companies were in fact in the game much earlier.

Affiliate marketing essentially started as a cooperative cross-promotion system between competing companies. A visitor to Danni's Hard Drive who opted not to subscribe would get a message as he tried to exit, including links and an invitation to visit other sites that might be more appealing. The surfer had already declined to give Ashe money, so she had nothing to lose by sending him elsewhere. Those other erotica sites would in turn direct their non-takers to Danni's site.

This informal cross-promotion was just the start. Pornographers figured out how to use the tools of the Internet to make such arrangements more systemized and complex. Software systems could track who clicked on what link, which allowed businesses to work on commission. Every referral that converted into a paying customer resulted in a kickback for the referring site (which came to be known as an "affiliate").

In pre-Internet days, the affiliate system took the form of "finder's fees" and commissions paid for recommending potential customers. Online, though, these programs could become much more sophisticated. Once money started changing hands, even the simplest affiliate system required complicated tools. How does a website owner know where a new paying customer was referred from? How does one affiliate know that others are being honest about how many referred customers have converted? Affiliate programs became a technological puzzle of accounting, tracking and reporting.

One of the most notable innovators in this area was a company called Cybererotica. In 1996, Cybererotica developed a web analysis tool called XXX Counter. It allowed commercial sites to establish credible traffic statistics, which they could then use to sell advertising. It also provided information about where traffic was coming from, what sort of search terms people were using to land on a page, and even what screen resolution and browser the surfer was using. XXX Counter gave adult-site webmasters a flood of new information that they could use to tweak their sites for user compatibility, search-engine optimization, and maximizing the prominence of their best-selling products. It allowed websites that had merely been devoted to selling adult content to do double duty as real-time market research tools, with up-to-the-second information on who was buying what. It also kept affiliate programs honest, ensuring that all paid traffic was reported and that no referring site was short-changed on its commissions.

Pornographers also pioneered the use of invisible pieces of software known as cookies, which are used to record information about surfers' activities. Cookies can track the meandering path of users from site to site, keep track of registration information and store users' preferences. Cookies in turn helped affiliate programs flourish by providing a simple means of keeping track of individual referrals.

The esoteric computer technology that originally merely allowed EuroNubiles.com to know when PantyhosePlanet.com had sent some customers their way is today a key part of how

Amazon, iTunes, eBay and thousands of other online retailers work. Each offers a commission system for referring sites that send paying traffic their way. They rarely acknowledge that this key part of their business model was developed and refined by the adult industry.

The adult world does not always help itself in its struggle for mainstream recognition. Today, Cybererotica is the parent company of an outfit called CECash, which specializes in affiliate programs for adult websites. Its slick online presence feels very corporate . . . in a Bizarro World kind of way. Its peculiar business marketing combines a hi-tech feel with a brand of directness that seems far removed from Wall Street or Silicon Valley.

On CECash's site is a short video aimed at enticing adult webmasters to sign up for its affiliate programs. The video features a man known as Tooshort (identified in the video as "Mr. Short, the Architect") speaking over driving percussion and horns on what looks like a low-budget sci-fi set. I include a transcript of Mr. Short's spiel, both because it provides an illuminating précis of the short and turbulent history of the adult web industry from an insider's perspective and because it illustrates the strange mix of corporate sensibility and coarse directness that is so typical in this world.

> In the beginning, you didn't even exist. There were no middlemen, no affiliates, no webmasters. The Internet was only for the big boys. They wouldn't even let a pimp in the game.
>
> In the mist stood a visionary. A real pimp who made it happen: CECash. The affiliate system was born, and it changed the Internet forever. This introduced a new breed of keyboard hustlers: you, the adult webmaster. Webmasters got paid like a motherfucker. They started partying with the bitches and hos. The profits saw no boundaries. And neither did the greed.

This was the beginning of the end. You know, somebody always gotta fuck the party up. Shit got oversaturated, too many fake-assed webmasters with no originality, the sponsors disappeared, corners were cut, the banks got burned, and worst of all . . . the customers lost faith, and the industry collapsed. The good old days were gone, the godfather had been forgotten, and the dream was lost.

We ain't goin' out like that, though. We started this. Fuck this shit. Fuck all the old shit. Get with this new shit. CECash 2.0. We're upgrading, baby. We're taking it to the next level.

Now we're creating a new era of webmaster affiliate relationships. Big pimping all over again, baby. Let's kick this money. All you have to do is click that button and choose us.

The person who puts a swear jar in that man's office would be rich indeed. The unselfconsciousness with which he employs an expletive-laden patois speaks to a fierce unwillingness to make any apology whatsoever for any aspect of the pornography business. But beyond its explicitness, this pitch has something important for mainstream media companies to consider. While newspaper, television and radio outlets search about for a business model that can carry them forward in a changing and fragmented media universe, while trend watchers and market researchers make shaky predictions about which way forward might lead to continued viability, and while mainstream media consumers hesitate to adopt any new technology for fear it will be outdated six months down the road, the porn industry just says, "Fuck all the old shit. Get with this new shit." It's not something you'd see as a bullet point in the strategic plan at Redbox, Universal or CBS, but it has a certain appeal. A willingness to leave behind the technologies and business models of the past is a powerful way to better prepare a company for the future.

———

Danni's Hard Drive and Cybererotica's XXX Counter were just two of the many pornography-driven Internet innovations of the mid-1990s—advances in technology and the art of moneymaking that would help fuel the euphoria of the dot-com bubble.

As bandwidth and technology continued to progress, a new, massively saleable online service became feasible: live shows. No amount of trade in static text and images could compete with a real person performing real erotica in real time. The trailblazer in the world of live webcams was a woman named Jennifer Ringley, who opened up her entire life to any voyeur on the Internet, billing herself as a "lifecaster." Her main product could not be stored, stolen or traded anywhere else, because it was live and always new. Ringley hooked up a webcam in her dorm room in 1996 and left it running for the next seven years. At its peak, JenniCam claimed a hundred million hits a week. It sparked a webcam revolution. And, while Ringley herself never got rich selling subscriptions, the "cam girls" who followed continue to make up a major part of the adult market.

The technology of Ringley's day was not spectacular. Her original camera uploaded a black-and-white still picture every three minutes. Furthermore, voyeurs were treated to very little in the way of actual erotica. She did do an occasional striptease, and in later years left the camera on during assorted sexual liaisons, but the vast majority of the webcast just showed her carrying out the commonplaces of everyday life. Yet people were fascinated. The peep-show nature of the medium meant that very little sex was necessary to get viewers turned on. Just having a window into a real person's life was plenty—people would pay for the occasional chance to observe Ringley's non-porn-star-like sex life, or to just catch her walking naked to the shower. The phenomenon of the technology itself was considered so sexy that Ringley barely had to perform.

David Dennis was one of many millions of men who were captivated by Ringley's performance, and her person. Today, Dennis runs a social networking website called amazing.com that is home to a small, close-knit community of online acquaintances—the sort of place for people who want to trade messages with three real friends rather than three thousand Facebook friends. (He also works as a mad scientist at a haunted-house attraction in Monongahela, Pennsylvania.) Dennis is a prolific writer, and scattered across the Internet, among his thoughts on technology, philosophy, love, dating and politics, are fragments of his bittersweet history with Jennifer Ringley and her revolutionary webcam. When I contacted him to find out the full story, he requested that we correspond only by email, giving him time to think through his answers to my questions.

"I became interested in her when she made a web page based on a tour of her body," he told me. "It was almost entirely clothed, but very creative and fun and a bit naughty." Dennis achieved in reality what so many others essentially experienced as a fantasy: he struck up a friendship with Ringley. Part of that relationship was based on the fact that he could offer her something she needed: bandwidth.

Dennis grew up in a technological environment. His father was a professor at the Massachusetts Institute of Technology, in Boston. In his pre-Internet days, Dennis ran a bulletin board system that focused on dating and discussion. (Dennis himself was among the beneficiaries of his own service. "During the years of David's Amazing BBS, I did better than any time before or since, because it was a local phenomenon," he said. "I tried to replicate its success a few times [on the Internet] but could not figure out how to market it successfully. My problem was that I wanted to give the customer a good deal, and so I could not afford the enormous affiliate programs needed to drive customers to sites like match.com and the like.")

His father's university position gave Dennis early access to ARPAnet, the precursor to the modern Internet. "When I learned about the Internet, it was a lot like going home," he said. He decided he wanted to become an Internet service provider, and began subscribing to many of the growing number of email lists devoted to the profession.

"I noticed there was no FAQ, or centralized information document, for the list and decided to compile one. I got a lot of help from various ISPs, and the document rapidly became popular," he said. "This got attention from a nice fellow named Avi Freedman, who ran a huge ISP called Netaxs. He had bandwidth to burn and so he gifted me my own server that I could use as I pleased. This was how I got all the bandwidth required for the JenniCam without my actually doing much of anything."

Dennis, Jenni-fan that he was, began hosting her site just when it was taking off. At that time, Ringley's lifecasting experiment was still free for the taking, though that did nothing to diminish its influence. A confluence of factors—a smart woman willing to bare everything about her life, a smart man with a passion and talent for computing, and a technology just at the brink of becoming something really interesting—led to a major shift in how the world thought about, and used, the Internet.

"Eventually, Jen had a friend set up a more sophisticated site with her own bandwidth. That was when she started charging for it," Dennis said. "I seem to remember that I could only ethically provide her with the bandwidth if her site remained free."

Ringley at first charged a pittance—$15 per year—but she soon had enough customers to cover her computer equipment and growing bandwidth costs, and to make a comfortable living.

Once the site became a business, things went a little sour for Dennis. Not only was he out of the hosting role but JenniCam Inc. also demanded that he remove the archive of images he had painstakingly collected and made available to her millions of fans. Her real draw was the live action, and Dennis's still freely available archive risked devaluing her newfound currency. His labour of love (or affection, at least) was subsumed by the very commercial demands it had created. Dennis lost a friend, but gained a place in technological history.

Soon, many other businesses were plying the trade route that JenniCam had opened. "Cam girls" became a buzzword among adult-content entrepreneurs. As a product, live web shows could offer a level of realness that other media could not. Comedian George Burns famously said, "The secret of acting is sincerity. If you can fake that, you've got it made." Porn producers big and small quickly came to a parallel conclusion about webcams. Ringley's appeal was that she offered people an authentic experience that could come only from capturing a glimpse of real, unedited, unpackaged life. The adult world quickly learned how to package that raw, authentic experience and sell it at a premium to men who were bored with standard pre-recorded pictures and video.

By the time JenniCam went dark, hundreds of other young women had gotten into the game, many as independent entrepreneurs. Often, rather than charging a membership fee, these girls used a lower-tech system of posting a "wish list" of items. Men who bought these items—ranging from books and videos to high-end electronics—could become the cam girl's "special friend." Cam girls turned intimacy (or the illusion thereof) into part of the pornographic product. Many sites charged anywhere from $2.99 to $6.99 per minute, and many clients spent $6,000 or more per month to interact with their chosen model. This phenomenon resulted from more than prurience. In *Obscene Profits*, Frederick Lane quotes one webcam entrepreneur saying, "They fall in love." The immediacy, this hauntingly realistic emotional connection, was an aspect of webcam technology first exploited, developed and commercialized by pornographers that would later become a device used by millions who might otherwise never have viewed a salacious image.

But first, the pornographic businesses would get bigger and uglier. Entrepreneurs like Jonathan Biderman set up cam-girl "portals" where customers could for a fee choose among dozens of feeds. His "Cam Whores" portal proved so popular among both male customers and women trying to get in the game that he had to open a second portal—"Cam Whore Wannabes"—for those who weren't good looking enough to go on the main site.

Webcams were mixed with instant messaging or "chat" functions, so that viewers could type messages to the girl on the screen and then watch as she typed responses. (The porn industry was also a very early adopter of instant messaging behind the scenes. It wasn't just for show—they also used chat to do business. One insider told me that a great number of people who work in adult still do business via ICQ, which was the first chat service not tied to a particular Internet service provider. Though the modern Internet boasts many such services, the porn industry sticks with the pioneering software for which they were the original business clientele. Many business cards handed out at porn trade shows include all the modern means of contact, but also include an ICQ address for those who have been in the business since the start of the boom.)

Dennis is philosophical about what he gained and lost through his JenniCam experience, and the inexorable evolution from Jennifer Ringley's relatively tame performance-art version of voyeurism to the Cam Whores and others who made the medium purely pornographic. "Sex sells," he said, echoing dozens of other interview subjects. "Men and women both need it, but men are far more willing than women to accept a commodified version of it. Technology early adopters are almost exclusively men. So in a world where women are rare, men are common as weeds, and an interest in sex way exceeds the ability to actually get it, the interest in pornography should not be in any way surprising."

Like so many aspects of the relationship between pornography and technology, though, the cam phenomenon was not always about selling sex. Mo, the Middle Eastern man who learned so much about sex and sexuality from Usenet, says that one piece of technology he remembers acquiring specifically to improve his porn experience was a webcam. He bought his first in 1995.

"I went through several webcams, upgraded from parallel port technology to serial port technology to USB," he said. "By far, the leading usage was porn. I remember seeing at a couple of companies I worked at these great Silicon Graphics desktop computers with webcams on the top, but they were all gathering dust. Not a single person used them. Webcams weren't yet ready for office use." Mo's webcam interests extended beyond sexual applications, but it would be more than a decade before any other use became at all viable. "I could find [webcam] communities online with people who wanted to take their clothes off if I did, and that was great. But what was frustrating was that until about 2007, there wasn't a single friend of mine I could have a video conversation with."

That's twelve years since Mo—and eleven since Ringley—first employed a technology that had virtually no use outside of sex, pornography and voyeurism. It would be more than a decade from the time early adopters started using cams for erotic applications until the mainstream caught up and caught on. Internet-based video conferencing is now common in the business world, laptops and desktops increasingly come with built-in webcams, and Internet-protocol-based telephone systems like Skype offer high-quality video call options. Pornography and erotica created the mainstream technology and infrastructure that a travelling mom now uses to say goodnight to her children, or that a CEO uses to keep in touch with branch offices around the world.

By the late 1990s, mature content was giving way to mature technology. Though Usenet still exists today in a state close to its original form, it also now has intellectual and technological descendants, many of them also driven by pornography. Currently, more than 120,000 newsgroups are available (for a monthly fee). The companies that hawk Usenet today acknowledge their marginal location on the fringes of the Internet. In fact, they try to give their off-the-beaten-track nature some cachet. "Now that you've discovered us, you could go back to the 'mainstream' Internet, or you can become a part of The Usenet Experience. Go ahead, tell your friends . . . or don't!" reads one pitch. They also make emphatic promises of anonymity. "Usenet is a private community when you use [our service]. We don't log your activity and neither can your ISP when you use our FREE SSL Encrypted Access."

For a certain market, untraceability is a crucial selling point. One of the great paradoxes of the Internet is that it offers unprecedented privacy and anonymity, yet at the same time a user's browsing history, email trails and downloaded files can almost always be uncovered by someone with sufficient technological expertise and processing power. A service that is supposedly undocumented and hidden away in a dark corner of the Internet where a prying investigator or spouse might never think to look becomes a prime place for secretive trading in pornography. The "Usenet experience" has always been predominantly a pornographic experience.

Today, though, millions more partake in modern, nonpornographic versions of the Usenet experience without even realizing it. The concepts and technologies of Usenet have moved into the mainstream, though they have evolved greatly from their primitive origins. At its core, the Usenet experience is nothing more than a large group of people sharing files, information and stories across a series of decentralized networked servers. Even if you surf without a Usenet, it's virtually impossible not to be a part of that legacy. Consider: twenty years after Usenet laid down the foundations and got people familiar with the novel concept of online communal living, a new application appeared on the scene that built directly on that concept. It was called Napster.

Abiding by a seemingly universal law of origins for Internet-based advances, Napster was created by two young male computer fiends, in this case a couple of Americans named Shawn Fanning and Sean Parker. It was launched in June 1999. Napster was a decentralized file-sharing system that was specifically designed for trading music files.

Napster revolutionized the music industry. For tech-savvy music lovers, it was sweet freedom at last. It was finally possible to acquire the latest hit or the most obscure sea shanty with a few clicks of the keyboard. You no longer had to buy a whole CD of so-so music just so you could listen to that one song you loved. The consumer was in control, and the big music companies had the wind knocked right out of them.

Nearly all Napster file sharing was in violation of assorted copyrights. Not only that, the system depended on central servers that kept track of where all those music files were hiding, awaiting download. These two things provided Big Music with the motivation and means to shut down the whole operation. Six months after Napster launched, the Recording Industry Association of America filed a lawsuit, which two years later resulted in Napster paying a total of $36 million in damages to compensate copyright owners for lost revenue. Napster tried to reinvent itself as a legal music-distribution network, but never made much of a go of it. The technology then took an odd lurch away from mainstream, back into the realm of porn. Napster was bought in 2002 for $2.43 million by Private Media Group, the largest adult-content company in Europe. Private Media planned to use Napster as a distribution service for porn, but it also couldn't make a go of it. Roxio, a software company best known for its CD-burning utilities, then bought Napster for $5 million—and also failed to do much with it. In 2008, electronics retail company Best Buy bought Napster for $121 million, and announced that it would reinvent the service as an online music store.

The journey from marginal to mainstream is not always direct. Napster's conceptual roots traced back to the pornography-driven Usenet. Napster itself wavered back and forth between mainstream culture and the shadow world of lawbreakers and pornographers. But despite its cycle of going bankrupt and then being sold for ever larger sums of cash, Napster was never more than a stepping stone on the journey to mainstream. The most relevant descendant of Usenet is Apple's iTunes—a service notable for its utter lack of pornographic content. In April 2009, *Forbes* magazine reported that 87 per cent of digital music buyers used iTunes to make their purchases. In some ways, Apple merely put the finishing touches and technological refinements on a concept that had begun with the trade and distribution of pornography.

Pornography Outstrips the Mainstream

As the Internet continued to develop in leaps and bounds, pornography solidified its reputation as a driver of technology. The adult industry was making the Internet profitable, and it was also the place where the greatest creativity and innovation were happening—this was the cutting edge. As a result, pornography companies started to draw in people from mainstream sectors who were looking for new challenges and opportunities.

In the late 1990s, Reena Patel was employed in the heart of Toronto's financial district. She was making good money, but the work was intellectually moribund. "For me, working in finance was a very corporate, structured environment," she told me. "I was using what was a very small sampling of my skill set from school. Very limited Internet or new media was happening at all, and it was just purely financial, crunching numbers and delivery of those numbers. I was ready for a change."

She took off for Los Angeles, to pursue a Hollywood dream of honing her strategic-marketing skills in an increasingly tech-oriented market. She worked for a start-up company, trading her marketing expertise for room and board. By the time she entered the world of Internet marketing, the tech bubble had already burst, but all that really meant was that people were starting to take a more rational approach toward making dot-com dollars. The industry still involved big risks and big opportunities. "I guess the Internet wasn't primed yet to enable some of the people in the business back then to be able to do the things they wanted to do," she said. "The consumers weren't up-to-date yet. You could be streaming media, but your bandwidth costs were through the roof and there were no consumers out there who could actually watch the video you were streaming."

Many struggling website developers in this period turned to the sector that had weathered the boom-and-bust cycle: adult. "I came across one company in L.A. that we hired to make the websites for [a client that sold] medical device products. They were sister companies with a gay magazine that was technology-based, called Cybersocket. It was a web magazine geared towards gay men. What that magazine found is that the only people that had money at that time in gay media were the porn companies. So their advertisers were substantially gay porn advertisers, and a lot of these advertisers—whether they were just studios or production companies or retail product companies or toys or whatnot—didn't have websites and were looking to develop a web presence out in the marketplace."

The magazine's sister company started to supply these websites, and Patel went to work for them. "We had a number of mainstream clients: a silk company, a big tire company, a couple of banks, real estate companies and whatnot, but in order to sustain us through that rough period, we started picking up a lot of these adult companies," she said. "Through that transition we learned the technologies of how to build membership sites and third-party processing that were coming out of the woodwork then. There was a lot of money to be made back then because there weren't that many good-quality sites that were processing accurately in U.S. dollars."

Third-party processing is an alternative to having your own online credit card processing service. A separate company deals with all the security, logistics and legalities of taking credit card payments over the Internet. It can be costly, but for many adult companies the service was particularly worth it because it relieved them of the responsibility of dealing with one of the great banes of the industry: chargebacks. Chargebacks happen when a customer claims (truthfully or not) that a transaction has been billed to his card that he did not authorize. Generally in such disputes, the customer wins. He gets his money back, and the seller pays the cost. Chargebacks are a very common way for porn consumers to defraud adult websites.

People tend to think of pornographers as the lawbreakers and dirty dealers, but it was the high risk of fraudulent *customer* activity that pushed many adult companies toward innovations in e-commerce. If a porn company received too many chargebacks, the card issuer would drop it and effectively put it out of business. There were other risks for companies that sold physical products online—if an adult-novelty outlet accidentally shipped a video or a sex toy to a state where that product was illegal, it could be enough to end their relationship with the credit card companies. Online sex-based operations were risky business. Sheer pragmatism drove the adult industry toward new technological solutions to minimize risk and maximize profits from selling online content.

Patel was in the vanguard. "The easiest thing for companies to do, if they had content or could purchase or license content which was available to them, was to get it online in some format and create a membership site," she said. "It was very easy to do. It wasn't very costly at the time."

Some technologies just weren't there yet. Streaming video was one of the holy grails of online content sales. Ideally, streaming video would allow thousands of customers to watch the same digitized movie via the Internet, each being able to start and stop the show at their own convenience. Such technology made great demands on processing power, bandwidth, data compression and encoding and more. The porn industry was ready, but customers were trailing a little further behind—technologically and conceptually.

Of all the ways pornography spurred the development of Internet technology, bandwidth is by far the most significant. On the face of it, bandwidth is a banal concept. It has none of the sexiness of a beautifully designed piece of consumer electronics. People give pet names to their iMacs, but not to their modems. A compulsive BlackBerry user needs to be connected to the Internet 24/7, but she craves the device itself rather than the behind-the-scenes technology that allows her to send and receive email, photos, documents and videos. Bandwidth is a mere conduit—like electrical wiring or plumbing and sewage pipes. It allows material to move from one place to another. More bandwidth means more people can move more digital information more quickly.

Digital images require more bandwidth than digital text. Video demands more bandwidth than images. Every step up in quality—higher-resolution photographs, better-quality movies—required increasing amounts of bandwidth. Pornography dominated the flow of images and video on the Internet, and because there was a perpetual demand for more, different and better pornographic products, bandwidth needed to grow.

"You had some companies starting to develop video-streaming products for content," Patel said, "getting the DVDs on there, so people could stream them and watch them online. But they weren't as successful just because people didn't have the capabilities to really view them or even to understand, 'How do I watch a video on the Internet? I don't get it.'"

Danni Ashe's DanniVision was one early attempt at video streaming. Another product came from a Dutch porn company called Red Light District, whose techies developed a simple, not-too-bandwidth-hogging streaming system in 1994, six years before the first shaky attempts would come from mainstream companies such as Miramax and Blockbuster. Red Light District's video-streaming system was literally built in a day—a testament to porn companies' ability to cobble together technological solutions quickly and cheaply. They also paid close attention to the technological capacities and limitations of their potential viewers—something mainstream companies seemed unable or unwilling to do. In 2000, mainstream movie companies were trying to sell humungous video files that could barely be squeezed through the fastest DSL connection at a time when only 10 per cent of Americans had high-speed Internet connections. Meanwhile, thousands of compressed, manageable full-length adult movies were already flowing through 28.8k modems.

Pornographers were running circles around mainstream media—streaming video was just the start. Patel found that the adult industry allowed her the opportunity to experiment with all kinds of new technologies. She found the exact kind of challenges she had been seeking when she left the world of finance.

"Flash was a big deal back then. We'd charge double for a Flash website. Now you see companies moving away from Flash and going back to simple HTML because it's better for search engines, but back then getting a glossy Flash website was a big deal." She also worked with a scripting language called PHP. "You could build really cool membership sites—if you knew how to customize the code. It was pretty straightforward and easy to develop these sites, but there was a lot of money to be made because you could charge thousands of dollars for a simple site.

"For me it was just fascinating learning about everything that was changing in technology on the Web and meeting all these brilliant people that were coding. We had hackers working for us, doing search-engine optimization. These were the guys that knew how to hack into systems, and we had them dealing with security of our servers. Learning about bandwidth, hosting, processing online. For me, getting into the industry was just all of that."

Until 2005, Patel worked for companies whose public faces were those of mainstream dot-coms but whose innovations and major revenue streams were quietly based in adult content. After 2005, she worked for a number of overtly adult companies, including Kink.com. While the technological challenges continued to keep her intellectually engaged, she found after a while that the fetishes she marketed got to be too much for her. This part of her story is typical. From the outside, it may seem that anyone who works in the adult industry is into everything, and that once you cross the first line, it's much easier to cross the others. The truth, though, is that everyone has lines they won't cross, limitations to what they enjoy, comfort thresholds beyond which it's just time to move on.

Patel ended up as the director of product development and affiliate marketing for Playboy Enterprises. Playboy's content, while trending sometimes harder and sometimes softer, is overall closer to Patel's comfort zone. Her portfolio includes adult. com and Club Jenna, the online presence of Jenna Jameson. While Patel sometimes contemplates leaving the adult industry altogether, she feels fortunate to have found a place within the industry where she was challenged technologically without having to experience an affront to her sensibilities.

Playboy itself is one of a handful of publicly traded adult companies that have become legitimate mainstream investment options. Intensely legal, transparent and accountable, such companies also work to make their products and brands as close to mainstream as they can. Though Playboy has made greater inroads into mainstream business and culture than any of its peers, many others play the same game. Barcelona-based Private Media, for instance, is also publicly traded, and did 19.7 million euros in sales in 2008.

I had this in mind when I attended the 2008 Barcelona Summit, the first major pan-European convention for adult webmasters. About two hundred web developers, wireless marketers, traffic dealers (who make their living shunting surfers via advertising from one porn site to another) plus assorted other techs, entrepreneurs and a few performers took over a hotel in this Spanish city for two and a half days of workshops and intensive networking. They came from more than twenty countries to attend sessions on search-engine optimization, country-specific marketing, updates on law and policy, and other conventional Web issues. It would have felt like any tech conference were the sessions not interspersed with, for instance, boot-fetish photographic workshops.

When the day's workshops were done, I was sitting at the bar listening to people in the industry mull over issues like whether they would put their pornographic credentials on an application for a mainstream job (consensus: the sexual stigma still outweighs the technological mystique), whether women actually find "couples-oriented" pornography erotic or just tolerable, the differences in pornographic demands among Europeans and North Americans and among gay and straight, and what fetishes were currently most marketable.

As the evening wore on, a middle-aged man who had been sitting at the bar not saying much was just getting up to leave when someone in my party thought to introduce me. He turned out to be Ilan Bunimovitz, the Israeli-born, San Francisco–raised pornography mogul who in 2009 was appointed CEO of Private Media Group. Though he is not as famous as *Playboy*'s Hugh Hefner or *Hustler*'s Larry Flynt (and does not exhibit any of their flamboyant showmanship), he is in their league as one of the world's most powerful pornography magnates.

In January 2009, Private acquired GameLink, a U.S.-based adult web portal and e-commerce provider that Bunimovitz had founded in 1993. As part of the deal, Bunimovitz became vice-president of Private's Online Media Division, and quickly moved into the top position. He now commutes between his long-time home in San Francisco and Private's offices in Barcelona. (He has no complaints about dividing his time between these two beautiful cities.)

In an industry that is often ahead of the curve, Bunimovitz has a reputation as a pioneer among pioneers. He settled back in at the bar and told me the long story of how he came to earn that reputation. As his story unfolded, it became clear that he personified many of the key moments in communications history where pornography showed the way.

"In 1993, a lot of chat rooms on some BBSs made money charging you a fee for connecting to the BBS," he said. "My business model was different. We sold porno."

The technology was far too nascent at that point to sell digital movies directly online. Bunimovitz's innovation was to create a digital catalogue of more than five thousand pornographic

VCR tapes. He sold the catalogue itself online, but people had to order the actual movies the old-fashioned way. He started this project in his spare time, but soon realized he could make enough money to leave his job in the hotel industry. "I was not particularly technological. So I had to teach myself how to use a computer, but I just fell in love with idea of doing the whole thing online."

Even as he discovered how readily possible it was for him to make a living selling pornography, he became aware that his business was also generating vast revenue for other people. "You look at the logs," he said, meaning BBS logs, "and you see the different calls, from Hong Kong, Singapore and Europe. People would spend hours on the phone going through the catalogue. And if you remember in 1993, a minute of long distance cost a dollar. And so I was like, 'Hey, those guys are actually spending more money on the phone bill then they're spending with me.'"

Someone might spend a hundred dollars exploring a catalogue Bunimovitz charged five dollars for. He came away from this experience with a lifelong conviction that if you can provide people with a compelling product, price will be no object. "It's a lesson that is exceptionally valuable today, because everybody is freaking out. There is free competition," he said. "Everybody says, 'What are we going to do?' What we are going to do is present a product that is compelling enough for people to pay for it, just the way that in 1993, my catalogue was compelling enough for people to spend a hundred dollars on a phone call to get what they wanted. Now what does it mean to have something compelling? This is the million-dollar question. But if you can answer this question, it can make your business."

In 1994, a friend showed Bunimovitz the Internet. It was slow, it was text-based, and it was his next business opportunity.

At the time, many BBSs were starting to provide the means to give their users access to the Internet. Bunimovitz used these gateways to draw people in the other direction—Internet users could now access the BBS where his catalogue resided, which meant that long-distance charges ceased to be an issue.

As his business grew, Bunimovitz realized that he needed to stay at the forefront of computers and the Internet, and to seek out new tools and new technologies to keep money flowing in. "I learned how to use a database. I found a shareware program on CompuServe—I still have the original program. It's a DOS program that basically allowed you to create a catalogue on a disk.

"I took the file with all my products from the BBS and reformatted it for this catalogue. You only have to insert the tags—it's like doing HTML. It took me a few nights of work." He ended up with a much more dynamic, searchable catalogue that made it vastly easier for his clientele to find exactly what they wanted.

He began advertising in men's magazines that had entire pages of ads for catalogues of pornography. Most of these ads included raunchy images evocative of the content. Bunimovitz's ad was a picture of a computer with the tagline, "The most discreet catalogue of all." He was soon selling five hundred catalogues every week.

"I would stay at home copying the disk manually on my computer—just sit and read a book and change floppy disks." He invested in other leading-edge technologies of the day, like a fax machine for taking orders and a manual credit card imprinter for processing. The next really big step, though, was to move the catalogue from the BBS directly on to the Internet.

"I went and bought, for eighty bucks, an unlimited licence to use the Zip program. I set up an account with an Internet service provider. I was customer number 37." He placed a few ads for just a few dollars on the major Internet hubs of the time, CompuServe and America Online, using the same slogan: "You can FTP the most discreet catalogue of all."

"Within three days I got a phone call from the guy that owned the ISP. He said, 'What are you doing?' I said, 'What do you mean?' He said, 'You saturated my FTP line. Nobody else can use it. And it looks like, if I get more lines, you'll saturate them too.' I was getting, by this point, like $5,000 a week in orders. People were faxing the orders all day long."

The push for increased bandwidth had begun in earnest. Bunimovitz paid the ISP to install more and more lines, widening the pipe through which pornography could flow. Bunimovitz was building the infrastructure of the Internet.

While many customers had the technological know-how to FTP a Zipped file, Bunimovitz had already realized that he would find a much larger client base through the more intuitive Internet interface known as the World Wide Web. He hired an expert to build a website for him, but quickly realized he could do it himself. At the time, the web was still text only—pictures were yet to come. HTML was a simple programming language that provided limited design options.

"It was all text. The fancy stuff was the logo, I used 'font=10,' so I got big letters. Then I learned how to do italics and was like, shit, you know italic *and* bold. I used *three different tags* at one time. But it worked. I had a catalogue with thousands of movies and a good menu system."

Given that the high-end technology in 1995 was a 1200-baud modem, it was still too soon to sell actual pictures. So Bunimovitz instead focused on giving customers ever greater ease with and control over their shopping experience. By this time, he had twenty thousand movies in his catalogue. He hired a UNIX programmer to create a more sophisticated and flexible online database, giving him one of the most technologically advanced websites of the time.

As his business kept pushing the technological envelope, it became time for him to bring the big porn companies on board in a more active capacity.

"A friend took me to Vegas and he introduced me to all the studios. He was a bigwig in the industry. And he said, 'Hey, this is my friend Einstein.' I had long hair at the time. He was telling them, 'He sells stuff online.' And they said, 'What's online?' And he said, 'Don't worry about it. My friend Einstein will make you money. Just work with him.'"

Work with him they did. He had each studio fax him their back catalogue, and he hired a crew of data enterers to incorporate all of this information in his online database. Nothing like it had ever existed before.

"If you look at the way the industry was structured at the time, the business was a new-release business. A typical store could carry a hundred or two hundred videos. A megastore could carry like five hundred movies. Just like the book business was before Amazon, just like every other business before the Internet, it was a small catalogue. Suddenly I had a catalogue with seventy thousand titles. For the consumer, it became like, somebody would say, 'Hey, I heard that my girlfriend from high school is doing porn.' And they would do a search for her name and find the movie and order it."

Studios had back stock sitting on shelves that they tried to sell in mixed bags at the rock-bottom price of $2 a title. Bunimovitz, who now had a tool that could connect individual customers with the exact film they were looking for, offered to buy up back stock at $3 a pop, knowing that out there somewhere was someone who would pay $30 or $40 for the exact movie he was looking for. The lesson Bunimovitz had learned examining phone logs in his BBS days paid off—money was no object for the right product.

"It became a very thriving business, and basically now they have a name for it. You hear about the 'long tail' and it's a fancy word. People write books about it," he said. The term "long tail" was coined by *Wired* magazine editor Chris Anderson in 2004. It describes a business model that provides a huge variety of specialized, hard-to-find items that are sold in very small numbers at premium prices to an equally huge variety of specialized clientele. "We had the long tail in 1994. There was no name for it. I just instinctively knew it would work."

Bunimovitz knew he had a technological lead over his competitors, and he also knew how quickly he could lose that lead and just become one porn-database provider among many. He kept moving. "Every business model that I had, I worked under the assumption that it was about to go away," he said. "The technology is very dynamic, customers are very dynamic, and you have to always look two, three years down the road. You have to try enough things that one of them will be the right thing for the future."

He did not do market studies or focus groups. He did not do SWOT analyses or develop mission and vision statements. He did not wait to see which way the technological winds were blowing before committing. He did what the porn industry does: he experimented, he left behind the old, and he employed new technologies based on nothing more than his own hopes and instincts.

In 1997, his staff employed a scripting engine called ASP, or Active Server Pages, to make their website more dynamic. Months after they went live, a developer walked smugly into his office with a new book that explained to programmers how to do exactly what the team had already done. The technological development cycle had picked up the pace, though, and soon

ASP was nothing special on the web. Bunimovitz still had the edge for a while, because nobody had a catalogue anywhere near as comprehensive as his. But once DVDs became standard, his vast repository of videotapes became much less valuable. Price became the only differentiating factor from one site to another.

"Suddenly you're selling for a dollar over cost," he said. "It was no longer an interesting business. I had to reinvent."

He moved to DVD along with everyone else, but was already looking ahead for the next technology that could put him out in front again. "This was 1999, and I figured I had to find something new. We decided to go after video-on-demand for broadband. At the time people who saw videos online had 56k modems. You'd get those little videos, postage-stamp sized and shaky, two frames a second," he said. "We went broadband-only from day one. Because I was like, 'Hey, we're going to differentiate ourselves.'"

Again he approached the studios, and again they trusted him to go out and make them money on the Internet, even though they (again) did not fully understand what he was trying to do.

"On day one, we put maybe a hundred movies online. We did a soft launch. We put a little tab on the side that said 'Video on Demand' and we sold the movie for $10. I figured that's a good price. We sold twenty movies the first day. Now, you don't get rich with $200, but I looked at it and said, 'You know, we have a business.'"

They bought up dozens of computer services and began encoding one to two hundred movies every week, turning them into files that could be watched at any time by anyone with a high-speed Internet connection. Very quickly, Bunimovitz had tens of thousands of pornographic films available online—his old catalogue had given way to direct access to the product itself.

"I believe I was the first to do this," he said. "Other people claim that they were the first and it's hard to tell if I was number one and another guy started a few months after me or vice versa. I'm not the only smart guy in the world. There are a lot of smart guys around. You've got to give other people credit too."

This was the first, or close to the first, instance of a working commercial video-on-demand service being piped into people's homes via high-speed Internet. And it was significant for three major reasons. First, it proved to entrepreneurs—adult and mainstream alike—that there was money to be made in selling content online. Second, it gave consumers a reason to move to high-speed Internet, which created increased demand for better Internet infrastructure. And finally, those consumers who upgraded their connection to get better pornography became part of a growing user base of people with all the tools necessary to use their new technology for purposes besides the porn that had brought them there. Only when the bandwidth and users were already in place was the Internet ready for non-pornographic services such as YouTube, CNN.com and Flickr, all of which depend on sending images, text and videos through the very pipelines that were created through the buying, selling, stealing and trading of pornography.

If bandwidth represents the mundane nuts-and-bolts contribution of pornography, some of Bunimovitz's other innovations speak to more sophisticated, creative and innovative influences. For instance, he had also been experimenting with technology that would analyze customers' purchase habits and recommend other products they might enjoy. Bunimovitz incorporated some of these pattern-recognition tools into his websites, but after a time found that their most effective applications were in email-based direct marketing campaigns.

He allowed one of his employees to spend six months developing a tool that would incorporate a recommendation engine into an automated email campaign. With a few keystrokes, the company could send an email to everyone in, say, San Francisco who had not bought anything in the last six months. Each customer would get new movie recommendations, individually tailored on the basis of what they had bought in the past. Today, such tools are commonplace—anyone who has bought a few books or DVDs from Amazon will receive from them often disconcertingly appropriate recommendations of other products they might like. But when Bunimovitz began using these tools, the concept was so new (and so profitable) that he had to restructure to make the most of this revolutionary marketing strategy.

"This was when I ended up letting go of my director of marketing. She came from direct mail. In direct mail they were used to using coupons. I don't like coupons. I think that if you give people something that has value, they will buy. Give them a coupon and you bribe them to buy. It creates sustainable business if you give people a reason to do business with you." His marketing director was only interested in discounts and rebates, which did not match Bunimovitz's ideas of how to use his new software tools. "She said, 'What kind of offer will you send?' I said, 'The offer is: Here are ten movies you're likely to like. This is the only text you're going to put.'" It turned out to be the highest-grossing mailing they had ever done.

Today, Bunimovitz runs a massive company in a heavily fragmented market, where early adoption happens more quickly and more widely than ever before. Taking risks and finding avenues that will set his product apart and entice customers to pay top dollar is that much more difficult. He has the advantage of strong brands—both his own and Private Media's—but in an age where getting free pornography is no longer the technological ordeal it once was, he has his job cut out for him to continue converting surfers into paying customers. He remains confident that, despite all the changes, the lessons he learned early on will continue to apply.

"Today, we're going into a world where content consumption will be very fragmented. It's going to be fragmented among consumer groups. Some will prefer Internet, others will prefer IPTV"—Internet protocol television, or digital television delivered online—"others regular TV, and others will still buy DVDs," he said. "It's also fragmented within the same customer. One customer might buy a movie through IPTV. And then next week, they're on the road in their hotel room and they buy the same movie or another movie on the computer. And they also find this movie that they love and so they carry a copy on their mobile device."

Bunimovitz sees two ways for adult companies to go. Small companies can specialize, offering niche products via niche technologies. Delivering the right product via the right medium will still prove popular. For a major company like Private Media, though, there is no longer a single "next big thing" in communications technology. Instead, there are lots and lots of small things, all of which matter.

"I'm looking at my business and I'm saying, my goal over the next year is to make sure that we are in every channel and in every territory," he said. "That makes your life very simple. You look at your business and say, 'Where are we now geographically and channel-wise? Where are we not? These are the holes in my lineup? I'll plug those holes.' It's a very simple business plan." A business plan that may well once again show the path to the future for mainstream media companies.

PART FOUR

The Strange Future of
Mass Communication

Words Get in the Way

C hange begets change. Ilan Bunimovitz's plan to be everywhere brought to mind another conversation I had had
on the other side of the world at a much larger pornography
event that happens each year in Las Vegas: the Adult Entertainment Expo, which is sponsored by the trade magazine *Adult
Video News*.

Every January, the kings and queens of the porn industry step
out from the "Adults Only" section of the video store to enjoy a
few minutes of mainstream fame. The AVN Expo is the world's
biggest convention for adult entertainment fans. The four-day
extravaganza draws thirty thousand people to the Sands Expo
and Convention Center.

For these few days, the face of pornography shifts from a
creepy old man in a raincoat to a glamorous celebrity in a gown.
It is a surreal mix of crudeness, business and technology, with
booths pitching everything from 3D video technology to UV
teeth-whitening services. Christian organizations hand out

temporary tattoos that say "Jesus Loves Pornstars," and vanity publishers sell books on building self-esteem. The sensory overload circulating around the floor is unlike anything else.

Many journalists have written accounts of their visits to this expo—one of the funniest and most perceptive has to be David Foster Wallace's essay "Red Son Rising," in his collection *Consider the Lobster*—though most focus exclusively on the floor dedicated to fans and performers. The AEE, though, is actually several events in one: at the fan expo, tens of thousands of porn enthusiasts line up for a chance to meet the objects of their desire. The clichés here abound, from the porn actress posing with a fan, whom I overheard saying, "You touch my tits, I break your fingers," to the sex-toy vendor wearing a T-shirt that said, "We treat objects like women," to the crowd of men gathered around the one screen in the whole place showing a football game rather than trailers for the latest porn releases.

Elsewhere in the convention centre was a B2B trade show, where the business and networking got done. There was also a series of seminars that were every bit as dry as those you'd get at an academic conference or standard marketing convention— nothing says conventionality more than a poorly stage-managed forum on search-engine optimization in a room with a bad sound system, sallow lighting and uncomfortable chairs. You could convince yourself this was a business like any other, were it not for the fact that a hundred yards away were booths staffed by women wearing nothing but high-tech paint-on "liquid latex," orgasm faking contests, and the kind of kerfuffles that could not possibly happen anywhere else. While I was walking past a booth hyping the latest in peep-show technology, a convention centre official took the booth owner aside to talk about the demo films he was using. "Sir, I'm sorry, but you can't show a woman being penetrated at the Centre—it's kind of a policy. If the penis is already in, that's okay, but you can't show it going in." The booth operator begrudgingly obliged—until the official was out of sight.

Not coincidentally, this event overlaps each year with the other big show in town, the International Consumer Electronics Show, which is one of the biggest mainstream electronics trade shows of the year. The running joke on the adult side is that it requires only a couple of their stars to saunter past the gathering of geeks and techies at the CES to boost attendance at the AVN Expo by thousands.

But not all those whose attention shifts down the hall are excited about the same thing. Many duck over to the porn convention to hear from pornographers about what the next big content-delivery vehicle might be.

I had noticed a man circulating on the floor of the AVN B2B area in a high-tech "standing wheelchair." It used the same kind of gyroscopic stabilizers that make a Segway scooter stay upright (they were created by the same inventor), which allows the user to climb stairs, travel over rough terrain and raise the chair up on two wheels so that its owner can have eye-level conversations. The chair's owner, Michael Kaplan, turned out to be a software engineer who specializes in closed-captioning and subtitles for films—a growth area in an age of increased internationalization, and one where the adult industry, perhaps not surprisingly, is pushing the technological envelope.

Stag films were essentially a local industry due to the cumbersome nature of the technology. Peeps and VCRs made adult movies a national concern, with some cross-border trade. The Internet opened up a truly global market with producers, distributors and especially customers in every country on the planet. The international pornography market was a reminder that the language of love is not actually universal. Michael Kaplan's company, Trigeminal Software, specializes in internationalizing and localizing software and other media, so that people around the world do not have to learn English in order to enjoy the full range of contemporary utilities and entertainment. His clients have included software giants like Microsoft and Adobe, as well as many adult film companies. His work in subtitling and captioning means his market also includes people who are hearing impaired.

"It's a very rich area because the technology is slowly coming along," Kaplan said. "I've found it's being driven much faster by the adult industry than by mainstream. Honestly, people seem to put up with a lot more outside of the adult industry: things don't work as well, languages aren't supported as well, whereas in the adult films people just want stuff to work. They don't want to have to think about it."

Some of the challenges are the same for any subtitling, adult or otherwise. Subtitles need to be easily readable without obscuring the images. You can't put white text against a white background. Because reading is slower than listening, some information will be lost in the subtitling process. There is also the challenge of ensuring that the closed-captioning (which is in the same language as the film and is aimed at the hearing impaired) does not interfere with the subtitling (which is in a different language from the film and is aimed at foreign speakers).

Kaplan says the innovations that the adult industry are driving are not so much aimed at improving the sophistication of subtitles and captions as they are at making the process cheaper and easier. The most expensive part of subtitling is the manual effort that goes into placement and colour adjustment on the screen—there is an art to adapting text to the content without creating a jarring reading experience for viewers. Kaplan's company is developing better ways to automate this process, reducing the overall costs of adding subtitles to a film.

Porn distributors, he says, "want to be able to sell their movies anywhere. They don't want language to be the blocker. Maybe they don't speak Hindi or Japanese or Romanian, but the words should be there so they don't have to think about them. So if it's easy and it's cheap, then it's, 'Yeah we want to add it to our movie.'" The cheap and easy innovations created for the pornography industry will of course make it simpler for mainstream movies to follow suit and access similar global markets.

Kaplan says viewers see a qualitative difference between watching an adult film and, say, watching a nature documentary. They both have action, which means they face some of the same logistical challenges. But because porn films rely on creating an immersive fantasy for the viewer, the stakes are higher to get things right. So, while viewers can and do put up with erroneous words and the occasional string of gibberish generated by auto-captioning systems for mainstream television and movies, such errors simply won't cut it with porn viewers.

"It's industry driven, but not in the way that things are usually industry driven," he said. "It's different just because they are trying make you feel at home with the movie you're getting, and they want 'home' to be any part of the world."

Cheaper, faster, easier and less intrusive: these qualities are all touchstones of pornography—the areas where the adult industry shows the mainstream world how to do it. And there is more. Sometimes, no matter how seamless the captions and subtitles are, they only get in the way of what's happening on-screen. Even people who like to follow the plot of their adult feature just want all the text to disappear during the sex scenes, when the nature of the communication is more self-evident.

"What about multiple levels of captioning where you can actually choose no captioning during the sex scenes?" Kaplan mused. He said his initial discussions with adult movie producers had already generated a lot of interest on this front. "It ends up in this very weird and interesting area."

Weird and interesting has always been Kaplan's bread and butter. A self-described "geek at heart," he arrived in the world of multilingual adult film subtitling by way of technology. "I guess I've just always been hanging around computers," he said. "I've always been intrigued by problems that are really complicated that people don't understand, so I kind of jumped into the international side."

Some years ago, he hired a woman to work on a website for him. When he offered to give her a credit on the site, she warned him that she was associated with the world of adult entertainment—she happened to be a former porn actress—and gave him the option of keeping her name out of his business. "I said, 'Where I work that is not a blocker—that is exciting,' and I gave her a little icon. She became the webmistress instead of the webmaster. From there, I ended up going to a few industry events and it just snowballed from there. People said, 'Maybe you can help with this project or that project.' They said, 'Hopefully you're not offended by that,' and I'd say, 'Are you kidding? I can brag about this later.'"

Kaplan's pride was typical, but not universal. In the same way that porn sometimes seems to be both everywhere and nowhere, it also engenders embarrassment or a whiff of scandal, even among those who recognize its influence on developments in the means of communication. This leads to a seeming paradox in which we treat pornography simultaneously as a widely known established truth and as a skeleton in the technological cupboard—one that can be spoken about only in a conspiratorial tone.

In June 2006, the online Electronics Design, Strategy News published a comprehensive analysis of the pornography industry's influence on emerging technology markets, focusing particularly on the growing market for next-generation cellphones. These phones have the processing power, display quality and Internet speed sufficient for adult applications. What is not surprising is that many adult companies have already jumped into this new market, quietly working with mainstream partners to provide pornographic services for high-speed smartphones. What *is* surprising is the article's headline: "Dirty Little Secret."

"The mobile Internet is the most recent example of the industry's dirty little secret," writes Bill Roberts in the article. "Pornography is an old friend of technology. Flush with content, pornographers can reap new profits from each new channel, and they risk being left behind if they don't adopt them. As risk takers, pornographers offer the heavy-volume usage that start-ups need in order to prove and improve their concepts. As prompt paying customers, by most accounts, pornographers provide important early revenue to technology partners."

There is a real question here about who is privy to this secret, and from whom it is supposedly being kept.

"Young males with cash to spend are repeating the boost they gave early multimedia computers, broadband and video-on-demand, by paying premium prices for advanced multimedia cell phones so they can surf for sex anyplace, anytime—to the benefit of ARM, Motorola, Nokia, Qualcomm, Samsung, SanDisk, Sony, Texas Instruments and a host of other companies," he writes, as though readers should be surprised.

Nobody he interviewed for the piece seems surprised. Ghatim Kabbara, managing director of the Barcelona-based software company Safira Solutions, says the first client for the company's cellphone content delivery service was Cherry

Media, a mobile pornography portal, and that half of Safira's mobile business still comes from adult content.

American forecasters were predicting revenues between half and one and a half billion dollars for cellphone porn in 2009 for the United States alone. Other predictions put the worldwide market at more than $2 billion, with more than 112 million users by 2010.

As with every number connected to the pornography industry, every analyst agrees that these ones are questionable. Industry players tend to exaggerate the numbers; users tend to lie in the other direction. Plus, however much money will be actually spent on pornography, no statistic can take into account the piracy, theft and consensual sharing of adult content among those who invest in new technologies but never spend or make a dollar directly from pornography.

Nevertheless, it is clear that mainstream industry watchers and entrepreneurs understand that pornography and erotica are a key part of the early market for a new medium such as high-speed Internet for cellphones. Even if the numbers are somewhat overblown, sex is still big business, made even bigger by the underground trade.

In the twenty-first century, the influence of the porn industry on new communications devices may still be dirty, but it is no longer a secret. It is part of the standard business model. The fact that it is still treated like a secret, even by analysts, journalists and media employees who have long understood that influence, indicates something beyond coyness or discomfort with the truth. People say it's a secret even as they shout it from the mountaintop.

Call it compartmentalization. Call it cognitive dissonance. Call it the interplay between subconscious and conscious motivators of technological progress. No matter how it is described, it seems as though people are very willing to utter the truth of the matter and then immediately file this knowledge away in the backs of their minds, separate from their day-to-day thoughts and experiences, stored away until the next occasion where it becomes necessary or desirable to once again disclose this same "dirty little secret."

Some people, of course, make a secret of pornography's role for less psychologically complex, more practical reasons—reasons such as having unexpectedly ended up in a professional role that requires them to deal with pornography, but not much liking it, and suspecting that their wife and family would like it even less.

"A lot of people will look at our content and say, 'This is obscene, it's disgusting.' I think to us it's just a business, you know?" a man I'll call Andrew told me. Andrew is the vice-president of business development for a mobile infrastructure company in England. His company creates software tools that allow cable television and other media companies to get their material onto mobile devices. The company that employs him actually has two identities: one for the mainstream world and one for pornography. These two companies do the same job, using the same technology. They only differ in the nature of the content.

"That's just our business model," Andrew said. "It's based on the fact of the popularity of the adult market, and the brands that we feel are really going to drive traffic and sales. We are a technology company, and the fact is that our technology is being used more for the adult industry than anything else."

That much is unambiguous. There are parts of this reality that Andrew finds murky. He has been working in the mobile industry since 2002 and joined his current company in 2008. He didn't know he would be standing with one foot in each world when he took on this position—he thought he would be dealing exclusively with non-adult clients. But the profit to be made getting porn onto smartphones proved seductive to his bosses, particularly when the economy collapsed around them.

"The company has sort of shifted away from what they were originally going to do to," Andrew said. There are degrees of extremity and legality when it comes to pornography, and Andrew's company doesn't stray anywhere near content that might get them in trouble. Still, "I don't personally feel 100 per cent comfortable with the industry. For example, my wife doesn't know everything that I'm doing, and that's hard for me. But I don't think she needs to know all the details. She knows I deal with a bit of adult because it's a big seller, but she also thinks I'm doing a lot of other things, and that makes me feel slightly uncomfortable."

Andrew was one of the few people I spoke to who did not want to be identifiable in any way. This was in part because of his concern about his wife and children, but it was also about his own comfort level. "None of us want our kids to see the stuff that I've seen," he said, "but *I* don't want to see half the stuff that I've seen."

It's also an issue for his employer's mainstream operations. They do not want their non-adult business to be tainted by their connections to the pornographic world. Despite widespread coverage of the influence of adult content on the development of wireless content delivery, this is one of many companies still maintaining its "dirty little secret."

Much of Andrew's work is devoted to creating multiple versions of websites, each optimized for a different smartphone, such as the iPhone or BlackBerry. (The iPhone occasionally makes news because, as yet, Apple has not allowed applications with adult content to be sold for their device. However, iPhone users can access pornographic content by browsing the web just like any other mobile device users.) "The mobile phone has taken adult surfing to a new level where you are answerable to no one. You take your mobile device anywhere you like and nobody has to know where you are, what you are doing or where you've been," Andrew said. "The success of the mobile is the fact that you can take it anywhere and nobody has to know and nobody can track where you've been. So that's why I think there is an ever-increasing demand for better quality mobile adult entertainment."

Even though increasingly infamous free porn sites are also available for wireless devices, Andrew sees proof every day that people are still willing to pay for adult content. The adult side of his business turns about $10 million in annual profit—and that is in a weak economy. That's enough of a reason for Andrew to stick with his current position at least long enough to weather the recession. And although it isn't what he would necessarily choose for himself, he does find the work challenging. "I don't regret anything I'm doing," he said.

He says that by working on adult content delivery, he's learned more about technologies like the iPhone than he ever thought he would. He believes this will serve him well when he moves into a position he's more comfortable with. "The truth is that this industry is unlike any other industry that you will ever find. People are very open and very friendly. They introduce you to anybody and everybody. It's quite a close-knit community." Given that his situation, bridging adult and mainstream, is typical, he expects the contacts he has made in the former will ultimately help him land a job in the latter.

When he does make the move, his CV will mention the mainstream company and not the adult—his personal dirty little secret will remain just that.

———

Even as pornography continues to push Internet technology in new directions, its earlier influences have already filtered into the mainstream. The cycle of early adopters giving way to mainstream users now happens more quickly than ever before. Technologies move from the margins to the mainstream with such velocity that people still marvel over these mind-blowing new tools of communication at the very same time that they can no longer remember what life was like without them.

Today, the mainstream Internet is Google, eBay, iTunes and Amazon. It is newspaper, television and radio institutions that recognize that their future—if they have one—is on the Internet. It is retail chains, banks, travel agents and software companies whose projections portend the demise of bricks-and-mortar businesses. It is dating, gambling and gameplaying, social networking and a blogosphere filled with voices that would never have found a platform in the previous century. It is a set of research tools equally valuable to academics, businesses, amateur logophiles, crowdsourcers, inventors, journalists and trivia enthusiasts. It is email, instant chat and Internet-based videophone calling—tools that make it economically and technological feasible to feel as though you're there when you're not. The mainstream Internet has changed the face of everything from celebrity gossip to political activism. The transformative power of the Internet has been commented on ad infinitum, and yet it never gets any less astounding. It is an explosion that continues to explode, with no decrease in sight.

Many Internet applications are only now starting to mature, as seen by their reduced reliance on the pornographic content that helped bring them into existence. Even today, though, porn still holds power over these technologies. About 12 per cent of all current websites deal in porn, with annual worldwide revenues pegged at about $97 billion in 2006. In one month, December 2007, thirty-eight million people—about a quarter of all surfers—visited a porn site.

It's interesting to think for a moment about those other tens of millions of Internet users who do not visit pornography sites. For them, it is now easy to go online and be blissfully unaware that the foundations of that world, the infrastructure that makes it possible to watch television, trade stocks, play games and do all the other bandwidth-hogging, processor-hungry activities of the modern Internet, were created to serve the needs of the pornography industry.

Following the pattern of dozens of pre-Internet technologies, a widespread scrubbing of pornographic roots has begun, with many mainstream companies lapsing into silence or denial of their erotic ancestry or their current relationship. Not least among these are the search engines that make everything else online manageable and useful. Google and other search engines do not disclose how much of their earnings or traffic have to do with adult content, leaving analysts and others to speculate. Everyone knows pornography is significant, but nobody can say definitively how significant.

In 2006, the American Department of Justice requested huge volumes of search data from Google and other services in the hopes that the information would provide support for President George W. Bush's Child Online Protection Act. The Justice Department was hoping to get sympathy for COPA by proving how easy and common it was for minors to access porn on the Internet. Google argued that handing over such data would compromise its users' privacy and reveal its own trade secrets. *Forbes* magazine suggested that the secret

Google really did not want revealed was its heavy dependency on pornography.

"Google and its competitors all benefit from porn sites, which help generate search queries and page views," wrote Chris Kraeuter and Rachel Rosmarin in "Why Google Won't Give In." "But Google is the only portal company that makes nearly all of its revenue from click-through advertising. Restricting porn and porn advertising—the likely aim of COPA's sponsors—could hurt Google disproportionately."

In fact, they went on to report, Google's reliance on pornography goes beyond the revenues it earned from people clicking on advertisements for adult websites. Google's brand is built on the idea that it gives users access to all available information, organized and catalogued, but not filtered according to politics, economics or any bias other than that of the users themselves. (The degree of truth behind that brand identity is another matter.) Google gives surfers filtering tools so that they can deny themselves access to pornography, but if the company were forced to do that itself, it would cripple its efforts to provide access and organization to all the available material.

Most analysts, academics and industry personnel I have spoken to are cautious about statements like "Without pornography, there would be no Google." All acknowledge, though, that pornography, erotica and sexual representation (and passionate love) do indeed deserve a special status as an engine of innovation in communication, and that without them, Internet technology would have developed much more slowly or even not at all. The adult industry made many innovations happen faster and better than they would have otherwise. Pornographers also helped the initial user base grow comfortable with the technology.

Google and most other mainstream Internet applications rely on pornography today, but even more important is the fact that without the last forty years of steady porn-driven technological improvements, many of these modern tools might never have been possible in the first place.

Out of the MUD

Today, the cycles of technological development, adoption and maturation have become a blur. It took thirty-eight years for radio to garner fifty million users. Television hit that mark in thirteen years. The Internet did it in four. Perhaps that means that people more readily adopt new technologies than they used to—technological change itself has become a more familiar concept, which diminishes the inertia that has historically dampened initial enthusiasm to trade old technology for new. That suggests that pornography could become less important to technological progress—that new technologies might be able to rely less on the special draw of pornography to develop their initial user base and infrastructure.

Many means of communication, though, still take their time moving toward mainstream consciousness, percolating for years and even decades on the margins. Some technologies remain difficult to use and still feel foreign and unnatural to broad swaths of society, simply because they are so different from what has come before. Video games and virtual worlds still fit into this category. For more than forty years, beginning with MUD1, virtual worlds have been edging toward the mainstream, but they have not arrived yet. They have become vastly more sophisticated than the text-based games of yore, full of graphics, animation, sound and music. But virtual worlds still take a considerable investment in time and energy just to make the least sense of them.

The complexity of a virtual world interface is compounded by ambiguity over what the objective of the medium is. Someone who cannot program a VCR still can easily grasp what the machine is meant to do. The purpose of a virtual world, though—particularly of the kind with no puzzles or quests—is less immediately discernible. These worlds are full of strange customs, foreign jargon and local shibboleths, and a visitor can wander around lost, bored or frustrated indefinitely. As with real-life exotic travel, the safest and most practical course of action is to enlist an experienced travel companion—someone who can translate the local dialect, who knows where the points of interest can be found and who knows how to stay out of trouble.

That's how I ended up exploring a sunlit shopping plaza with a computer programmer named Randal Oulton. Oulton had agreed to show me some of the ways that sex and erotica are actively shaping the technology of virtual worlds. His tour would take us into some pretty strange territory, dealing both with some fairly serious kink and with some issues of love and other emotions that are on some level more disturbing than sexuality on its own could ever be. Considerate guide that he was, though, he eased me in slowly, giving me a chance to acclimatize. We were exploring one of the most famous virtual worlds, called Second Life. Like LambdaMOO, Second Life is a place for socializing and sex, rather than swords and sorcery. Unlike LambdaMOO, Second Life is also a place to do business.

As we walked around the plaza, we passed a rug shop, greeting card store, art gallery, offices for an AIDS education charity and even a retail outfit that sells diagnostic scanners and other medical equipment. (An MRI machine sold for about $6 U.S.) We didn't have all day, so we opted to fly instead of walk. (One of the perks of virtual worlds is that you can mess with physics.) With a little jump, we were airborne. Before we entered any shops, we flew up to the mall roof, where Oulton wanted to show off his latest acquisition: a lighter-than-air ship. He uses it for hosting parties in the sky to promote his Second Life businesses.

"I make sure that I socialize and network, because it's a big part of branding and marketing," he said. "I sponsor a lot of club openings with prizes, money, that kind of stuff. I make sure my name is out there, and that it's a trusted name." He's doing okay, too. He owns the mall we were flying around. It sits on an island he bought for about $700 U.S. He rents out many of the shop spaces and runs several of his own retail businesses here.

"Sadly, airships are banned in this mall, so I will take it away before anyone notices," he said before causing it to wink out of existence. "Let's do another tour of the mall."

Among the shops selling picture frames, clothing and bric-a-brac, we passed a store that sold chest and body hair. Some was thick and curly, some thin and wispy. Many versions covered the pecs, with a narrow trail running down the abdomen. Some packages also included arm, armpit, leg and pubic hair, along with chin stubble.

Self-representation has evolved since the first multi-player online games. Avatars in MUD1 days were nothing more than textual self-descriptions created by the author. If a player wanted her avatar to have body hair, she simply wrote it into her profile. Now, not only has text given way to sophisticated 3D graphics but avatar customization has become big business. In shops like this, scattered throughout the virtual environment, you can buy not just body hair but cleft chins, aquiline noses, rippling biceps, tattoos and piercings and whatever else you need to get your online representative looking the way you want. The people who come to Second Life make major investments—personal *and* financial—in their avatars. They are not there to battle giant spiders or shoot aliens. They are there to meet other people, make friends, fall in love and have sex. Items such as body hair help increase the intimacy between player and avatar, which helps set the stage for, and maximize the emotional engagement in, more explicit products and activities.

Oulton and I wandered into a second-hand store filled with tchotchkes, gewgaws, knick-knacks and curios. "I guess it's 'Welcome Mat Month' here at the store. Everything is very tacky," he said, as his avatar poked around a selection of carpets. Hovering the mouse over an object brought up its product name and description. A click gave the price. Mixed in with virtual lamps, mats and tables were a set of blue spheres whose function was unknown until Oulton moused over them. Oulton was blasé. "I'm not really in the market for anal orgy balls, but let's see how much he wants for them," he said. They were 65 Lindens for a set of six.

Lindens are the currency of Second Life. Like any other foreign currency, virtual Lindens can be bought online with real-world currency. To buy his island, for instance, Oulton had to exchange real dollars for virtual Lindens.

The economy and trade in a virtual world is puzzling for many reasons. For one, the very concept of a second-hand store makes no sense. Unlike real-world items like cars and computers, a digital item does not decay or decline in quality over time or through duplication. A second-hand item is identical to when it was new. Somehow, though, an object in Second Life is still worth less if bought from a previous owner rather than from its creator.

The transactions within Second Life are not imaginary (or at least no more imaginary than a real-life cash transaction). Some people make their entire actual living within the virtual world. Others, like Oulton, merely supplement their incomes by doing business in Second Life.

Knowing what the blue spheres in the second-hand shop were called did not really explain what they were. A "ball" is a specific thing in Second Life—one of the basic units of creativity in that world. Also called "poseballs," they are generic objects that an enterprising programmer can transform into saleable products by assigning them certain properties. Value can be added only through creativity and programming expertise—there is no actual physical resource.

Objects created in Second Life often come with qualities other than size, shape, colour and texture; they can also have animations attached to them. These animations are a major way in which players interact with virtual objects and with each other. It starts with one's own avatar—the graphic depiction of "you" in the game. A new Second Life player sets out the basic parameters of his or her avatar—sex, skin, hair and eye colour, physique and clothing. He starts with a default set of animations—hitting the arrow keys on your keyboard causes your avatar to walk around—knees lift, arms swing and virtual feet move one in front of the other. Another keystroke causes the avatar to fly. Type a message to another player and the avatar makes typing motions with its hands.

Stay with the basics, though, and millions of Second Life residents will never see you as anything other than a newbie. For a businessman like Randal Oulton, that simply will not do. "You're making sure that you brand yourself by looking good, by your avatar looking good," he said. "Because if people see you and you look like a newb, you're going to look bad."

You can tell just by looking at him that Chaz Longstaff (Oulton's Second Life avatar) is a worldly and stylish man about town. Chaz appears to be a good ten years younger than Oulton and to have lived a much more athletic existence than his creator—or any other regular human being. His deep-blue plaid shirt and fitted trousers show off a buff physique that borders on comic-book proportions. Not only did Oulton pay for those clothes, he paid for the body underneath—he bought a bottom, some abs, a more sophisticated skin tone ("Good skin costs money," he says) and a hint of facial hair. He also bought a more natural and confident walking style for Chaz—this is one of the basic types of animation that entrepreneurs create and sell. The fact that Chaz walks differently from a basic avatar reflects both on himself and on Oulton. For Chaz, his particular gait is part of his character. For Oulton, this animation sends a message that the man behind the image knows what is what in this virtual world. Most SLers quickly learn how to correct other default anatomical deficiencies.

"When you're born in SL, you may notice that you have no bits," Oulton said. "It's one of the first things that guys notice. It is something they consider rather important to their identity, and it is missing. So, you want to get bits. Many people make bits and sell them. Some people give them away for free, but the undisputed owner of the bit business in SL is a place called Xcite. One of the first stops every newbie who is going to survive in SL makes is at the Xcite store. So we'll go there now." Using the in-game interface, we teleported to one of many Xcite retail stores within Second Life. As our tour continued, I was reminded of Brenda Brathwaite's words: "If you give them tools, they will make penises." Linden Lab, the San Francisco–based creator of Second Life, gave them tools. Xcite did the rest. The store we were in had row after row of displays promoting bottoms, breasts, vaginas and penises of every size, colour, shape and species (feline, canine, dragon). Users can buy a single set of bits, or even acquire a variety to be used as appropriate to a given situation. Like all virtual body parts, these bits could be attached and detached from an avatar with just a few mouse clicks. The Xcite products are for more than just show, of course: thanks to the addition of animations, their bits do things.

"The thing about Xcite is that your penis will react to somebody else's clit—it's compatible. You will arouse each other," Oulton said. "Since everybody has Xcite, you're going to want Xcite, because you want your bits to interact."

Oulton is an authorized Xcite business partner. That means he has limited legal access to programming code that allows him to make his products Xcite-compatible. He's not actually making penises—he says there's no way to compete with the major players in that market. He acquired this code to use for a line of "sexual furniture products" and is looking into whether he can apply the same code to create other lines of Xcite-ready products. Competition is stiff, though—Xcite is constantly improving its own products, always providing upgrades and new features and rolling out new products. A promo in one of their stores read: "Technology for your derriere: the X3 ass for the next evolution for the buttocks body parts, providing you with the best technology and compatibility related to the X3 technology, so you can easily combine and control everything from a visible anus to a wide variety of anal toys without sacrificing attachment points." That is one high-tech rump.

We moved on from the Xcite store before things started getting too weird.

Animations don't always belong to an avatar, or even to that avatar's add-on anatomical parts. They can also be attached to external objects in the game. For instance, the MRI machine in that medical supplies shop has a built-in animation that allows any avatar to lie down and be scanned. (You may ask, "Why?" To which neither I nor Oulton has an answer. But, given that the Xcite store had virtual condoms for sale, one just has to accept that not everything is going to be 100 per cent intuitive.)

Programmers design animations and attach them to virtual objects of all sorts. You could program a little sphere so that when a player activates it, her avatar dances, does a handspring or high-fives. You can group these objects so that a number of avatars become part of a single animation—do a line dance, say, or form a human pyramid or take part in an orgy. Usually, especially if you're planning to make money from the animation, the activity will be closer to an orgy than a line dance. The anal orgy balls in the second-hand shop would be used by six consenting avatars who wished to get up to virtual hijinks.

Objects can be sculpted and given colours and textures to make them much more than abstract shapes. The visual experience can be made to match the embedded animations. For instance, you can create or buy beds, couches and furniture of all sorts with appropriate animations built in. Players buy a bed that comes with sexual animations, place that bed in their home on their land, and then they have a place to invite others back to for sex.

While the animation is going on, the players interact with each other by typing or via live voice. This feature has led to a booming prostitution sector within the world, through a combination of animation, voice, text and trading of photographs. (So-called "voice escorts," of course, require higher bandwidth and more powerful computer processors than text-based sexual services, which further helps to drive the upgrade cycle.)

Sex is "the undisputed number one factor in the economy" of Second Life, says Oulton. (Gambling used to be a contender, until Linden Lab cracked down on that front.) Oulton is a small player in the virtual world, making about $1,000 a month in adult content. (He earns additional revenue from selling virtual elevators, greeting cards and other items, as well as by collecting rent from his mall tenants.)

"I came in through the gay community. That's my peg," he said. "If you're gay, and you move to a new town anywhere in the world, you know the gay community is highly organized. They've got health, they've got finance, they've got clothing—it's like the velvet mafia. If you're into that, they'll take care of you. It's the same in SL. I found that they'd hand out free packages for newbies on how to get started: here's a free kit with okay-looking clothes and stuff, here's where to go, here are the clubs and that kind of thing. So that gave me a kickstart."

In the real world, Oulton is a computer consultant and entrepreneur who has been involved in maintaining a gourmet food website, programming databases in Lotus Notes and other conventional computer geekery. He had never visited a virtual community before he logged on to Second Life in 2006.

"I had read a newspaper article about how Second Life was the next big thing for the Internet, and so I created an account for myself. I picked that stupid name of Chaz Longstaff because I thought I was going to be in and out in half an hour. I just wanted a preliminary look so that I could say to clients, 'Yeah, I had a look at it. There was nothing there, so don't worry about it.'"

It didn't work out that way. Instead, he found a pixellated land of modest opportunity. Oulton likes the community he's found in Second Life, but he's clear that it was the business opportunities that kept him there. He is adept at ferreting out such opportunities, identifying needs and selling solutions. For instance, the wedding of visuals and animations sometimes causes problems. Suppose a customer buys a bed from Toothfairy Tizzy (an Israeli woman who reputedly makes six figures a year—in U.S. dollars, not Lindens—selling Second Life sex products). Suppose then that six months later, the customer still loves the sex animations that came with the bed, but she's changed her décor and now the bed no longer matches the boudoir. Buying a whole new bed would be costly.

Oulton created a line of invisible objects—called mats—that you lay on top of a bed (or other object). The erotic animations are attached to the mat, rather than the object, so that you can swap out the bed and keep all your favourite naughty moves.

"With my stuff, you preserve your investment in animations because you just move it to another bed. You buy a new bed— very cheaply because there are no animations—and then just drop the mat on the bed. They're selling like hotcakes. I'm surprised I don't have any competition yet."

It is no coincidence that the drive to innovate, the impetus to deliver new products that make the medium easier and cheaper to use, comes from the world of erotica and sexuality. Virtual worlds are a living example of a technology still in transition, still dependent on sexual applications for the marketing innovations that will ultimately make them ready for the mainstream. The cycle is not yet complete—both the technology and the user base are still developing—but every new penis, every invisible sexual furniture product, every orgy ball speeds the evolution of virtual worlds into a mainstream medium.

When Oulton and I were nearing the end of our Second Life tour, we started talking about another aspect of virtual sex—making friends, falling in love and sharing emotional intimacy. Even after you've accepted that people can get turned on by the virtual actions of distant lovers, it might still be difficult to comprehend concepts like getting married and settling down in a virtual world. There are even those who raise families.

Here's how having a Second Life family works: If a couple wish to have a child, one of the partners agrees to become pregnant. You buy a "pregnant suit" for the gestation, with options for slow growth or instant bulge. Either way, that avatar is pregnant. Then you get to what Oulton calls "the controversial bit."

"There are people who want to be children in SL. They want to be child avatars," he said. "There's a big movement against them, but they are fighting to protect themselves. They're saying, 'What's wrong with it? We're not doing anything sexual. You might be thinking that way, but we're just wanting to be children.' And usually what you do is you get one of those persons to agree to become the child that is born. That person agrees to become part of your family."

This type of agreement raises many questions: What if any of the three players involved decides they don't want to play any more? What if the couple splits? What happens to the estate? Possessions in the game carry real dollar values, so how do you divide property? When does it become worth it to involve lawyers?

Such questions speak to the issue of exactly how far virtual worlds can extend into real life. The barriers to the expansion of virtual worlds—technological limitations and difficulty of use—are disappearing quickly. When these hurdles become sufficiently small, mainstream users will be sucked into virtual realms in as great numbers as they have been to email, surfing, Facebook and so on.

Before virtual worlds hit the mainstream, they will also likely be scrubbed clean of any vestigial sexual overtones. As with today's mainstream Internet, sex will still be a presence, but it will be once again pushed to the margins, compartmentalized in ways that won't make the rest of the virtual world feel uncomfortable.

It is more difficult to predict what will happen to the other, related aspects of virtual worlds—the intimacy and personal connection users have to the medium. It is, after all, the essence of what makes virtual worlds so powerful as a means of communication.

As Oulton and I spoke, I was reminded of one of the stranger (at least from an internal logic perspective) things I had seen for sale on our tour: those virtual condoms. Why, in a virtual world, would you need protection from either disease or unwanted pregnancy? I asked Oulton whether virtual sex was necessary for a virtual pregnancy.

He said it was not. As our conversation continued, though, he started thinking about how he might *make* it necessary. Ever the entrepreneur, he leapt straight past the questions of logic and taste to the possible business opportunities.

"As a business partner I have access to scripts to make stuff Xcite-compatible. If a couple decide they are going to do the impregnation thing, I could probably make a stomach that would react to the Xcite scripts in the penis, which would then pronounce, 'Okay, you've climaxed, impregnation has just happened.' Maybe you start swelling and then it could grow over time. What a great idea. It's exciting to think that you could make this and sell it. Oh my god, you're going to make me rich."

I have been using Second Life as a stand-in for all the other virtual worlds out there—from expressly hard-core worlds like Red Light Center, to MMORPGS like World of Warcraft, to kids' worlds like Club Penguin. I use it partly because it has received some media attention, meaning it might be more familiar, and partly because it is a direct intellectual descendant of LambdaMOO—it reflects many of the same principles of community and in-game player control that characterized that earlier world. Second Life shouldn't necessarily be voted Virtual World Most Likely to Succeed, but it does typify the general direction that technology is moving.

Linden Lab claims that more than six million people have signed up for accounts on Second Life. Many people are deeply skeptical that this number remotely reflects the number of players who log on regularly (reportedly about six hundred thousand), let alone those who spend money there, let alone those who *make* money there. In the real world, Second Life employs about three hundred people. Even the biggest virtual world of all, World of Warcraft, hasn't made a mainstream dent; its 11.5 million monthly subscribers may look like a lot, but that's small potatoes compared to the hundreds of millions using email and surfing the web.

From an economic perspective, virtual worlds seem almost as marginal as some of the sexual activities found therein. But that is the precise reason why it is so interesting. Currently, the interface for a world such as Second Life is difficult to negotiate. There's lots of waiting for images and information to download, navigation makes no initial sense, it's nearly impossible to find anything without the help of an experienced friend, the means of interaction seem strange and off-putting to the uninitiated, and the primary activities all seem to centre around sex.

Yet that is how, with minor modifications, we would have described the World Wide Web a decade or so ago. Or the Internet itself not long before that. Many experts concur that virtual worlds are where email was ten or fifteen years ago: they have become part of the general discourse and expanded beyond the core geek community, but they have yet to go mainstream.

A number of things still need to happen in order for virtual worlds to hit the big time the way other Internet applications have. Mainstream users will require a vastly simpler and more intuitive interface. We'll need another leap forward in bandwidth and processor power—current lag issues might be bearable for diehards, but not for the rest of the world. The percentage of non-sexual activity will need to grow. That doesn't mean that erotica will go away, but as happened with the VCR and many other Internet applications, other content will expand more quickly. In all likelihood, virtual worlds will require an analogue to the back room of a video rental shop—the adult content will have to be sequestered for those who choose to see it.

All these things, in fact, are already happening in Second Life and elsewhere. Any particular world might wither and fall victim to the vagaries of technological and social change, but virtual worlds themselves are clearly on the ascendant. Already, university courses are being taught in virtual worlds. Real countries set up virtual embassies to take questions about visas. Therapists in virtual environments treat people with phobias. Hollywood blockbusters have been screened in Second Life. And business people and academics are finding ways to turn virtual worlds into collaborative laboratories and meeting places. A concept that began with some sentences strung together in a database more than thirty years ago is poised now to shake up the fundamentals of how we communicate with one another.

sixteen

Emergent Sex and Non-emergent Technology

N ot all virtual environments take the approach of Second Life, which is to rely on emergent sex as an engine of change and creativity. Some virtual sex comes from games' creators rather than the users. Given how ubiquitous sex is in general-interest games, pornographic games intuitively strike one as a natural business opportunity. In reality, though, adult video games are the domain of a very few companies and individuals who are able to invest in an area where the track record is one of limited success (and some spectacular failures).

Video games earned a reputation as entertainment for kids and teenagers. Some people suggest that this association explains why an adult video game industry hasn't sprung up on the same scale as pornographic movies. This can't be the whole story, though. After all, other so-called kids' mediums had X-rated counterparts. Superhero comic books, for example, existed alongside "Tijuana Bibles"—illicitly sold pornographic comics, often featuring unauthorized depictions of celebrities.

Two other factors limit the number of video games made expressly for pornography. First, making a video game is not like making a movie. One guy with a camera can shoot a scene for a porn flick, but a video game demands time and expertise that is not nearly so cheap or common. Producing even a simple game—even one as simple-minded as Custer's Revenge—requires a major investment. No one can churn out thirteen thousand video games every year the way "the other Hollywood" does with porn movies.

The second limitation brings us right back to the power of the word "you." The effect of being immersed in a video game is qualitatively different from any medium in which the consumer is just a spectator. You don't feel as though you're pushing a button on a controller—you feel like you're blowing up a tank. Translate that into sexuality, particularly acting out sexual fantasies, and you are playing with a power that few companies have been willing or able to harness. Although the explicitly erotic video game sector remains relatively small, it is still a driving force in the field.

One of the few success stories in the adult video game genre is Virtually Jenna. Developed by Thrixxx Technologies (slogan "Simulates what stimulates"), whose Vancouver-based operation is run by Brad Abrams, this game has the advantage of trading on one of the most famous names in pornography, Jenna Jameson. As the eponymous title suggests, the game involves a computer-generated version of Jameson, along with those of many of her "friends." Essentially, the game allows the user to be a porn-film director, setting up virtual scenarios and then playing them out. There are many options for different positions, toys, numbers of partners and so on.

"The challenge," Abrams said, "is that people's imaginations are so extensive that in our role-playing games, even when you do all the animations, create all the scenarios, create content, outfits, you can't match everybody's fantasy."

I asked him whether creating an erotica game had any unique technological demands. It turns out there are many—most centred on disguising the computer-generated aspect of the avatars. "If you take Quake or whatever other kind of [mainstream] game," Abrams said, "those engines are made for running around, shooting, explosions and all that kind of stuff. So when you get down to creating sex, they just don't work. You basically have a lot of different, subtle nuances that you want to try and create. For instance, in those games a character's face isn't really that important. Our eyes twitch and move and gleam and all this kind of stuff. They have a lot of life, because we're trying to create that intimacy. In traditional games, too, you're going to be using a lot of polygons for backgrounds and so your polygon budget is used differently. Our models are about six thousand polys, and so they are a lot higher definition."

Polygons are the basis for many modern video games. They are simple two-dimensional shapes (usually triangles) that are combined into three-dimensional objects like cubes and pyramids. These shapes are called polygonal wireframes, and they can be rotated, stretched and otherwise manipulated to create movement and animation. The more polygons devoted to an object, the more sophisticated and realistic it can become.

"We spend a lot of time on, I don't know what to call it, some kind of boob physics or whatever you want to call it," Abrams said with a laugh. "I have no idea what would be a great name for it, but basically our boobs bounce. There are so many little details that we go into to create a little bit of life in a character which are typically ignored most times in other games."

Do adult video games have no more to contribute to the medium than "jiggle physics" (as Brenda Brathwaite calls it)? Yes, actually.

Though adult video games will not likely ever outstrip the graphics innovations of major mainstream game and animation studios, they are contributing more than just convincing pertness.

Abrams believes that adult games can improve mainstream games simply by making it okay for sex to be part of the narrative. "To me, sex and video games is the last frontier in storytelling, because it's been such taboo, because people think video games are for kids. But now the average age of video gamers is twenty-eight years old. In Mass Effect, they have a situation where there's an alien commander and a female commander and they're kind of getting all nice and cosy and it's a cut scene just as they are ready to kiss. And God of War had a scene where this warrior grabs a girl by her hair and shoves her head down into his crotch. Cut scene. You can see it's all there in the storytelling, but they just can't do shit.

"It's always been sort of a goal of mine to get mainstream traction," he said, though that wouldn't be simply in a bid to legitimize his own products. "More just to legitimize the fact that sex in video games and the storytelling experience is a valid part of the whole overall experience."

The battle over this taboo is not restricted to video games. Comic books, movies, television, all have faced public outcry because of sex and violence. A common refrain among those who work in adult industries, though, is that the protests always seem to be much more about sex than violence. Abrams has no patience for it.

"All these people just get out on their high horses and say, 'Sex in video games: it's evil incarnate.' And I'm going, 'Okay, well then how come people can go out and blow people's heads off and you can see the blood spatter on the screen and then it dribbles down the screen. It's ultra-realistic, ultra-violent.' And I'm going, 'That's okay?'"

And, he adds, it's not as though the content of video games is in any way unique. "You read the Old Testament and you see whose cousin is marrying whose cousin and whose half-sister is having that kid, and the adultery and all that shit. Don't come down on video games for having anything new and original. It's all been done before in the Bible." Abrams's feelings about religious hypocrisy around pornography conjure the ghost of Pietro Aretino—he carries on the centuries-old tradition of pornographers who are outraged by the hypocrisy they see in their puritanical critics.

But he doesn't expect pornography's technological influence to change people's attitudes. In fact, he says he is "pretty jaded" about the idea of pornographers as early adopters and pioneers of technology. When it comes to improvements in Internet infrastructure, he says that Thrixxx is more of a beneficiary than a driver. "I mean, right now the beauty of the Internet for us is that ten years ago you could have never done this," he said. "Even if the technology was advanced enough to create good sex sims back then, the distribution pipelines weren't in place. We don't need retailers right now; we don't need mainstream distribution. People can find us and buy it, download it and it's a done deal."

He says adult producers are now leading the way in marketing and business models. "I think adult is one of the most pure forms of free enterprise I've ever seen. If you have something people want, if it's good enough, people will pay for it. If you don't have something that people want, they don't pay and you're done. The marketing, doing everything online, and payment processing: that is where adult is the strongest. Setting up the pipelines, adult is really strong and good at that."

These may seem mundane aspects of communications, but without them, nothing else can develop. People tend to be nervous about giving out their credit card information online—doubly so when the product is taboo. One of the biggest challenges of e-commerce is making customers comfortable with a new way of paying.

"The adult side of the business has actually done a really good job of generating trust from the general consumer," Abrams said.

Other people in the industry remain more optimistic about the adult world's capacity to continuing innovating on a technological front as well as a business front. Among those with a cheerier outlook is Jenna Jameson herself. She has heard the pessimistic chatter, but does not buy into it.

"We always hear that the adult technology lead is slowing down," she told me. "Not in my opinion, though, as every time I turn around, this industry is still at the forefront of the next new thing. I think we will continue to see the adult industry spearhead the development and use of technology."

Jameson may have more reason to be optimistic than most. Not only is she one of the most successful, famous and rich X-rated stars of all time but she has also become an iconic entrepreneur whose brand has crossed over into mainstream culture. Her autobiography spent six weeks on *The New York Times* bestseller list, and she has appeared on billboards in New York's Times Square promoting her website. Her brand includes a line of sex toys produced by Doc Johnson (a company founded by Reuben Sturman of peep-show notoriety) as well as ringtones ("moantones," actually), purses, guitars, perfume and more. She has done commercials for Adidas and People for the Ethical Treatment of Animals. She has attained such celebrity that I was not allowed to contact her directly: my questions and her answers filtered through her handlers.

Long before Jameson secured her place as a bona fide mainstream celebrity, the former stripper who graduated from soft-core to hard-core, and from stills to film, was already pulling the technological levers that would catapult her to stardom. In those days, though, it was more about survival than getting ahead. "Being in the adult industry means always having to fight: fight with government, media, ISPs or other regulators in both public and private sectors," she said. "In order to survive and deliver what our customers wanted, while working with these restrictions, we had to be better, cleaner and smarter in being able to adapt and constantly look for new and intelligent ways to deliver new media."

Two-thirds of the way through her autobiography, Jameson has a single line about the porn world generally being ahead of the pack technologically. I wanted to know whether she was just repeating a truism, or whether this was something she had actually experienced working in the industry.

"I have seen this throughout my career, especially in the advances in streaming video. Big mainstream studios were always watching what us little adult companies were up to and a perfect example is shown in the adult world bringing video to the web before the rest," she said. "In my business, keeping ahead of the game in technology just made sense so we could satisfy our surfers and customers with new and exciting media. We started off with photos and stories, but to give customers a true experience, the next natural step was to provide video content. Once video was commonplace, the demand was to meet enhanced and higher-quality video requests, and so on."

The demand for "more," "better" and "new" never abated. As the push moved beyond video toward more interactive media, the technological demands made by Jameson's fans began to feel more like personal demands.

"Fans never had a forum with which to interact with me before the Internet," she said. "And then, with my participation, they were able to email, chat, submit artwork and send mail directly to my computer in a way that was easier than ever before. They couldn't get enough. The more I made myself available, the more they asked. I had to learn to draw the line in order to keep my personal boundaries intact."

In some ways, Jameson was becoming the highly commercialized version of Jennifer Ringley. As lucrative as it might have been, though, there was to be no JennaCam to replace the long since defunct JenniCam. "As I made myself more available on web chats, I had many member requests to install a 24/7 webcam into my bedroom," Jameson said. "That's an area where I had to draw the line."

With Thrixxx's Virtually Jenna, Jameson commercialized another piece of Internet technology that had until that point been a deeply personal aspect of many people's online experience: the avatar. I have described some of the ways people have developed intimate relationships with their own avatars and have built up infrastructures of sex, love and marriage with others through MUDs and modern virtual worlds. Jameson's avatar, though, commodified this intimacy in the form of a pornographic fantasy world in which you could buy, interact with and control the online version of a real person. (Of course, "real" is a tricky concept in this case, as the "real" Jenna Jameson, as with any porn star, is also mostly fantasy.) Given the personal relationship so many people have with their online presence, and Jameson's limits as to how much privacy she will give up, it seemed as though creating a virtual Jenna might be a bit too much for her. She said, though, that other projects have felt more intrusive.

"When Doc Johnson approached me to create a full body mould of myself, it was exciting to be at the forefront of this type of interaction, but it took a little bit of getting used to knowing that someone was probably using a mould of my entire body for their pleasure," she said. "When it came around to creating my avatar for VirtuallyJenna.com, not only was it easier but it was exciting to be at the top of this new technology and a lot more fun to be able to make facial expressions and movements that would be linked to my image."

She said having a virtual version of herself feels "kinda like being cloned." In this, she has realized the dream of many a science fiction fan—creating a clone of one's self to do all the work, while the original human being sits back and reaps the rewards.

Jenna Jameson confirmed to USMagazine.com in August 2007 that she was "done with porn forever." In one sense that's true—she does not have sex on camera any more. But her virtual counterpart continues to be the main player in thousands of user-generated sex scenes, and the resulting revenue helps feed the $30-million-per-year Club Jenna juggernaut.

Usually when people think about having artificial entities to do humanity's work for us, it's in the context of robots, and it usually has to do with manufacturing or the military. But for entertainers—adult and mainstream—virtuality may be where the greatest threats and opportunities lie. Should it become the norm down the road that Hollywood celebrities maintain a virtual version of themselves to build their fan base or entertain the masses, there is a real chance that nobody will remember or acknowledge that this was another technological innovation first proved viable by the pornography industry.

One of the other major players in the adult video game scene is a product called Bonetown. Unlike Virtually Jenna, which is basically a create-your-own-porn-scene application, Bonetown has gameplay and a narrative arc. It plays more like a traditional first-person shooter or sci-fi game. The driving forces behind this game have none of Jameson's celebrity or mystique—they are a group of rough-looking twenty-something boys who clearly can't quite believe their own good fortune to be working at the intersection of pornography, video games and their own business enterprise.

I met Bonetown's creators at AVN Expo in Vegas. Scruffy and gregarious, they appeared fresh out of school, familiar with the rules of the marketing game but playing it for the first time.

Their booth had the game running in the background, demo copies for fans and full versions for the press. Their operation befit any slick start-up video game production company. I thought I was about to have a straightforward interview, the kind one might use as the basis for a newspaper business feature showcasing an enterprising group of young men who found a lacuna in the market and a means to fill it.

Then they started talking.

As with Ugly George Urban, Hod (Bonetown's CEO) and Max (its marketer) can be understood best through their own words, describing the virtues of their product from a creative and technological perspective:

Author: So talk me through the premise of the game.

Hod: The premise of the game is you start as a newcomer to Bonetown, which is an island city, and right off the bat you are introduced to someone who tells you about "The Man," which is a company that is trying to moralize it. She lets you know that Bonetown is a place where you can have sex wherever you want, drugs are everywhere and now this company called The Man is trying to make drugs illegal and make sex in the streets illegal. So the whole purpose of the game is to save Bonetown from The Man.

Max: You start out as, like, a tiny little wimpy guy who isn't real good with the ladies, so you've got to start with ugly, nastier, fatter girls and then as the game goes on, you can get better and better and bigger and bigger balls. [A set of testicles in the corner of the screen grows over time to mark your progress in the game.]

Hod: You get buffer too. Your character actually gets stronger. You go from our small, wimpy model to our big buff model by the end of the game.

Author: Okay.

Hod: At the end of every mission, which is how you grow your balls bigger, we put special sex scenes that only happen in the mission. To fill in fetishes we have the threesomes, the foursomes, the fivesomes, we have a hooker giving you a blowjob with no teeth. Since we really feel like we're the first adult video game, we wanted to fit all the different fetishes into the game, so we could represent the industry well, in this one game. So the missions we fit into a lot of the niches in the industry, so people can see what they want to see.

Author: So it's all about sex and drugs and violence.

Hod: No violence.

Author: Is that right?

Max: There's fighting.

Hod: There's no blood, there's no death. There's no implied . . .

Max: It's the same type of violence you'd see on a Walt Disney cartoon with the Road Runner type shit.

Author: Is it designed to be erotic?

Hod: It can be. We started out wanting to make an erotic game that you could pleasure yourself to and I think, depending on what you're into, I think you can to our game. But the more important goal is a fun video game. That was the number one goal of the game, was make a game that is fun.

Author: Right.

Hod: You can be Jesus, you can be Moses, you can be all these religious figures and you can have sex with girls as Jesus and your pickup line can be "Suck my dick, in the name of my Dad."

Max: Or, "I'll cleanse you with my jizz."

Hod: Moses says, "I'll part your legs like the Red Sea."

Author: And these things are all embedded in the game?

Max: After you beat a guy, a character, you beat him up, you assume his identity.

Author: So you have to beat up Jesus before you can be Jesus?

Max: Yep. The other unique thing about our game, you can change identities and outfits and all your accessories change on the fly. There's no load time for when you're changing outfits. You can be anyone you want, you don't have to stop the game and load up a new character.

Author: So, tell me about the technology behind it, because that's really where I'm going to want to go.

Hod: We bought a [game-creation] engine and we created a random character generator within this engine that had been an idea from the start for this game. We knew we had to create lots of people for this to work.

Author: Why?

Hod: So, if there are five girls, after you've had sex with those five girls, why do you want to play the game any more?

Author: That's an interesting thing, because when I'm writing about the special demands that come from adult content, I guess variety is one of those things?

Max: Yeah, in a game like Grand Theft Auto, all the characters are the same height. They can make them fatter, but actually what they do is they use the same skeleton. They don't actually change the breadth of the shoulders or the height of the characters. They just change the skins on top of the skeletons.

Hod: Yeah, you'll see one guy walking down the street and you can see that exact same guy fifty places around the city. In ours, everybody is different. Another technology that we put in that is starting to be in more games now is hue shifting. We actually hue shift them on the fly in the character generator, so one cyan

T-shirt could actually be a thousand different-coloured T-shirts. So, two people could be exactly the same and have the exact same clothes and look completely different because their clothes are different colours.

Author: What about creating the environment itself, the world that it's in?

Hod: We actually had a level designer who did almost all of it. He actually went on to work on the next Call of Duty. He was the lead level designer for the multi-player levels.

Author: And this is interesting, because part of what I'm writing about is how the advances from the adult-content type thing, like your character generator, are going to have applications in other mainstream games.

Hod: Oh yeah.

Author: And one of the things I have been told is that companies like Google and Disney will hire from within the adult industry because they think they are ahead of the curve.

Hod: Yeah. They think we have little more information on the technology.

Hod: The funny part is that our designer definitely did not leverage that this was an adult game when he went on to Call of Duty. We changed some things on our website and on our MySpace page while he was applying for the job because he was concerned that the adult aspect was not going to help him get the job.

Author: And this is apparently a big debate: What do you put on your CV when you're looking for a job outside of the industry?

Hod: I would not play up the fact that it was adult. I definitely don't think that the fact that I made an adult game would wow them. I think that would scare them more than anything else. I would use the information that would wow them, which is that I was the project manager and things like that. In the video game industry there is a big taboo about the adult industry.

Author: Someone said you've had one negative review so far. But you have to imagine there's going to be a backlash against this kind of game.

Hod: We planned for it. The game was made expecting that backlash to happen.

Author: So you'll benefit from the controversy in some ways—you'll get publicity that way.

Hod: The thing is I could stand behind everything in our game. Everything in our game I could solely stand behind. We're waiting for the backlash to come.

Author: And, I guess, you'll know you've made it big when that happens.

Hod: Exactly.

Author: So, all the fights, is it men against men? Is it ever men and women fighting?

Hod: Nope, we don't support violence against women. You can walk up and hit a girl. She falls to the ground and then runs away. That's it. We don't glorify it. You can run after her and hit her, she gets down, you know and eventually she'll sit there and, like, shake on the ground, like, "Get away from me." At that point you can't hit her any more. But there's no purpose to it, there's no goal, no reward. We don't glorify it at all. We put it in there just because it was a by-product of the game that you could hit them, but we always made sure that you couldn't abuse it. And actually, after you've had sex with a girl, good or bad, whether you get her off or not, you can't hit her after that. So after you've had sex with a girl, there's no violence that you can do towards her. So, you know, if you can't get her off, you can't be like, you know, "Bam!"—all pissed at her. We really didn't want to do anything violent. We wanted this game to be thrown in the face of the rest of the video game industry that "you think you're so high and mighty but look at the violence that you have in your game." And you're saying this is worse, that sex and drugs is worse than killing women and children.

Author: Where do you sell this game?

Hod: Right now we're selling on our website and in adult stores. Actually, worldwide—we have them pretty much around the world right now.

Author: And in the adult stores, have you had trouble getting it placed there? I mean, it's not like any other product, right?

Hod: Yeah, you know, the adult stores actually, most of them, have been very helpful for us. They are tired of just selling DVDs, and DVDs aren't doing well any more because of the Internet. All of them are more than happy to find something new to try and make money off of. We're really hoping to get some more marketing out there to help out the stores that we send to, because I don't think they're doing very well. People don't know to go to adult stores to get an adult video game.

Author: Right.

Hod: So it's really our website where we get most of our sales right now. And international is our biggest. We're getting a lot in Europe. Japan is selling well. Really, around the world, we're doing pretty well. With the little bit we've done, you know, our marketing is in its infancy right now.

Hod and Max represent some of the more uncomfortable and uninspiring links between pornography and technology. Their motivation appears to come less from visionary creative drive than from a mundane and pragmatic desire to find a market for their particular brand of pornography. They are not inventors: their changes involve tweaks and adjustments to existing techniques and technologies. In many ways, they come across more as cavemen than as the forward-thinking pioneers one might intuitively associate with technological progress.

But however you might recoil from their primitive attitudes toward sex, violence and women, they still are responsible for pushing the technology of video games in new directions, experimenting with alternative marketing plans and generally helping the medium to develop.

The Law of Unintended Consequences

For some people, it's hard enough just to acknowledge the technological contributions of those pornographers who work within the law and with some modicum of professionalism. Beyond these boundaries, though, lurk darker beasts whose pornographic endeavours go beyond offending people's sensibilities to all-out assaults—sexual, physical, emotional, intellectual and financial. These people do not flog their products at trade shows or join online affiliate programs. They work through back channels and the underbelly of the Internet, plying their trade in places where law enforcement has trouble following. Such people do not deserve sympathy or legitimacy, and I offer neither when I assert that they too have played a role—albeit often an indirect one—in the advancement of communications technology.

Pagejacking. Unauthorized credit card charges. Spam. Chargebacks. Copyright infringement. Piracy. Fraudulent websites. Fraudulent customers. Cybershoplifting. Hacking. Selling pornography to minors. *Making* pornography with minors. There is no puzzle about why people would be reluctant to acknowledge that such activities might have contributed to something positive. And when many of these stories are broken down it actually turns out that the technological advances resulted from the *response* to such activities rather than from the activities themselves. The "arms race" between criminals and the law, spammers and anti-spammers, fraudsters and watchdogs has sometimes had surprising benefits for the rest of us.

In the pornographic trade, the wrongdoers are the customers as often as they are the suppliers. Adult webmasters have had to deal with every ill imaginable on the web. While cybershoplifting (the act of buying something online, taking receipt of the product and then denying ever having authorized the purchase) and other forms of digital theft are endemic, many people in the adult industry say that people just seem to think it's *more* okay to steal pornography than the latest hit from MGM or U2. Patrons of adult websites cause countless headaches, whether it be fraudulent chargebacks or stealing content and posting it to "tube sites" or other freely available venues.

So-called tube sites are the pornographic equivalent of YouTube, where users upload video clips they have made, bought or stolen, creating vast online libraries that contain more free pornographic video than even the most obsessive addict could conceivably watch in a lifetime. Tube sites are gutting the profits of the adult industry, and are one of the main reasons why so many insiders are pessimistic. They feel as though the industry is being devoured by the very technology it helped create.

Mainstream online content providers contend with the same issues as the adult world, but not to the same degree. Adult sites are more likely than mainstream sites to be hacked, have passwords stolen or face fraudulent chargebacks. This could be a result of the same motivation that prompts honest people to pay more money for pornographic content than anything else—hackers pay a different kind of premium, allocating more time and energy to attacking porn sites than they do other targets. Another oft-bandied theory is that people simply perceive the porn industry as a more justifiable mark for theft and mischief. Because pornographers are seen as morally questionable to begin with, stealing their content has just a touch of twenty-first-century Robin Hood feel about it.

Regardless of the reasons why pornographic web businesses face so many challenges, they have no choice but to deal with them. (Particularly so given that credit card companies and banks actually hold adult companies to a higher standard than the mainstream when it comes to fraud and chargebacks. Financial institutions find the adult industry so distasteful to deal with that a relatively small problem is enough justification to revoke an account. In 2000, American Express opted not to deal with adult sites at all. Though it claimed this was a business decision, pornographers viewed it as a moral judgment.) Adult webmasters often seek technological solutions to their problems, and many of the results have application beyond the world of porn. The entire web is a more secure place thanks to the by-products of the ongoing contest between would-be scammers and those who work to stymie them.

Sellers of pornography have been known to perpetrate their fair share of fraud against their customers (though online auctions, general merchandise sales and many other mainstream businesses have far worse records). Some early trickery was both mundane and low-tech—for instance, offering a free trial membership that automatically converts to a paid membership, and then making it impossible to get to the page that allows the user to cancel. (One scam actually involved a line buried in the terms of service that said that when customers cancelled their account, they were actually triggering an upgrade to a more expensive membership.) Such scams were a short-term proposition, because when customers could not get a response from the website, they went to their credit card companies to complain. The credit companies repaid the customer, reclaimed the money from the porn company and charged the company a hefty fine. Once the chargebacks started soaring, the credit card company would sever its relationship with the webmaster, which meant the jig was up. This didn't stop a few porn-site operators in the late 1990s from bilking customers out of tens of millions of dollars before they got shut down.

Pagejacking was another trick used by unethical pornographers—it involved creating a duplicate of a real mainstream web page but modified with a bit of code that forwarded surfers to adult websites. These modified pages were then submitted to search engines that couldn't tell the difference between a harmless page and its evil twin. When a user did a search for, say, sports sites, the engine would spit out links that would take the user straight through to a gateway to sex. People found themselves at websites they had not sought. The unwitting sports enthusiast did not even need to make a purchase in order for the porn scam to be profitable—the operators could sell the "exit traffic" of disgusted dupes to other sites, which meant that all you had to do was get people to the site, by hook or by crook, in order to make money. Not only was this annoying and offensive, it caused office workers to inadvertently violate their employers' anti-porn policies, and landed unsuspecting kids face-to-monitor with nudity.

The criminal element earned the adult industry a reputation as a cabal of hi-tech thieves and scoundrels who would tell any lie necessary to separate fools from their money. That such dastards plied their online dirty dealings in significant numbers is indisputable, but that does not tell the whole story. Alongside those who looked to scam $10 million before disappearing forever were those who were trying to turn an honest dollar selling a legal product, and perhaps earning a million or two a year. Thus it is that legitimate operators of pornographic websites, to ensure ease of cancellation, pioneered services such as intuitive, reliable cancellation web links, 1-800 numbers and instant chat customer service. Not only do these moves appease the financial institutions but they also distance the legitimate companies from their ne'er-do-well colleagues, which in turn helps assuage their customers' concerns about fraud. Porn sites, through business necessity, have become the model for how to keep customers comfortable with and secure in their online transactions.

Credit card companies themselves have made some effort to reduce Internet fraud. They have experimented with hardware solutions such as home credit card readers that plug into a computer, forcing customers to physically insert their card to make a payment. They have also tested elaborate software solutions such as digital verification certificates. Although such systems made fraud more difficult, they were clumsy and slow to catch on.

Adult sites could not wait for mainstream companies to solve the problem. They were running a perpetual risk of fees in the tens of thousands of dollars should their chargeback rate go too high, and were always in danger of losing their authority to process credit cards entirely, meaning that a site would have to shut down no matter how profitable it was overall. So they became pioneers of self-protection strategies. They designed, from scratch, Internet-based transaction systems that would satisfy both their jumpy clientele and anxious financial institutions. They experimented with systems where the customer gave credit card information over the phone to pay for online services, or filled out a digital form that someone at the other end would process manually. The telephone system, first used in 1994 by a Netherlands-based porn company, had the advantage of keeping credit card information off the web, which at that time had little in the way of data encryption or other security measures. This additional interaction and record keeping also made it more difficult for customers to falsely deny their purchase later. Overall, though, such systems were cumbersome, and they also violated the spirit of anonymity that online customers appreciated so much.

In 1994, a company called CyberCash set up an e-commerce system that was simpler for customers and did not require merchants to jump through so many hoops with the banks and card companies. CyberCash was a third-party system that took a commission for facilitating secure credit and "e-cash" transactions online. CyberCash's first forays in the field were almost as ungainly as the credit card companies', requiring users to install browser plug-ins before they could do business, and requiring a degree of time and technological expertise possessed by too small a percentage of their potential market.

By 1997, the company was up and running with more technologically streamlined products, as well as refined services that made smaller payments—under $10—more feasible. CyberCash's then-chairman and CEO William Melton was clear about where he expected the company's services to be in demand. "Revenue from gaming and adult entertainment will be substantial in the early stage," he said. "These people tend to be impulse buyers and less price-sensitive." He went on to talk about how pornography (and gambling) consumers craved the anonymity that CyberCash's system offered, and how adult-content merchants craved the instantly completed transactions that made the potential for chargebacks much smaller.

CyberCash faced some difficulties in the ensuing years, including claims in 2000 by an eighteen-year-old Russian who went by the name of Maxus that he had hacked one of the company's credit card verification applications and stolen more than three hundred thousand card numbers along with other data. CyberCash denied its culpability in the breach, but the damage was done. Because of this and other setbacks (including a Y2K bug that resulted in billing errors), the company went bankrupt the following year.

That was not the end of the story, though. CyberCash's assets and name, built up in the porn market, were bought by another e-commerce company, VeriSign, which was in turn acquired by PayPal, which today is one of the financial backbones of the modern commercial Internet. (PayPal came into existence only in 2000, the result of a merger between two other electronic payment companies, Confinity and X.com. These two companies had only been around themselves since 1998 and 1999 respectively. The first major non-adult third-party payment system, run by Yahoo!, launched in 1997, three years after the adult industry had begun demonstrating and refining how it was done.)

The arms race continues to this day. Businesses and financial institutions continue to implement new-and-improved security measures, while hackers continue to pull off the occasional high-profile identity heist, sometimes siphoning the credit information of hundreds of thousands of people. Pornographers are still faced with the doubly difficult task of making their customers confident with a technology of questionable security and confidentiality, and comfortable with an industry of shady repute. They need to do everything in their power to make the interface simple, reassuring and reliable.

———

It happens that consumers of pornography are an excellent test market for a product that could have ramifications for hundreds of millions of people around the world. Antoine Metivier refers to his company's client base as "the digitally nervous, and the digitally excluded." Metivier, a transplanted Frenchman now living in London, is the head of European sales for a company called uKash. His is one of two companies pioneering the use of cash transactions on the Internet. For suppliers, cash transactions have the benefit of zero risk for chargebacks. In turn, customers can be sure that their payments are untraceable and that there is no danger of unauthorized debits from their credit cards or bank accounts.

As with so many other technologies, cash-based Internet transactions did not begin in the adult world, but the adult world is the proving ground where the system is prepared for mainstream use. The gambling industry was the first to implement the system—online gamblers liked how nobody knew how much they were spending, and nobody knew how much they were winning. Spouses, tax collectors, creditors and anybody else who might lay claim to the spoils of a lucky wager had no way to follow the money.

Gambling and pornography are often lumped together as "vice industries" by people who are involved with neither. Within these two sectors, though, not all vices are equal. The gambling industry does not care to have its reputation sullied by an association with porn, and many in the porn world view gambling in the same light.

"I used to work for a company that was specializing in the gambling industry," Metivier told me, "and the first thing I told them was, 'Why don't we do adult?'" But the company was reluctant to tarnish itself by allying with purveyors of pornography. (Those in the porn business see their own industry as the morally superior of the two. "If you're addicted to gambling, you can lose your house," one adult webmaster told me. "Even if you're addicted to pornography, that's not going to happen.")

Metivier's company's gambling clientele was largely based in the Middle East and South Asia, where gambling was better tolerated than pornography. It took an economic downturn and some changes in leadership before the company was willing to explore the pornographic markets for online cash.

Once it made the move, it found that anti-pornographic sentiment actually worked to its advantage. Many countries limit the scope of the pornography industry through financial regulations that affect the use of credit cards and bank accounts. Cash is much more difficult for a government to control, and is therefore much more appealing to customers. Metivier sees client comfort level as the most important value point of his company's system.

"This is where I think we have a role to play with security. People might be reluctant to put their credit card details on a foreign website: 'What are they going to do with my credit card? What are they going to do with my name? Am I going to receive an XXX magazine promoting the services of [a porn] merchant? I don't want my wife to know.' This is where we try to bring our expertise in. You want to spend the money, you want to use your cash like you do in the sex shop where there's no trace. I like to use this example because everybody talks about the French and their mistresses: how many times have I seen guys in a sex shop buying two different sex suits, one for their wife and one for their mistress? Everybody loves this example because it's true."

The system is simple: a customer pays cash at a bricks-and-mortar store and gets a card with a code—like a long-distance phone card. They can use this card at any website that takes uKash. This form of e-commerce is in no way traceable back to a bank account, credit card or any other information that could identify the customer. It offers a kind of security that appeals to more than just those who are worried about being caught buying porn.

With identity theft and credit card fraud weighing ever more heavily in the public consciousness, the term "digitally nervous" applies to more and more people. "My mother wouldn't use a credit card," Metivier says. "Her bank keeps on saying, 'Have a credit card!' She'd rather be using cash. Seven years ago her credit card was stolen and she lost about six thousand francs."

And then there are the "digitally excluded"—people who simply do not have access to a bank account or credit card. That includes about three-quarters of the world's population, including an estimated twenty-two million Americans and about half of all Europeans. Of course, there may be some correlation between not having a bank account and not having Internet access (or reason to conduct business transactions there), but that does nothing to change the fact that cash-based e-commerce can serve many markets that have nothing to do with sex—once the pornography industry has proven that the technology works and has refined it to a sufficient level of user-friendliness.

"We are trying to push as much as possible to make sure that anybody, anywhere in the world, can pay online," Metivier says.

Metivier's company provides a possible holy grail in a quest that has occupied a certain sector of society for hundreds of years: the search for a means of consuming erotica completely anonymously.

Consider the case of Pierre de Marteau (literally, Peter of the Hammer). De Marteau was a fascinating man for many reasons. Throughout the seventeenth and eighteenth centuries, the imprint of his publishing house in Cologne, France, appeared on hundreds of controversial books—many were politically or religiously subversive, and many others were smutty or pornographic. The most interesting thing about de Marteau, though, was not the apparent fearlessness with which he published books that were panned and banned by governments and Christian leaders alike. The most interesting thing about him was that he did not exist.

De Marteau was partly a publishers' inside joke and partly a very practical means of disguising who actually was publishing pornography. Respectable publishers from England to Germany credited de Marteau's publishing house for many risky books that might bring ill repute or punishment upon their own.

"There were lots of names like that," literary historian Ian Moulton told me. "Some of them were used in a systematic way, others were just a useful name. There was a lot of stuff—most of it political or religious, but some of it erotic—that was published with false printers' names and false locations: 'Published in Cosmopolous,' 'Published in the City of Joy.' A lot of them claim truly or falsely to have been published in Amsterdam, which was a huge clearing house for all sorts of goods."

Anonymity has remained at the nexus of freedom of political and sexual expression from then until now. The *technology* of anonymity cuts in more than one direction, providing liberation for some and empowerment to commit crimes for others.

There are three ways to anonymize the pornographic experience: disguise the producer, using a cover identity like Monsieur de Marteau; disguise the user, as happens when people cover their downloading tracks on the Internet; or disguise the product itself, which is what hotels do by not including the names of the pay-per-view movies their guests have ordered. (Hoteliers are cagey about what percentage of their in-room video-on-demand usage is adult movies, but acknowledge that this is yet another technology that owes its very existence to the demand for pornography.)

How times change: four hundred years ago, producers of sexual material desired anonymity to avoid censure, while their publications were widely purchased and discussed. Today, adult industry moguls like Hugh Hefner and Larry Flynt and porn stars like Jenna Jameson and Ron Jeremy are mainstream cultural touchstones, while consumers increasingly embrace modern technologies in large part because of the anonymity they afford.

It is not at all surprising that porn consumers crave anonymity, even when they feel no shame about their activities. Consider the story of an acquaintance who pursues the decidedly non-sexual practice of knitting. She purchased a few skeins of yarn and a set of needles at a yarn shop. In under an hour, she discovered that her credit card was frozen. To get it unfrozen required a Visa representative to ask her a number of uncomfortable questions about the purchase. (Uncomfortable for the Visa agent, that is.) This was all over a purchase measured in the tens of dollars. The reason for the fuss? The name of the yarn store was The Naked Sheep.

Like pornography itself, the technology of anonymity really came into its own concurrently with the development of the Internet, which was striking, given how eminently trackable most online activity is. (The Internet *feels* anonymous to a lot of people, but remember the story of a MUD operator tracking Buffy Childerhose down and phoning her at home. Those who know what they're doing can find out a startling amount of information. Some years ago, another acquaintance started with a telephone number from an online personals ad and, using simple tools like an Internet-based reverse telephone number look-up and MapQuest, emailed the placer of the ad a digital map with a star marking her home. He included a note that said, "This is what you look like to a stalker.")

Real online anonymity requires technical know-how—a kind of know-how first mastered by the pioneers of Internet pornography but useful today for anyone wishing to escape persecution. One of the basic tools of being unidentifiable online is a service called an "anonymous remailer." With a remailer, users don't send their emails or Usenet posts straight to the recipient, but instead send them through a server that strips out all of the sender's identifying information and then releases the message to its destination. Return messages pass through the same server back to the original address with the digital tracks covered the same way. Anonymous remailers make it easier for people who deal in illegal forms of pornography to ply their trade without getting caught.

The law often lags behind technological developments, and the early Internet was no exception. Child pornography, bestiality and images of rape and torture were all common on the 1990s Internet, and police and governments were flummoxed as to how to deal with them. Ultimately, their response was itself technological. Anonymous remailers had a major weakness: in order to route messages back and forth, the remailer must keep a table that ties an identity to each anonymized message—otherwise return messages would be impossible. That meant it was possible to extract information that would connect an illegal pornographer to his product. As soon as police and lawmakers began exploiting this weakness, though, lawbreakers began to get more sophisticated.

They achieved greater levels of anonymity by sending their product through a series of remailers—potentially located all over the world—before it reached the recipient. For real security, though, they began encrypting their messages and files. Encryption encodes the message in such a way that only the sender and recipient can read it—at any interim step along the way, the message is undecipherable. An undeciphered message wouldn't be identifiable as illegal matter, let alone provide information about where it came from.

As in Pierre de Marteau's day, anonymity is inextricably linked not just to sex but also to politics. While law-breaking pornographers hid from cops behind walls of encryption and mazes of circuitously routed messages, and while cops grew ever better at decryption and digital tracking, both sides were honing tools that would be of use to political revolutionaries (and those who would oppress them). In his book *The Politics of Internet Communication*, Robert J. Klotz writes, "While software to enhance privacy has often struggled to find a market in democratic nations, it is in great demand from dissidents in nations limiting political freedom. Indeed, human rights organizations quickly identified the Internet as crucial to their efforts to disseminate information about repression. Originally released in 1991, the seminal encryption software Pretty Good Privacy was created by Phil Zimmerman with the explicit goal of assisting human rights organizations."

Unfortunately, child pornographers were some of the early adopters of that technology, and to this day, the same tools of anonymity that promote political freedom also enhance the ability for buyers and sellers of criminal products to find one another and conduct transactions with impunity. Investigative journalist Julian Sher has pieced together some of the most comprehensive profiles of these modern villains.

"Burt Thomas Stevenson"—not his real name—"was a software engineer at one of the many firms in the Raleigh-Durham high-tech golden triangle. He frequently worked at home," Sher writes in his book *One Child at a Time*. "Earning a comfortable $91,000 a year, Stevenson was typical of the new face of child abuse in the twenty-first century: not dirty old men in parks but tech-savvy young professionals from suburbia." This man locked his six-year-old daughter in a cage in his basement, where he sexually abused and tortured her. He distributed images of his activities via Usenet and other Internet distribution channels to tens of thousands of pedophiles around the world. He wrote his own encryption software and digitally altered hundreds of photographs to obscure his own identity. For a time, he ran technological rings around the police who were trying to catch him and rescue the girl known pseudonymously as Jessica.

Stevenson was part of a loose alliance of child pornographers that could not have existed before the Internet. "Online predators had been cooperating for years, exchanging not just photos but security tips, encryption software and warnings," Sher writes. Law enforcement needed to fight fire with fire. "Could the police create the same kind of web to catch the porn merchants at their own game?"

They could, and they did. An alliance of North American and European police began collaborating on the Internet to use a combination of traditional investigative methods and technological solutions to locate and arrest dealers in child pornography. They tracked chat room conversations and traced the flow of photographs from server to server. They used cutting-edge software to enhance minute details in photographs that might provide clues about where the picture was taken. In Jessica's case, in one photograph she was wearing an orange wristband that looked like it came from a chain of amusement parks that operated in only five states. In another, she was wearing a dress that appeared to be a school uniform—the cops delved into websites of companies that sell such uniforms, cross-referencing with other information. Ultimately each digital clue narrowed the search, until they found the right school. At that point, it was a simple matter to identify the girl, find her home and take her father into custody. Even then, Stevenson's computer drives were so heavily encrypted that the police had to call in more specialists to decode and reveal the hundreds of thousands of digital images that would provide the evidence to convict him of his crimes.

This was an arms race in which the criminal faction had a healthy head start. The police were starting to catch up with the criminals, but neither side could ever have the technological advantage for long—every enhancement in anonymity or subterfuge for one side led to a technological response from the other.

One of the large impediments to tracking pedophiles through the Internet is that police forces are tied to a geographic location—a city, state or country—while criminals operate globally. Many police organizations keep databases of known pedophiles, but each uses its own system that can't easily be connected to any other. Pedophiles were coordinating with one another around the world, while an investigating officer in New York City might have no idea that someone in the next county over was pursuing the same quarry.

To work around this obstacle, a new partnership sprung up between the world's largest software company and a number of police forces. John Hancock is a Microsoft software engineer who worked with the police to help develop a powerful tool called the Child Exploitation Tracking System. At its heart, CETS is an information-sharing utility, which might not sound like much in the grand scheme of technological innovation, but it has revolutionized how the police chase criminals online.

Before he got involved with this project, Hancock had worked in the area of "business intelligence," helping clients customize Microsoft software to extract useful information from large datasets. He had the right skill set to work on CETS, but he didn't at first think he had the temperament. "They came to me and said, hey, we have this great new project we'd like you to volunteer for; it's about helping Toronto Police with child pornography. I thought for fourteen seconds and said, 'Thank you, no.'

"I could not imagine myself going in to help these people if I had to deal with the daily subject matter that they deal with," Hancock said. "But I went home and I thought about it some more and I talked to my wife. Over a week I came to realize that this was a chance to do something important. Any tiny little thing that you can do to help these guys makes you feel like you are actually having a significant impact on the world."

This is why I had approached Hancock for an interview. I wanted to know how it felt to be one of the people who turned the technology back on the criminals—who used the Internet to fight crime rather than perpetrate it. When I spoke to him by phone, he said that the hurdles he had to overcome were at least as much about police culture as they were about technology.

Many police forces had a well-established culture of jurisdictional independence—nobody liked having another police force (or the FBI) horning in on a big case. Images of child pornography changed that culture, though they did so by perverting one of the common influences of conventional pornography. With media from cable television to BBSs, pornography was the compelling product, the "killer content" that drew in early adopters and made them master the new technology. Child pornography images were the opposite: they were so heinous and repellent that police forces all over the world were driven to transcend their territorial instincts, and to cooperate and share information on a deeper level than they ever had before.

"Pedophiles have always had this culture of adopting brand-new technologies," Hancock said. "They would cross all boundaries to do what they do, whereas police officers have always had a jurisdictional approach. These jurisdictional conflicts, they happen all the time. The only difference in this area is that all of the police officers who are doing the work are sitting there staring at images of babies being abused. So this area, like no other, lets them overcome those legacies. We could never have built the Child Exploitation Tracking System if it was going to be used for conventional policing because there would not have been the incentive for people to overcome the cultural barriers. It's only because it is this particular topic that we managed to get the results that we did."

CETS is a powerful information-sharing tool that is now used in more than half a dozen countries. It works like this: Suppose the police department in London, England, get a report from a parent saying someone has been instant messaging their child and it looks as though it isn't the twelve-year-old-boy he claims to be. With CETS, the local police can quickly and easily find out whether the same suspect is being investigated in Bristol or Birmingham, or even in Barcelona or Buffalo. Forces can then share information and coordinate their investigations, creating an international law enforcement network that can match the global scope of the criminal activity.

As CETS expands to more countries around the world, it is starting to spread to areas of police culture beyond the world of pornography. Hancock said that thanks to the success of CETS, online information sharing has taken on a greater role in planning, hiring and training at many law enforcement agencies. "People get it," he said. "Whether it is terrorism, whether it is child protection, or whether it is car theft." The technology and the techniques that were driven by some of the worst crimes imaginable are now finding wider purchase as police forces increasingly see the benefits of better information sharing.

The police are not the only people with an interest in fighting crime online. Software and media companies are concerned about a different kind of criminal activity: digital piracy. Here, once again, you can find examples of important technological advances whose roots lie in pornography.

One of the major software tools for fighting digital piracy, in fact, was pioneered by a company based in Los Gatos, California, called BayTSP (that's TSP for "tracking, security, protection"), who created the product to help police catch child pornographers. Some of the original investors in the company were police officers. BayTSP's software can extract salient and unique information from a computer file—its metaphorical DNA—and then search the nooks and crannies of Usenet, Internet Relay Chat and peer-to-peer file-sharing networks to find copies of it and identify who posted it. Even if a photograph is cropped or a video clip edited, the modified version can still be traced back to BayTSP's database record. It was a powerful product that could be very effective at tracking down at least the distributors, if not the creators, of child pornography images. Unfortunately, the company discovered that that the people who could most use it weren't in a position to make it profitable.

"The market for it didn't pay out because law enforcement really didn't have a lot of budget, and then 9/11 happened," Jim Graham, a spokesperson for BayTSP, told me. All resources were being shunted toward anti-terrorism initiatives. "So BayTSP went looking for different markets. The one that turned out to be the most lucrative was the entertainment industry, where you have people uploading movies online." Software companies faced similar problems, with thousands of people illegally uploading and downloading Photoshop and Office and other major programs.

BayTSP keeps its client list secret, but online complaints and other available records speak to the company's "takedown notices" dealing with products from Paramount Pictures, Adobe Systems, Activision, Microsoft and others. Though they have been modernized and optimized over time, the tools BayTSP developed for catching online distributors of child porn are "100 percent the same" as those for nabbing mainstream digital pirates. BayTSP's services include everything from sending cease-and-desist notices on behalf of clients who simply want to quash all illegal downloads, to merely tracking download data for companies trying to figure out how to adapt their business and marketing strategies to the current file-sharing landscape.

In addition to the police and the corporate world, there is a third major group with a strong interest in stamping out images of child exploitation: the pornography industry. The industry also wants to prevent children from accessing its products: a 2001 study found that seven out of ten Americans between the ages of fifteen and seventeen had viewed pornography online.

In 1996, the founder of XBIZ, one of the pornography industry's major trade journals, started a non-profit organization called the Association of Sites Advocating Child Protection. The ASACP's funding comes from those in the industry—owners and operators of pornographic websites—and is devoted to ensuring that everyone involved in the porn industry—producers, performers and consumers—is of legal age.

There's a clear element of self-interest for such an organization. Nobody running a legitimate adult website wants to run afoul of the law, and neither do they want their brand conflated in the public mind with illegal activity. The tools and self-regulations offered by ASACP can help porn purveyors blunt the attacks of critics who attempt to flatten the entire continuum of erotica into a single plane of amoral depravity and exploitation.

The group is more than a craven PR gambit, though. Many people working in the industry are genuinely concerned about protecting children. This is not to ignore reality: if you imagine the worst possible form of degrading, exploitative, damaging pornography, somebody out there will inevitably be ready to sell you something ten times worse. Estimates place the illegal trade in child pornography (primarily involving girls between the ages of eight and twelve, but with a significant portion of children under the age of four) at about $3 billion per year worldwide. But that does not mean that all or even most mainstream pornographers would sell child pornography if it weren't illegal. A great number of people in the porn industry—women in particular—are quite certain of what they do and do not find acceptable. It is neither true nor productive to treat the tens of thousands of people who work in the adult industry as though they were all cut from the same cloth.

Former sex therapist and ASACP's CEO Joan Irvine monitors emerging technologies to help the adult industry set up best practices early on to ensure that children and pornography stay in their separate corners. She is American, but we met in Europe and Canada—she spends much of her time on the road working to establish consistent international standards for the industry. One of the first things she wanted to talk to me about was her concern over a perfect storm that was brewing around the confluence of high-speed wireless Internet access and GPS-enabled smartphones. Internet access means a pedophile could reach children whenever and wherever they were. And the GPS means that the pedophile could pinpoint his target's location.

"It's frightening because they are actually looking at developing some applications on social networking groups so that you can use the GPS to find out, 'Oh, my friend is around here,'" Irvine said. "Well, could you imagine if you as a parent don't know who these people are? You could have a pedophile tracking your child. The phones are already built with this capability. It just has to be turned on." Through ASACP, Irvine is working to anticipate these kinds of dangers, and trying to collaborate with the consumer electronics industry to develop systems to protect children. They have already gained ground with some earlier projects.

One of the technological solutions she is most proud of is something called "Restricted to Adults," or RTA, tags that can be entered into the metadata of a website. Metadata is information about a website that doesn't show up when a page loads but which allows the site to be searched, sorted and categorized more efficiently. RTA tags make it easier for search filters and other parental controls to sort out what is inappropriate viewing for underage surfers. Used consistently and widely, RTA tags could make it simple to block pornographic content from those who should not see it. (Cruder automatic porn-blocking tools have trouble analyzing the difference between, say, a pornographic site and a sexual health site. As a result, important information can be erroneously blocked from those who can and should have access to it.)

Buy-in in the adult industry for RTA tags has been positive—more than two million websites now carry the tags, and the technology has started to move into other areas. In fact, Irvine said, ASACP deliberately named its product "Restricted to

Adults," rather than giving it a name referring specifically to pornography, so that it would have a broader application.

ASACP is trying to expand the use of RTA tags to other "sin" industries that come with age restrictions: gambling, alcohol and cigarettes. This is just the beginning, though. Potentially, mainstream media rating companies like the Motion Picture Association of America and the Entertainment Software Review Board, which assign age-appropriate labels for movies and video games respectively, could use the same technology to create more layers of filtering. It would be possible to refine the tags so that one could search only for G-rated material, for instance, or PG-13.

RTA tags can also be attached to an individual file rather than an entire website. That makes it a powerful tool for all kinds of categorization, sorting and searching. ASACP has licensed the tags to a company called Secure Path Technologies, which works with media organizations to register movies, podcasts, games and other files with a Geneva-based organization called the ISAN International Agency. ISAN stands for "international standard audiovisual number." It is the video equivalent of the ISBN, or international standard book number, a unique number assigned to each published book.

ISAN-IA is creating a similar cataloguing system for digital media files. It happens that the RTA tags are compatible with its cataloguing system, which means that the pornography-inspired RTA has become a contributor to a technology that is helping to make the explosion of the entire modern mediaverse—not just the adult-oriented parts—more manageable, searchable and usable.

Down but Not Out

F or forty thousand years, pornography, erotica and sexual representation have shaped the tools human beings use to express themselves. If anything, pornography's influence has increased over time. Millennium by millennium, it has grown in power, exerting its greatest influence on the technologies of this century and the last. The formula is hard to improve upon: pornography, a possibly addictive product, supplied to a near-insatiable market, jumps up in value each time it is recreated or repackaged for a new medium. It is a low-cost, high-return means of drawing in early adopters, who will do or pay anything to receive their adult content in a new, better, faster, clearer, easier way. Pornography bears all the hallmarks of an unstoppable force in technological development.

Yet a surprising number of people in the industry—people who a decade ago would have been only too happy to sing their own praises on this subject—think the glory days are over and that pornography's influence is waning.

Playboy's Reena Patel is among those who question whether the adult industry still leads the pack. She is one of many who think it was true ten years ago, but not any more. "At this point, I think that people that were leading the technology in the past are trying to figure out ways to use the social networking platforms or other technology out there to make money on the web," she says. While many of these Web 2.0 applications benefit from the same kind of emergent sex that helped shape the early Internet, pornography businesses are now scrambling as much as any mainstream media company to understand whether and how they can capitalize on these latest trends.

The pace of technological change confounds pornographic and non-pornographic media companies alike, but purveyors of pornography have also seen a powerful resurgence of an old threat to their livelihood: free porn. And unlike in the days of the early Internet, free online pornography has proliferated at a level of quality and convenience that matches the pay sites.

The web-ranking site Alexa.com keeps track of the most visited and used sites on the Internet. At the time of writing, tube sites occupied positions 47 and 51 on the list. (Google.com holds the top position, with ten more Google sites also placing in the top 50. Yahoo!, YouTube and Facebook hold positions 2, 3, and 4, with Microsoft, MySpace, several blog clearing houses, photo-sharing sites and a number of Russian and Chinese social networking sites making up the majority of the top 50.) These tube sites are far and away the top-ranked pornographic sites and among the most visited destinations on the web. Tube sites' traffic dwarfs that of fee-based porn businesses.

After such a long history of mutual benefit, technology now seems to be turning on pornography. It is happening in many ways. Newer versions of the major web browsers—Explorer,

Firefox and Safari—all include a "privacy mode" (often referred to as a "porn mode" by the blogging classes) that can delete all history, including cookies, at the end of a browsing session. The obvious purpose of such an option is to cover one's tracks after visiting pornographic websites. But those tracks also contain the information necessary for affiliate programs to work. With privacy mode enabled, adult webmasters no longer have a record of who referred customers to their site.

On an entirely different front, pornography has suffered from its early adoption of high-definition television. When the industry moved to hi-def formats like Blu-ray and HD DVD, porn stars discovered that hitherto invisible "flaws"—from moles and wrinkles to razor burn and surgery scars—were suddenly visible to audiences. This forced actors and producers to take all manner of compensatory action, including changing camera angles, increasing makeup, changing diet and exercise habits and even undergoing cosmetic surgery to remove the smallest imperfections. The technology had created too much clarity for the fuzzy fantasies that are at the heart of pornography.

Things were looking so grim in early 2009 that *Hustler's* Larry Flynt, *Girls Gone Wild's* Joe Francis and others in the industry appealed to the U.S. government for a $5-billion "porn bailout." This (unsuccessful) bid for government aid demonstrates more than the dire situation faced by America's porn moguls. It points to the mainstreaming of the porn industry. Yet this move out of the margins is also damaging in some ways, diminishing pornographers' power to experiment and innovate. Pornography's traditionally marginal existence places unique exigencies on them. They have contended with prosecution, persecution, censors and censurers, and many of their technological leaps were a result of these struggles. Those companies that become more mainstream necessarily lose that edge.

Christie Hefner gave a lecture in 2008 (at IdeaCity, an annual speakers' festival coincidentally founded and organized by Citytv maverick Moses Znaimer) in which she spoke about the empire created by her father, Hugh, which she was running at the time. (In 2009 she stepped down as CEO of Playboy Inc., a position she had held since 1988.) After her talk, I caught her in the hall and explained my research, in the hopes that she could offer some views on the concept of the adult industry as tech pioneer. She shut me down immediately. "That's not Playboy," she said.

Though its revenue still comes from erotica, Playboy is far from marginal. Well before Christie Hefner took over the company, Playboy was already a publicly traded, multi-million-dollar operation. Under her leadership, the company moved ever closer to the mainstream, seeking a brand that was sexy in a more publicly consumable way. Playboy faced the inevitable consequence that comes with mainstream legitimacy: increased risk aversion. When you're answerable to shareholders, you don't mess around with content that might run afoul of the law, and you don't experiment with new technologies that demand large investments for questionable payoffs. Playboy would no more be out on the fringes of some experimental medium than NBC or Universal.

In some ways, anti-pornography activists and lawmakers actually play a role in keeping the industry at the forefront of technology. Attempts to limit pornography and drive it from the mainstream can inadvertently force it to innovate. Financial and legal suffering sometimes breeds great technology. Of course, this doesn't stop some pro-pornography activists from advocating movement in the other direction.

"Pornography, far from being an evil that the First Amendment must endure, is a positive good that encourages experimentation with new media," writes American lawyer Peter Johnson in

"Pornography Drives Technology," in the *Federal Communications Law Review*. "The First Amendment thus has not only intellectual, moral, political, and artistic value, but practical and economic value as well. It urges consenting adults, uninhibited by censorship, to look for novel ways to use the new media and novel ways to make money out of the new uses. Therefore, while it may be politically impossible and socially unwise to encourage computer pornography, legislators should at least leave it alone and let the medium follow where pornography leads."

Ultimately, legislation governing pornography is not based on whether technological development can best be served via greater or lesser freedom; it reflects what society finds acceptable or offensive. It does seem, though, that the porn industry gets more innovative when it is forced to struggle. Legal, cultural or even financial struggles just seem to make the industry stronger.

"A primary reason for the profitability of so many online sites is the lack of available outside investment capital," writes Lewis Perdue in *EroticaBiz*. "There are no venture capital firms with deep pockets behind adult sites. Most are bootstrapped by small entrepreneurs or built as an extension of an existing print or video porn business. As such, profitability, cost cutting, and serving the customer's desires have always come first for adult webmasters."

While it might provide no comfort to pornographers, some experts think the adult industry's expertise in cost effectiveness is more relevant to the mainstream than ever. Erotologist C. J. Scheiner said, "I've actually been trying to talk some of the people I know who made films in the adult industry into considering trying to get jobs in the television industry because TV right now is trying to cut back their costs all over the place. The people who have been making erotica really know how to do things very efficiently."

I asked Lewis Perdue, who has done so much innovative analysis of the adult industry, whether he thinks pornography's power is waning. He told me he hasn't seen anything that makes him question the industry's robustness. "As for the adult industry being a 'has been'—the fact that they still make money selling content while *The New York Times* and others are still struggling speaks for itself," he said in an email. "The adult industry is being hit hard by an avalanche of free porn which is hurting profits and making it harder to make money. However, they still manage—as a whole—to stay in the black. Their business models are evolving and that is where I see their innovation plowing new ground for the Internet as a whole."

So perhaps these dark times do not signal the end of the pornographer's role as technological pioneer. This may be a dip rather than a decline. Pornographers are already fighting back on many fronts. Some use "legal tube sites" to post promotional clips—titillating trailers for full-length films. They hope surfers will be intrigued enough to pay for the full feature. They are embedding digital watermarks and other identifiable properties into their products to help them better track and catch pirates. Some are specializing, leaving the vanilla porn to the tube sites while trying to attract a small but passionate market that is dedicated enough to a specific fetish to pay the cost of admission.

These measures may stanch the bleed. And if they do, mainstream media will no doubt adopt them to combat their own declining revenues. Such innovations, though, have to do with reaction and damage control. They are not the kind of bold advances that gave the pornography industry its technological mystique. Those kinds of innovations are more difficult to predict.

I asked *Porn and Pong* author Damon Brown (who also writes for *Playboy*) how he thought the adult world might next lead the mainstream. He wisely declined to make specific predictions, but did suggest where the next big ideas might come from.

"Because of our limited capacity, we don't know what's supposed to be next," he said. "What I will say is that I don't think it's going to be from the bigger companies. I don't see that happening. It's going to be someone or a small group of people who are not going to be of the mindset of today. I think there's a reason why the younger generation comes up with innovations. I don't think it's ageism. I think it's just that as we get older, we tend to look at things from a different perspective, within a particular paradigm. The porn industry, at least the modern one, is getting into its forties now. I do have confidence that some interesting things will come out of the porn industry, I just don't think it's going to come from the big guys."

Dunia Montenegro is neither big nor a guy. She is a Brazilian-born porn performer, producer and entrepreneur, now based in Spain. Her career is in many ways a product of technology: she is one of a growing number of female performers who work for themselves rather than trying to make a go of it in the traditionally male-dominated porn-studio world. She runs her own website, which includes her own photos and movies along with those of a growing stable of other female performers. She also blogs and uses other interactive tools to maintain a more intimate connection with her customers. By using the technology to create a dedicated fan base, she is maintaining her customer base and dissuading them from drifting over to the tube sites. She has found a way to make the latest web tools profitable.

"I love working on my website," she told me. "I have done my blog every day for three years, and every day eight or nine thousand people in Spain and South America visit it. It's very important to me."

Connecting directly with her fan base does more than foster an emotional bond that builds customer loyalty. It allows her to customize her product to meet her audience's needs. "Every day I ask my fans, my customers, 'What do you want? What can I shoot tomorrow? Give me a test.' The fans tell, I do, and the people buy the videos." The requests range from shooting a black-and-white movie to doing a scene with one of her fans. She fulfills almost all requests.

She says her fans see her not as a celebrity but as a regular human being they can relate to and imagine themselves being friends with. "People want to see normal people," she said. (That is vastly more true in Europe than in North America, where preferences lean more toward a surgically sculpted professional "porn-star look." Montenegro's perceived normalcy might explain why she has so little following in the United States, which is home to nearly forty-five million Hispanics.)

Montenegro profits from Web 2.0 technology with textbook proficiency. She could teach any mainstream media company a great deal about how to draw revenue via the interactive web applications. She is in control, and making far more money than she would have in a traditional porn career. Without her website, she would have to shoot scenes for other producers, and leave distribution and marketing to other people. She would get paid a few hundred dollars for a day of having sex on camera, and would never see another dime of profit.

"In porn, the money is a big cake and the [large] companies eat it all. The porn actress gets nothing," she said. "I said no, I want this cake." She maintains the copyright on everything on her site. "In thirty years, when I am old, *I'll* get money, not just the companies."

Montenegro is one of a growing cohort of women using technology to run their own show. Like so many others, Montenegro cites Jenna Jameson's autobiography, *How to Make Love Like a Porn Star*, as inspiration for her own career, something that pleases Jameson to no end.

"This is fantastic to hear," Jameson told me when I mentioned that she appears to have inspired many women like Montenegro to make the most of the technological developments they helped create. "One of my major concerns when I started doing what I did with Club Jenna was to teach girls how to be the captain of their own ship. I wanted them to think out of the box and be independent. This is how I ran my career and I wanted to share my experiences to inspire others to choose similar paths. There is nothing more empowering or linked to success in this business."

While some suggest that the Jameson archetype might just be another fantasy concocted for the modern male sensibility— "For the man who loves porn but hates to think of women being exploited, we give you the Technologically Empowered Porn Actress! She loves what she does and she's getting rich doing it, so you don't have to feel bad!"—Montenegro and others I spoke with rarely waver in their enthusiasm over how the technology has improved their careers, and their lives. They are proud to carry on a tradition of using pornography as a proving ground for the commercial viability of new media tools.

A Touchy Subject

While many in the pornography industry still make money via current media, others are exploring what sexuality can do with more experimental technologies. One research area that shows promise is a field known as haptics—the technology of communicating tactile information. Temperature, texture, motion and pressure are all examples of haptic stimuli.

The technology has a whiff of science fiction about it. Many haptic applications are extensions of virtual worlds, and they hint at a virtual reality that is vastly more real than anything currently in existence. In fact, one of the first inventions designed to transmit tactile data bears an unmistakable resemblance to one of sci-fi's most iconic creations.

The permanent collection at the Museum of Sex in New York City includes a mannequin dressed in what appears to be a modified Borg costume (the most notable modification being the addition of a black leather penis pouch). More black leather and chrome cover various body parts, and a mass of wires extend from various nodes, giving the suit a sado-masochistic aura.

Created by experimental media artists Stahl Stenslie and Kirk Woolford in 1993 (four years after the Borg race made its debut on *Star Trek: The Next Generation*), CyberSM suits were one of the first forays into the haptic field known as teledildon-ics—the science and technology of remote-controlled sexual stimulation. Each partner created an online persona, which appeared on the other's screen. As the avatars had sex online, the suits replicated the relevant tactile stimuli for the users.

Teledildonics deals with motors, heaters and other non-communications technology. But at its heart, it *is* a communications technology. Haptics feels different from the usual forms of communication, for good reason. Human beings have five basic senses, but almost all conventional communications technology deals with only two: sight and sound. Taste and smell are not part of any major medium, and touch has found no purchase beyond the Braille language. Forty per cent of the human brain is devoted to processing visual information, which gives some idea how much of what we know about the world comes to us through our eyes. Auditory information is almost as important.

It is reasonable to think, though, that if one more sense is going to be added to the tools of communications, it will be touch. It is a powerful means of human communication and it lends itself particularly to sexual communication.

In day-to-day life, of course, haptic information is not lim-ited to sex. Think of the information conveyed through the strength of someone's handshake or the way a friend puts her arm around your shoulders during hard times. Think about testing the ripeness of an avocado, or sinking down into a couch. Think about trying on clothes, or test-driving a new car or giving someone a wedgie. All these experiences involve sending and receiving tactile information. Tactile communications technology could change how we shop, work and interact with others. There is some way to go before people start buying groceries from a haptic-enabled virtual fruit stand, but the journey has begun. In fact, it has already made it to the infomercial stage.

The woman and the man in the promos for the RealTouch have the kind of polished perkiness one associates with late-night ads for stain removers and egg slicers. Their product costs a little more than the usual easy payment of $19.95. The RealTouch mechanical vagina/anus—which comes with a USB cable and a list of minimum system requirements—goes for $200 U.S. Then again, according to the pitch, it will "revolutionize the way you think about sex."

There follows a lengthy explanation of how to connect the RealTouch to the Desktop Electronics Unit, which connects both to the power outlet and to a computer; how to register online; and where to access the video-on-demand library to download adult films with haptic coding. "RealTouch does all the rest!" About the size of a football and with a slight hourglass shape, the RealTouch is "perfectly weighted for hands-free enjoyment!" Three servomotors, two heaters, moveable bands of a "supple, skin-like material called Versaflex!," a high-tech orifice and a "lube reservoir" round out the mechanical aspects of this piece of simulation technology.

The hardware is only the beginning, though. The real sophistication lies in the software, which automatically captures on-screen motion in a pornographic video and replicates it in the device. The makers of the RealTouch have a growing library of encoded films, allowing the consumer to feel what he sees. The makers are already working on an upgrade that will capture real-time motion for use with haptic webcam services.

This is a technology that many people may find repellent (particularly if they watch the instructional video on how to clean the RealTouch, which shows the device being rinsed out in a *kitchen* sink). Yet the business model is shrewd, building in a high level of customer loyalty: when a buyer acquires a RealTouch, he is committed to getting his value-added pornography from the same source.

Haptic technology will not likely be ready for the mainstream for some time. (At least not in any way more sophisticated or intimate than a game controller vibrating when your car crashes into a mountain.) Teledildonics, though, is already providing the proving ground that will demonstrate whether such technology is commercially viable.

Which makes it all the odder that in 2009, when *Wired* magazine convened a team of futurists to peer into their crystal brains and speculate about the next forty years, they did not foresee the advent of teledildonics until 2018.

This came as news to engineer Kyle Machulis, who has been creating teledildonic technologies for years. For Machulis and his ilk, teledildonics is an established technology that has already passed through several generations of refinements and added functionality. His cluster of blogs is a kind of clearing house and focal point for a scattered community of experimenters and inventors tinkering with haptic interfaces for sexual Internet-based communication—the exact kind of maverick community from which one might expect to see the next technological leap forward.

Machulis's work is far enough out there that even *Wired*—a magazine that is supposed to deliver the future now—isn't ready to acknowledge its existence. His machines exist in quasi-obscurity not only because they push the technological envelope but also because they tend to push the boundaries of the human comfort zone. The discomfort comes not from any physical horror or danger, but simply because touch-based inventions demand much more intimacy than most people have with their consumer electronics. One of the lessons of pornography, though, is that sexual applications can help make new technologies less alienating.

Machulis is keenly aware that his experiments are still far from the mainstream. "When you have as many vibrators as I do, and you have the technological knowledge that I do, you get bored," he told a crowd at the 2007 Arse Electronika expo in California. (If the name is not self-explanatory, Arse Electronika is a symposium that explores all aspects of the relationship between sex and technology.) That boredom has led to some interesting projects:

• An exercise bicycle wired to a vibrator so that pedalling harder increases vibration.

• The "Sex Box." Microsoft's video game platform, the X-Box, included a feedback system such that, when a player crashes a car, blows up an alien or otherwise does something momentous in a game, the controller vibrates. Machulis took out the vibration motors and hooked the system up to a sex toy. "That makes any single video game environment a sexual environment," he said.

• An experiment in "Twitterdildonics," in which he created an interface between the micro-blogging website Twitter.com and a vibrator. He used the ASCII values of the text from Tweets as vibrational intensity indicators—the higher the ASCII number, the stronger the motion. (A discovery from this experiment: Tweets in languages that use non-American alphabets—Cyrillic, for instance—resulted in more intense experiences, as the ASCII values for these characters are much higher.)

• A "force feedback reality" device, which uses a light sensor to control the intensity of the vibrator. Walking outside with the sensor in a shirt pocket caused the sunlight intensity to change as the cloth of the pocket shifted with each footstep—so the vibrator picked up on the gait of the user.

• Biofeedback to control sexual experiences. This could be as straightforward as, say, using someone's own pulse rate as a motion controller, or as complex as recording someone's muscular activity during a sex act and then transmitting that information to a remote partner who can recreate those sensations via an artificial device. If that sounds too weird, remember the story of webcams, which for the greater part of their early life were almost exclusively used by people taking their clothes off, but which now are used in an increasingly mobile society to allow loved ones to stay in closer contact. Imagine recording a hug and sending it to a friend. Or a massage therapist logging some therapeutic movements that could be replayed to treat a chronic sore spot. Or an urban surgeon performing an operation in a remote area with tactile feedback making the job as effective as if the doctor were in the room.

These are some of the places that Machulis's strange inventions might lead. For now, though, he is just experimenting, seeing what can be wrought from his ideas and expertise.

"I grew up out in the country in Oklahoma and always sort of worked alone," he told me. "Now I live in the Bay Area and I still work alone. It's always been sort of basement development aesthetic." His isolation does not extend online, where his extensive writing, photographs and videos made me feel as though I already had a pretty good sense of his ideas, temperament and sense of humour before ever we spoke.

Machulis's work falls somewhere between hobby and commercial enterprise. Teledildonics has never earned him money directly, but it has been key to advancing his career. "The way that I work," he said, "is that I publish all the stuff, and then find work through the press that that gets me. It's gotten me the job that I just had before my current one, at Second Life in Linden Labs. That's what got me out of Oklahoma. It's really just working off of the social links and the infamy, I guess, and seeing where that gets me."

Machulis sells himself a little short. He also has a long history of creating virtual worlds, though his natural inclination is toward the text-based form. He is still very active in the modern MUD community. "Some people just communicate better through text and some people need the visual help of virtual worlds with the full 3D system," he said. "The thing I think makes text so sexy is that, as long as you can use words you can do anything. The problem with SL and worlds like that is you're given all of these prerequisites like a sky and ground and physics."

At Linden Labs he adapted easily from text to 3D visuals. He worked on both sexual and non-sexual products there, including an (unrelated) exercise bike that allowed players to cycle their avatars around, and teledildonic products that were compatible with Second Life animations. Today, he is gainfully employed as an engineer at a (non-dildo-related) California robotics firm, but continues to be a teledildonics guru in his spare time.

"I seem to have taken the lead in this sort of underground building group. There's just tons of garage builders out there," he said. His own research is focusing less on the actual machinery at the moment. "I've been looking at software development. There's hardware out there, but most of the software for it is pretty bad. It's not cross-platform, it's not really user friendly. The user interfaces for them are laughable."

Often, when people really start thinking about user interfaces, it is an indicator that the technology is getting ready for a wider audience. People have talked about teledildonics since 1993, but this technology—and the haptic virtual environment it portends—is only now starting to pack its bags for the first leg of its journey to the mainstream.

The main challenge to developing an intuitive user interface is the sheer complexity of the devices. Machulis is convinced that the solution will demand attention to both simplification and intuitiveness. And for him, intuitiveness goes hand in hand with personalization. Nothing is more personal than one's own body.

"Right now my focus is mainly on biometrics," he said. "If you tap into the numbers that are coming off your body, you have as intimate a physical interface as you're going to get with a computer. There's no typing, there's no button pushing. You are taking your pulse or taking a galvanic skin response reading and it becomes a natural interface. And then the question then becomes, how we actually turn that [data] into something that, when sent to someone else, will do something interesting for them. That's the part that I'm working on now."

Results thus far have been intriguing for the teledildonics crowd, though possibly frustrating for the test subjects. "I created an interesting teasing technology. It is just a simple feedback loop of pulse and a vibrator. To make the speed of the vibrator go up, you have to keep your pulse below a certain level. It's very simple feedback loop, but there's so much going on in the physicality of that feedback loop that it actually becomes an interesting system."

Even a man of science like Machulis describes some of his own work as "scary as hell." He knows he's playing with power, and he knows that, although people's comfort limits have changed over time, they have not disappeared. He says that virtual worlds in their current form represent the "maximum immersion" the real world can handle right now, but that sex might change where people draw the line.

Machulis cites the "genetic imperative" for sex and reproduction as the mechanism that drives the cycle of technological innovation and adoption. Perhaps that is why he is already a step ahead of Randal Oulton on the virtual pregnancy front. Among his many other activities, Machulis is a technology reporter for MMOrgy.com, a blog dedicated to reporting on sex in massively multi-player virtual worlds. In 2006, he posted an essay on the subject of teledildonic conception. The essay deals with many logistical, technological, ethical and emotional issues, but here is his basic concept:

1. John and Jane decide they want to have a baby in their virtual world relationship. They contact BabyCorp.

2. BabyCorp requests that each of the parent-customers send in a real picture of their faces. After this, the more the couple spends, the more they can customize. Otherwise it's left to "Nature" (Nature being the name of BabyCorp's server farm).

3. As part of the package, the couple is sent the BabyCorp hardware/software package, consisting of male and female teledildonics equipment. . . .

4. The couple copulates, using the BabyCorp package. The software relays the depth of the male stroking, which controls the speed of the woman's vibrator. For sake of argument, let's say the vibrator also contains a pump, fluid storage unit, and heater. At the time of John's orgasm, the pump goes to work on Jane's side.

5. Over at BabyCorp, the servers pick up that conception has happened, and Nature goes to work. Combining the pictures sent in by the couple, along with aging algorithms and a few mutations thrown in for good measure, the baby's facial textures are formed.

6. After the gestation time selected by the couple (Once again, depth of immersion in gestation time [ultrasound, virtual la maze classes, etc.] is figured by parental monetary investment), a bouncing virtual baby is born, possibly with mom's nose, or dad's eyes.

All of the technology exists now, or could easily be manufactured, to make this theoretical model a reality. And given the number of virtual conceptions already happening, it appears there is a market.

On occasion, Machulis himself is overwhelmed by the implications of his own ideas. He winds up his disquisition on virtual pregnancy, clearly having explored the subject past his own comfort level, with these words: "I'm going to go spend the rest of my evening in the bathtub, crying. This is a crazy world we live in, and it's just getting crazier. It's hard to deal with this shit when other people do it, much less be the one coming up with it. I'd quit this stuff and go make flying cars, but people would probably just crash them."

There is another reason why an obviously brilliant inventor like Machulis might choose remote-controlled vibrators over flying cars. The history of recorded human communication, from those first ice age drawings and sculptures to the electronic marvels of the twenty-first century, is full of echoes of R. Dale Guthrie's "universal human behaviour" and Brenda Brathwaite's tools-and-penises maxim. Whatever the next technology is—be it a virtual reality that feeds all the senses, or something else entirely—there is every reason to believe that pornography, erotica and passionate love will have dominated its formative stages, and that it is in these areas where you will find creative minds at work. The impetus to find new ways to depict sexuality has recurred so often, in so many places and in such variety that it seems impossible that it could be tied to a particular era or culture.

At every stage in every age, there seem to be creative people— artists, writers, engineers, businesspeople—who are drawn to the sexual applications of new forms of communication. Perhaps the most striking aspect of this ubiquity is the sheer variety of media for which it holds true. Woodblock prints, VCRs and Internet chat rooms have almost nothing in common with one another except that they have all been used for creative expression. Yet these and dozens of other equally improbably related technologies have had their development shaped by the desire to employ them as media for erotica.

This drive is often onanistic, but it is more than that too. There is a deep impulse at work that is fundamentally tied to a need to connect with others. The longing to communicate about sexuality is often a reflection of—or a desire for—passion or intimacy. Our bodies have not changed much since humanity developed the first tools of communication. It's not just that our endocrine system and sensory organs closely resemble those of whoever actually drew those penises on cave walls. It's also that those ancient artists shared our modern, sophisticated emotional capacity. The entire complex combination of motivations that gives sexuality its distinct power to change how we communicate has been there since the beginning.

One thing that has changed over time is our understanding of the phenomenon. Though people continue to treat pornography as technology's dirty little secret, they now recognize its influence well enough to use it in a calculated way, building it into launch strategies and business models for new media.

I believe that the more powerful force, though, remains the kind of compulsion that drives people like Machulis and so many others—the drive to seek out emergent technologies so as to experience sexuality and express passion in ways that nobody ever previously imagined were possible. This drive occasionally strays into the realm of addiction or obsession, and it sometimes feeds on people's darkest impulses, but it is the real source of power behind the technological creativity that has given us so many innovations in communication.

As the current travails of the porn industry show, smut is not an infinite market. Even with pornography, there are limits to what people will pay for, particularly when they can get the equivalent product for free. And yet, the cycle of technological evolution moves more quickly than ever. As quickly as communications technology marches on, sexual applications always seem to remain in the vanguard. Even while the porn industry goes through some difficult moments, the deeply rooted human desire for new forms of sexual representation has not diminished. Love it or loathe it, the Erotic Engine that has been a driving force for millennia shows no sign of losing its power.

FOR FURTHER READING

BUSINESS ANALYSIS OF THE PORNOGRAPHY INDUSTRY

Eroticabiz: How Sex Shaped the Internet, Lewis Perdue, iUniverse Publishers, 2002

Obscene Profits: The Entrepreneurs of Pornography in the Cyber Age, Frederick S. Lane, Routledge, 2000

GENERAL OVERVIEWS AND HISTORIES

Pornography and Sexual Representation: A Reference Guide (Volumes I, II and III), Joseph W. Slade, Greenwood Press, 2000

Pornography: The Secret History of Civilization (Documentary series), Channel Four Television Corporation, 1999

Pornography: The Secret History of Civilization (Companion to the documentary series), Isabel Tang, Channel 4 Books, 1999

Pornography: A Groundwork Guide, Debbie Mathan, House of Anansi Press, 2007

The Encyclopedia of Erotic Literature (Vols. I and II), edited by C. J. Scheiner, Barricade Books, 1996

Encyclopedia of Erotic Literature (Volumes I and II), edited by Gaetan Brulotte and John Phillips, Routledge, 2006

Utterly Without Redeeming Social Value: Obscenity and Pornography Decisions of the United States Supreme Court, edited by Maureen Harrison and Steve Gilbert, Excellent Books, 2000

OTHER

The Nature of Paleolithic Art, R. Dale Guthrie, University of Chicago Press, 2005

Sex or Symbol: Erotic Images of Greece and Rome, Catherine Johns, Routledge, 1999

Pornography and Representation in Greece & Rome, edited by Amy Richlin, Oxford University Press, 1992

The Invention of Pornography, 1500-1800: Obscenity and the Origins of Modernity, edited by Lynn Hunt, Zone Books, 1993

The Secret Museum: Pornography in Modern Culture, Walter Kendrick, University of California Press, 1987

The Reinvention of Obscenity: Sex, Lies and Tabloids in Early Modern France, Joan DeJean, The University of Chicago Press, 2002

The Gutenberg Revolution: How Printing Changed the Course of History, John Man, Bantam, 2009

Taking Positions: On the Erotic in Renaissance Culture, Bette Talvacchia, Princeton University Press, 1999

Before Pornography: Erotic Writing in Early Modern England, Ian Frederick Moulton, Oxford University Press, 2000

Sex and the Floating World: Erotic Images in Japan 1700–1820, Timon Screech, Reaktion, 2009

Bookleggers and Smuthounds: The Trade in Erotica 1920–1940, Jay A. Gertzman, University of Pennsylvania Press, 1999

Erotic Comics: A Graphic History from Tijuana Bibles to Underground Comix, Tim Pilcher, The Ilex Press, 2008

The Flash Press: Sporting Male Weeklies in 1840s New York, Patricia Cline Cohen, Timothy J. Gilfoyle and Helen Kefkowitz Horowitz, The University of Chicago Press, 2008

Industrial Madness: Commercial Photography in Paris, 1848–1871, Elizabeth Anne McCauley, Yale Publications, 1994

Reefer Madness: Sex, Drugs and Cheap Labor in the American Black Market, Eric Schlosser, First Mariner Books, 2004

From Betamax to Blockbuster: Video Stores and the Invention of Movies on Video, Joshua M. Greenberg, The MIT Press, 2008

How to Make Love Like a Porn Star: A Cautionary Tale, Jenna Jameson, HarperCollins Publishers, 2004

Black and White and Blue: Adult Cinema from the Victorian Age to the VCR, Dave Thompson, ECW Press, 2007

The Big Book of Porn: A Penetrating Look at the World of Dirty Movies, Seth Grahame-Smith, Quirk Books, 2005

Dirty Movies: An Illustrated History of the Stag Film, 1915–1970, Al Di Lauro and Greald Rabkin, Chelsea House Publishers, 1976

The Cybergypsies: A Frank Account of Love, Life and Travels on the Electronic Frontier, Indra Sinha, Scribner, 1999

My Tiny Life: Crime and Passion in a Virtual World, Julian Dibble, Henry Holt and Company, 1998

Porn & Pong: How Grand Theft Auto, Tomb Raider and Other Sexy Games Changed Our Culture, Damon Brown, Feral House, 2008

Sex in Video Games: Advances in Computer Graphics and Game Development, Brenda Brathwaite, Thomson Learning Inc., 2007

"Big Red Son" in *Consider the Lobster and Other Essays*, David Foster Wallace, Little, Brown and Company, 2005

One Child at a Time: The Global Fight to Rescue Children From Online Predators, Julian Sher, Random House Canada, 2007

ACKNOWLEDGEMENTS

My contributions to this book were only possible thanks to those of the dozens of people who have been so generous with their stories, ideas and analysis. I am deeply grateful to all of you who agreed to be interviewed for this project—I hope that readers will be as intrigued and entertained by your experiences as I have been.

Throughout the making of this book, many people helped open doors and make introductions on my behalf. In particular, I owe a great debt to C. J. Scheiner and Reena Patel for connecting me to so many of their contacts and associates. My thanks also go to Brenda Brathwaite, Joan Irvine, Sarah Jacobs, Natalia Kim, Annalee Newitz, Sofia Ramirez, Paul Saffo and David Wills for opening their address books to me.

Many thanks to my editor at Doubleday, Tim Rostron. His thoughtfulness, humour and intelligence are manifest throughout this book. Thank you also to Shaun Oakey, whose copy-editing resulted in a thousand improvements of clarity and brevity. Amanda Delong provided great research, transcription and enthusiasm. Shaena Lambert was my sounding board for all things related to writing. My agent, Anne McDermid, and her associate Martha Magor gave me invaluable encouragement, counsel and the occasional stiff drink.

Andrea Addario edited many drafts of *The Erotic Engine*, and provided feedback that made the book smarter, more authoritative and more fun to read. Researching this subject area was often challenging, and Andrea made me think and made me laugh at all the right moments in all the right ways.

INDEX